ne Way From Me To Us

A Memoir

MIKE COLEMAN

For more information contact:
Riverdale Avenue Books
Magnus Books
5676 Riverdale Avenue
Riverdale, NY 10471

www.riverdaleavebooks.com

Design by www.formatting4U.com
Cover by Scott Carpenter

Digital ISBN: 9781626016569
Paperback ISBN: 9781626016576

First Edition: June 2023

Nashville Banner articles reprinted by permission of the Nas
Library, The Nashville Room.

Praise for The Way from Me to Us

"Thoughtful. Sincere. A romantic and relatable love story—no matter which way you roll. Mike's stories are entertaining and heartbreaking. I only wish our global community had made more progress since his coming out four decades ago. These stories are still relevant, still raw, and will remind you what love looks like—from any angle."

~ Sarah Elkins, author of
Your Stories Don't Define You, How You Tell Them Will

"*The Way from Me to Us* is that rare delight—a love story with a happy ending. But this engaging, beautifully written memoir is more than a tale about two good people who are lucky enough to find each other. Mike Coleman's compassion and understanding, his passion for family and community, reminded me of what a privilege it is to have our brief time on this busy planet, and what a wonder love can be. Through a wealth of vivid details, each of which furthers the narrative or its many portrait sketches, Coleman resurrects a life of love and work and fun and heartbreak, from his secret childhood admiration for the men in TV ads for Brylcreem to holding his ailing mother's hand in a hospital despite their unresolved issues. Among its many strands, this beautiful memoir quietly celebrates the kinds of bravery required of everyday human beings who must resist those who act as if the world is so rich in love that we can afford to disdain some of its wonderful flavors. It isn't and we cannot."

~ Michael Sims, author of
Adam's Navel and The Adventures of Henry Thoreau

"Reading like a novel, *The Way from Me to Us* is—at its core—a double love story; one about two men making a life together in uncharted waters, and one about learning to love oneself, perhaps the harder of the two. In this entertaining and deeply moving memoir, Mike Coleman has provided not only insightful commentary about his life and those with whom he interacts but also provided a testament of hope and inspiration for younger gay men; they are not alone, deserve acceptance, equality, and, most importantly, their own love stories."

~ Jeff Clemmons,
author of *Rich's: A Southern Institution*

To Cory and Jeremy Douylliez-Willis

and

Dave Tello Isla and James Langill

Your fearlessness inspires me

Come, my friends, 'tis not too late to seek a newer world.

—Alfred, Lord Tennyson

Author's Note:

This is a work of creative nonfiction. While the stories are true to the best of my memory, some names and details have been changed to protect the privacy of the people involved.

Table of Contents

Acknowledgments

I am grateful for the kind and generous support I received in creating this book. More than a few family members, friends and colleagues deserve special thanks.

In their own individual ways, my brother-in-law Charlie Durham and long-time friends Neill Little, Vicki McMorrough and Dale Russakoff nudged me, after decades of successful corporate writing, to put something from my own heart on paper. Their voices were with me when I sat down Monday morning, April 13, 2020, to start this book. Thank you, all.

Annmarie Anderson, Ellen Schlossberg, Jeanie Daves, Vicki McMorrough, Linda Harding, Jeff Nakrin, Sheryl Roehl and Anna Robertson were an enthusiastic team of readers, offering critique, insight and encouragement at various stages of the book's development. True to their spirit as founding members of the Nashville Writers' Alliance, Madeena Nolan and Alana White detected veils in Draft 2 that I bravely lifted in Draft 3. Their comments also helped me trim pages and pages from the manuscript. In the process, I discovered the true line of my story.

In addition to her photography, Becky Gibson Portwood's proof-reader's approach to a near-final draft helped make these pages better.

Thanks to the many Facebook friends whose positive responses to posted excerpts of the book kept me going. They were my beta test, my focus group that helped me see that "maybe I have something here." Their enthusiastic comments, even on excerpts that I thought too lengthy to draw much response, were like cupcakes at the end of a long day, steaming cups of Starbucks that drew me back to my desk each morning.

Heartfelt thanks to my editor, David T. Valentin. What a joy to find that he grasped the essence of my story better than I did when he first took interest in it. I greatly appreciate his keen eye and gentle nurture. But most of all, I treasure the fact that he found relevance to younger readers in my work. That's music to a Baby Boomer writer's ears.

My biggest debt of gratitude is to Ted Brothers, love of my life, for giving me the space and the time to write this memoir. Drafting most of it during the early days of the Covid pandemic, I found it a welcome escape into the past. Ted graciously stood back and let me make the trip on my own, God bless him, although he did enjoy our *do you remember?* conversations when I struggled to fill in details of our early years together. He even patiently endured continuous loops of Mott the Hoople, whose music transported me to my college days while I wrote those parts of the book. Even all these years later, their songs capture it for me. "All the Young Dudes," indeed.

I am also grateful to Tara Westover for her powerful memoir, *Educated.* Reading it made me want to write my story. But even more than inspiration, her book gave me permission. It helped me understand that hindsight doesn't have to be 20/20 to write a memoir. Sometimes it's more interesting when it's not. Our rearview mirrors all reflect things differently over the course of our lives, and that's okay.

This book is what I see in mine.

Thank you for reading.

Chapter One: Willkommen

Bath time in Columbia, Tennessee, early 1950s

I had open-heart surgery in 2019 when I was 67. It was my first hospitalization in more than six decades; I had my tonsils out in 1957 when I was five. The world had changed a lot in the years in between. So had I. So had surgery.

1957: A dour nurse in a starched white cap wheels me into a green-tiled operating room, where a black vortex sucks me in after the surgical team puts the ether mask over my face. "It smells like bananas," my mother had said, and it does.

2019: A cheerful nurse anesthetist in pink scrubs asks what kind of music I'd like to hear as she wheels me toward the operating room, and when we get to surgery, another tech commands the Pandora app on the big-screen TV to play music from the show I requested, *Cabaret*. I hear nearly half of Alan Cumming's version of "Willkommen" before I skip the ether vortex and go directly to sleep while they prepare to saw my breastbone in half.

What stumps me today as I compare these two experiences is that there was life before *Cabaret*. How did people live in 1957? How did I? Maybe that's why the nurse in the starched white cap was so dour as she rolled my gurney to the operating room. She hadn't heard a song by Kander and Ebb.

I didn't know I was a Broadway show queen when I was five, but I did know I was a little gay boy. I didn't have a word for it, but I knew how it felt. I knew I liked men. This book is the story of how, like many men born in the 1950s and many thereafter, I've fought and embraced, embraced and fought that desire throughout my life.

It's a story of how I've made peace—not always perfect peace, but peace nonetheless—with my homosexuality, and found happiness with a guy named Ted, with whom I've spent the past 44 years.

It's also a kind of prayer that, one day, being homosexual won't require a peace treaty.

Mine is not always a pretty story. There's fire. Death. Family curses. Wishes to flee. Unprotected sex and its consequences. But there is also a splendid summer with 35 handwritten love letters between Ted and me when we were not only in the pink cloud of early romance, but also trying to figure out what a life together might look like.

The letters provide the strongest clue as to why our relationship has lasted as long as it has. Their passion—coupled with their earnestness as we wrote about building a long-term relationship—astounds me.

I am unable to read one of the letters without my eyes filming over with tears, the words going blurry on the page. Ted and I had known each other only a matter of months, yet he enclosed a detailed, scale diagram of "a house I would like to share with you." It even includes his ideas on where we'd put the furniture.

Let me state for the record right now: When my time comes, when they roll my used body into the cremation oven, I want that letter and diagram under my folded hands.

Though the road has been rocky at times, with its share of bad choices along the way, little moments remind me again and again of the best choice I've made in this life. Moments like the one after my heart surgery, when I woke up in the ICU, groggy, intubated to the gills and feeling as if a car had backed over my chest during the night. My first sight was a patch of morning sun in a grid-like pattern on the gray-blue blanket at my feet.

"Hello, sunshine," said Ted. I lifted my eyes. He sat in a chair by the bed, his trusty iPad in his lap. He smiled at me.

* * *

One evening several months after my surgery, our nephew phoned us. Sometimes people want to know, when Ted and I speak of our nieces and nephews, "Whose are they?" This was one of Ted's sister's sons calling. Chris and his wife and two teenage daughters were arguing at their dinner table in Charlotte, North Carolina. We were well over a month into 2020's Covid-19 lockdown; nerves were a little frayed.

"How did you and Ted meet?" Chris asked me.

His wife, Laraine, thought we'd met on a cruise. One of the girls, I think the older one (it was hard to tell; Olivia, 15 at the time, and Sarah, 13, frequently talk over each other), thought we'd met in a bar.

"You're both right," I said, pleased to have an answer that would make them all winners. I adore this family. "We met cruising in a bar."

"I thought you met on a real cruise," Laraine said.

"We were too poor in those days," I said.

Chris provided the recap. "Ted was still in school then, right? And you were working?"

He was correct. Ted was in grad school at Vanderbilt and I was in the first year of my job as a reporter at the *Nashville Banner*, the city's afternoon daily at the time. It is long gone today.

On the evening in question, Ted and I met in a bar called the Other Side. It literally was on the other side of the railroad tracks that divided downtown Nashville from a rough industrial section east of the city. In 1977, at least for this 24-year-old newspaper reporter on the verge of engagement to a young woman I had dated since college, going to the Other Side was frightening and thrilling at the same time, an act of courage or stupidity, depending on my mood. Images of being arrested, of losing my job spun through my head as I pulled my maroon Toyota Corolla into the bar's gravel parking lot the night I met Ted.

It might be difficult for young people today like our great-nieces Olivia and Sarah, who speak so freely about their boyfriends' boyfriends and girlfriends' girlfriends, to understand why going to a gay bar was risky business in 1977. Let me sketch a quick picture: The easy candor and openness of *Will & Grace* were light-years away. The sitcom *Soap,* which featured Billy Crystal as one of the first openly gay characters on American television, would launch in the fall of 1977; THAT was a big deal. Groundbreaking as the show was, its producers obeyed network powers-that-be and never permitted Billy's character and his boyfriend to touch on screen. God forbid.

The producers' response was no surprise, given how the decade had begun. In late 1969, a major weekly newsmagazine ran a cover story about homosexuals in America. (Queers! On the cover of *Time*!) It was a bold move for a mainstream publication to devote so much ink to the taboo subject, even though the article sounded as if it were describing creatures in a zoo.

Around the same time, a bestselling book about sex took a similar approach, with a focus on the more bizarre and dangerous activities homosexuals engaged in. (There was heavy emphasis on the "they" in both these publications—homosexuals as an odd subset of American life.) One section described the dire straits of gay men who showed up late at night in big-city hospital emergency rooms with light bulbs and other household items lodged in their rectums.

Grimly, I read the book by the light of the Ethan Allen early American eagle lamp on my bedside table when I was a senior in high school. Nowhere did it address the things I was curious about: love between men, romance between men. Yet the author had a monster hit on his hands. A frequent guest on TV talk shows, he was hailed as a sort of messiah of straight talk about sex. Sadly, nothing of equal popularity came along to present a kinder, more enlightened view of homosexuality in the decade that followed the book's release.

This was the zeitgeist, then, the climate that made me damn sure I entered a gay bar under cover of darkness in 1977—and so it was the Sunday Ted and I met. It wasn't only public attitudes that made me afraid. It was what was going on in my personal life, too. I had a bright future ahead of me. A storybook future, some might have called it. Going to the Other Side put it all at risk.

It was Mother's Day, a fact that usually gets a laugh when Ted and I tell the story today. I had spent the day with my parents at their apartment across town, and my maybe-soon-to-be wife, Maggie. She had to go to work in the morning, so our evening had ended early. I had the Monday off, a comp day for the extra hours I had accumulated covering stories. I could stay out as late as I wanted.

It was a perfect setup. A night and day of freedom. I didn't have to be accountable to anyone—for a while.

* * *

That Mother's Day night, I wanted something that had never quite been there for me in my 24 years on this earth.

I know, too, that I felt as if I were on an accelerating treadmill. I wanted to get off. I just didn't know how. The Other Side offered a terrifying glimpse of what might happen if I did. Did I really want to be one of those people?

Still, the place intrigued me. As I got out of the car and walked across the gravel to the Other Side's entrance on that warm spring night, I thought: *So, what if I throw it all away?* I had a decent job at the *Banner*; $10,000 a year felt like high cotton after my meagerly paid stint at the *Alabama Journal,* the afternoon paper in Montgomery where I'd had my first job after college. The *Banner* had been purchased by the Gannett publishing company, a fact that—in my opinion at the time, at least—gave the paper a modern, up-and-coming vibe, something the *Journal* lacked.

On the other hand, in Montgomery I'd been in the middle of an important developing story I had cracked at the paper—the wrongful police shooting of a young black man named Bernard Whitehurst and the subsequent cover-up of the shameful facts, a case that eventually led to the resignation of Montgomery's mayor and police chief, and, in later years, helped shift the city's attitudes on race. It was Pulitzer Prize material, "Alabama's Watergate," some called it. Maybe it had been a mistake to leave the story in its budding days, I was thinking that Sunday night.

The move to Nashville was for much more than a better-paying job. Was supposed to be, anyway. I was *going home.* Mom and Dad had retired to Nashville a year earlier. I had gone to high school there. Maggie had a good job there, too, teaching English in a private school.

We had begun our life as a family together in the same city. There'd be a wedding Mom could fuss over. There'd be children—grandchildren for the parents. I had set that future rolling by moving from Montgomery. And now that it was gaining momentum, I wasn't sure I wanted it at all. I had never been sure.

Chapter Two: The Bitch of Living

A new bike for Christmas, 1962

One summer morning in 1958, I kissed Luke McCoy. I was five years old.

I was stretched out on the living room rug eating peanut butter toast and thumbing through a copy of *National Geographic* (I liked the pictures) when farmer Luke grabbed my attention during a black-and-white rerun of an episode of *The Real McCoys*.

I shuffled on my knees to our console TV. There was a big close-up of Luke. I put my lips on his, my fingers outstretched on his broad shoulders on either side of the screen.

Just then my mother entered the living room to water the philodendrons.

"Michael!" she said, her voice sharp, filled with alarm.

I'd been so into Luke that she surprised and scared me. My little heart racing, I scooched away from the set, sat back on my open-toed sandals.

I knew she was angry by her firm strides to the TV, the way her hand moved quickly to turn it off, the staccato click of the clear plastic knob beneath her fingers. Most summer mornings, the TV stayed on while my older sisters got up and had their breakfast.

"Would you like to tell me what you were doing?" she asked.

"Just acting silly, Mama." Actually, I wasn't quite sure what I'd been doing. I just knew, at the tender age of five, that Richard Crenna, the actor who played Luke, was hot.

"Well, this isn't silly." She used the spout of the copper watering can to point to the smears I'd made on the dark TV screen. I must have had peanut butter on my fingers. "Daddy's not going to be happy when he comes home and sees our new television all smudged."

My tummy felt like it was full of wiggly tadpoles. I didn't like it when Mama sounded so cross.

She said, "Take your plate to the kitchen and bring me a dust cloth and the can of Windex from under the sink. Please."

I did as I was told, hoping that maybe the only reason my mother was mad was that I'd smudged the glass. Like a game of Let's Pretend. It felt better to think of it that way, to turn my thoughts from the other reason: Mama hadn't liked my kiss with Luke. I took the cloth and Windex to her, then picked up the *National Geographic*, closed the cover and set it on top of the other magazines on the lower shelf of the coffee table.

"Thank you, honey." She sprayed Windex from the metal can and wiped the glass. She sounded less angry now. But there was still something different about her voice. Something sad, disappointed, like when one of my sisters beat her at Parcheesi. "Why don't you take Scout outside? It's such a pretty day. Then you can get your crayons and color while I work on Mrs. Staunton's portrait."

"Okay." At the sound of her name, our beagle had roused herself from her bed by the upright piano at the other end of the living room. Tail wagging, she followed me through the kitchen and the screened porch to the back terrace, already warm in the morning sun.

Scout took off chasing something, a squirrel probably, in the blue-green recesses of the backyard, where hackberries, Osage orange trees and honeysuckle vine made an earth-scented adventure-land that stayed cool all day long.

"Luke?" I said, imagining his smiling Real McCoy presence beside me, taking his hand while we walked across the grass. "What would you like to do today?"

The tadpoles started wiggling again in my stomach. I wondered if Mama would tell Daddy that night what I'd been doing with Luke on the TV, or if she'd tell my sisters. Maybe she wouldn't tell anyone. Maybe she'd keep it our little secret.

* * *

Through my kindergarten and grade school years, we lived in Columbia, Tennessee, a small town about an hour's drive south of Nashville. I was six months old when we moved there from Buffalo, New York.

After WWII, when my chemical engineer dad's stint with the Manhattan Project was over, he had resumed his work with DuPont. In 1953, the company transferred us and other northern DuPont families to Columbia, where low taxes and cheap labor enticed the company to build a cellulose sponge plant on a bluff overlooking the Duck River, a muddy tributary of the Tennessee. Some of the northern transferees, with Lake Erie or the Hudson River or the Delaware their frames of reference for natural bodies of water, called it jokingly, "The Mighty Duck."

The town on the Mighty Duck was home to my family for over 10 years. There were five of us, including my parents and two sisters, nine and six years older than I. Maybe the female majority in my family influenced how I grew up. Theories abound on whether nature, nurture or a combination of both have an impact on one's sexual orientation. Speaking for myself, I have to say I was attracted to men before there'd been much time for the nurture side to get its hands on me.

It sounds funny now, but in addition to Richard Crenna, the TV ads for Brylcreem were a favorite of mine. The men in the ads were truly debonair, as the jingle for the hair cream went. They had an impeccable part as straight as the edge of a sheet of notebook paper in their dark hair. Women were flirting with them and touching them; I pictured something wild and forbidden happening once the ads were over. I wasn't sure what it would be exactly, but I knew the neat parts in that Brylcreemed hair wouldn't survive it.

Around the same time—I guess I was four or five—I went downtown with my mom one morning so she could buy paint at the Sherwin-Williams store off the square. While she made her choices, I sat outside on the stoop and watched the men walk by. I already had a rudimentary rating system—who was the best looking, who would I like to hold me, who unlike my dad was ugly or dirty or toothless or in some other way unacceptable, and yet, at the same time, deeply intriguing.

* * *

My best friend during those years was a red-haired, freckle-faced local boy named Terry, who lived within an easy bike ride of our house.

To this day, I can recite Terry's phone number. He and I loved to talk on the phone, even though we saw each other frequently during the week, riding our bikes together after school, having sleepovers at his house or mine. Some of my most vivid memories of Terry involve a heavy snowfall in Columbia when the schools were closed for days. One morning, Terry's mom made snow cream, an exotic treat that was a cross between a snow cone and a bowl of vanilla ice cream. I thought it was marvelous.

Another morning, he and I explored the snowy woods that bordered our neighborhood. Deep in those woods was a pond that gleamed in the winter sun. Ice crystals made lace across its surface. We ducked under a barbed wire fence to reach its edge.

"Do you think it's frozen enough to walk on?" I asked him.

"We can try," he answered.

One of us tapped the ice with one foot, then pushed. Hard as glass. Second foot. So far so good. In a few moments, both of us were inching forward on the ice. Did we consider prudently staying on the outer edges? Not once. The exhilaration was too much for us, sending us straight toward the middle of the pond. It's hard to judge distances in childhood memories, but I estimate the pond was between 25 and 50 yards across.

It was glorious, walking on what in the summertime was muddy and uninviting, transformed this day into a sparkling gem. We pretended we were the ice skaters we'd seen on ABC's *Wide World of Sports*, sliding and spinning on the ice.

It's a memory that horrifies me today. It hadn't been that long or cold a winter—not like the winters my Yankee mom and dad told me about. The pond was a good hike away from any of the houses in our neighborhood. There was no way anyone would have heard if one of us, or both, had fallen through. I suppose our footprints in the snow would have led a search team to the site of our demise, but hadn't more bad weather come that afternoon? We and our footprints might have vanished without a trace. Or the theory might have been that little Michael and Terry were kidnapped, though that kind of thing was practically unheard of in post-WWII Columbia.

Nonetheless, it was a magical morning with the blue sky overhead and my best pal by my side. Danger simply didn't enter our minds.

We went back to my house, had a contest to see who could make the better snow angel in the yard, then drank hot chocolate with marshmallows to celebrate our adventure. We must have had some inkling of the risk we had taken, though, because neither of us told our parents about our morning on the ice.

* * *

I was a ham in my grade school years, enthusiastically performing in skits at church and school. In a production of Phyllis McGinley's *The Plain Princess* at Theater Rondo, an in-the-round community theater in Columbia, I played a page who runs onstage in the first act and bangs a gong (a gas station road sign spray-painted gold and black) to announce the king's arrival. On opening night, an aristocratic elderly lady everyone called Miss Camille sat in her usual seat on the front row, dressed in her schoolmarm black dress with a white lace color, a little black hat and white gloves.

She seemed ancient to me. I was afraid if I struck the gong too loudly, the way I had rehearsed it, poor Miss Camille would have a heart attack. Her seat was right next to my gong. What to do? When it came time for my entrance, I hightailed it to the gong, heaved back my mallet to give it a mighty whack, then gently gave it a little tap. The audience loved it, including Miss Camille. I got a huge laugh.

From that point on, the theater bug was in my bloodstream and, especially in my 50s and 60s, I enjoyed letting it transform me once in a while.

There was a show at our school around the same time. Terry and I weren't in it, but we'd seen two girls in our class rehearse the duet dance number they were going to perform to "Ballin' the Jack." In his basement after school, pretending to make our stage entrances on either side of the family ping pong table, we'd walk through the dance steps the little girls rehearsed. Maybe we provided our own rehearsal track by singing, too. I loved those times. They were the best kind of afternoon play, in my book.

What I wasn't as fond of? Terry's older brother joined a boxing club and had an extra pair of gloves for Terry to use. He wanted to take turns sparring with Terry and me. I hadn't a clue about boxing, and I doubted my father—an expert tennis player and ice skater and decent weekend golfer—would be any help, but what did it matter? Boxing wasn't something I wanted to learn. It seemed senseless to me. Why would anyone want to do that, punch somebody with a padded glove? Terry, I was dismayed to see, seemed to enjoy it and was pretty good at it.

On my next sleepover at Terry's house, the gloves came out again. I remember feeling that Terry's interest in boxing meant he was leaving me in some way, starting down a road that I didn't want to go down, or didn't belong on. It was an odd, discomfiting feeling. I wanted to go back to dancing to "Ballin' the Jack," but it appeared that was no longer in the cards for us.

* * *

DuPont moved families around a lot when I was a kid. I guess they still do. When I started 6th grade in 1963, the company sent my dad to Newburgh, New York, for a year to work on a new project—the launch of its Corfam imitation leather product. Come summer of 1964, we'd be moving from Columbia to Old Hickory, Tennessee, outside Nashville, where Corfam would be mass-produced at a larger plant there.

1963 was an off-kilter year for me. I guess it was for everyone. It was the year JFK was assassinated. After the initial shock of that event, it seemed the whole country was shrouded in grief. But I had personal reasons, too. I missed my dad. I struggled with long division. And I didn't like the thought of leaving Columbia and my friends.

At the end of our sixth grade year, Terry and his parents threw a going-away party for me—a cookout.

After dinner, we gathered in the same basement where Terry and I had "balled the jack" and attempted boxing. There was cake and ice cream and dancing to the music of that long-haired new group from

England, the Beatles. Then Terry gave me a going-away gift—a white Sunbeam electric alarm clock.

"Something to remember us by," Terry's mother said.

"We're not going that far away," I replied, as if to reassure myself that the move wasn't such a big deal. But I knew when I plugged in the clock, the hands would start moving forward, quietly and efficiently toward moving day. A homesick feeling washed over me. And something else: fear. The thought of starting junior high in a whole new place terrified me.

That night, I danced my last dance with Teresa, a girl whose hand I had held during a hayride earlier in the school year. We had danced the twist together at a Christmas party at the Presnells' white-pillared mansion on the highway to Nashville. On Valentine's Day, I had made a card for her with red construction paper and candy hearts.

"I'm going to miss you," she said to me now, kissing my cheek with a light, bubble gum-scented smack.

"I'll miss you, too." I thought I meant it. Teresa was a pretty girl with dark hair, milky skin and a dusting of light brown freckles on her cheeks. We danced to "This Boy" with my arm around her waist, her hand on my shoulder. It was never an unpleasant experience, being close to her.

Still, I knew saying goodbye to her wasn't going to be all that difficult. But leaving Terry? That's what I dreaded most. How in the world was I going to say goodbye to my best friend?

* * *

A few days after the going-away party, Terry came to visit as we started packing the house for the move to Nashville. My room was still intact, so that's where we headed—up to my room.

Let me set the scene: Turquoise was considered avant-garde as a room color in the 1960s. All the walls in our house had been the traditional 1950s celadon green, but when Mom redecorated, the main rooms of the house were painted white. Gold carpet went down over the hardwoods in the living room and upstairs hallway. Pat got a pink room; Marsha an icy blue. Mom chose turquoise for me. I thought it was way out. (For a short time in the early '60s, *way out* meant groovy, cool, the bomb.)

My parents had friends who had also redecorated and had a double bed they wanted to get rid of. Mom and Dad had purchased it at a friendly rate. We had moved it in and set it up in my turquoise room in Columbia. The headboard was a blond wood bookcase with an open section in the middle and doors that slid open on either side. My mother called it—inaccurately, I think—a Hollywood-style bed. I didn't care if it was accurate or not—the name stuck with me. I had a Hollywood bed!

Behind the sliding bookcase doors was storage space for my expanding *Hardy Boys* collection, the paperbacks I got from Scholastic Books, the comics I liked—*Archie*, *Little Lulu*, *Casper the Friendly Ghost*—and a recent addition now that I was old enough: *Mad* magazine.

Terry and I had shared that bed on sleepovers at my house, but there had been nothing physical between us, except a little roughhousing with the pillows one morning while my mother cooked pancakes downstairs. Oh, and we did take turns scratching each other's backs one night, but it hadn't led anywhere.

On this summer afternoon in 1964, though, I wanted more.

Sitting side-by-side with Terry on the foot of my bed, we read one of my favorites—*Mad* magazine's comic book-style spoof of the recently released Hitchcock film, *The Birds.*

"Tipsy Headrinse!" Terry said. That was the magazine's name for the movie's lead actress, Tippi Hedren. One of the funniest drawings was of Tipsy in her mink coat, a big black crow smashing into her forehead as she rowed solo across Bodega Bay.

Terry laughed and laughed. It was the perfect opportunity. I put my arm around his shoulders, moved in and planted a big smacker on his lips.

He jerked away. The magazine fell to the floor.

"What are you doing?" Terry wiped his mouth with the back of his hand.

"I just wanted to—"

"Wanted to what?"

He wiped his mouth again, made a "bleh" sound. My face went hot.

"Nothing," I said.

"It didn't feel like nothing."

"Haven't you ever thought about it?"

"No, I haven't thought about it." He shuddered. "It's wrong. I can't believe—that you're like that." He stood, a look of unwavering certainty in his clear green eyes.

"I'm not like that." Afraid someone might hear us downstairs, I softened my voice. "I'm going to miss you, that's all."

"Miss me?" He said it as if I'd given a new, horrible meaning to those words. "I better go."

"You're not going to tell?"

We were opposites now. I was nearly whispering. He spoke louder than he had when all this started, sure of himself, unsure of me. "Why would I want anybody to know?"

He kicked the magazine out of his way. It landed by my rubber tree plant, pages scattered along the baseboard. He was out the door and gone.

I wasn't sure if I was going to cry or throw up. I just sat there on the bed, swallowing the saliva that welled in my mouth. That happened sometimes when I was sick to my stomach, but the feeling passed after a few moments, leaving only a sense that doomsday had arrived, thanks to me. The bomb had dropped. How could I have ruined everything so quickly?

I stood, my cheeks throbbing. No one had ever slapped me, but I imagined this was how it felt.

I picked up the magazine. The cover was torn. Several pages with Tipsy Headrinse on them had come loose from the stapled binding. I put it back together as best I could and hid it at the bottom of the stack in the headboard cubbyhole. Then I straightened the bedspread at the foot of the bed. Everything back in its proper place. As if nothing had happened.

But something had happened. I caught my reflection in the mirror over my dresser. Who was that boy? Why had he done that? How could he have been so stupid?

I think Terry's mother might have been downstairs with my mother. This might have been the day she came to our house with Terry to bid us goodbye before our move. If it was, I don't remember whether I went downstairs or stayed in my room while she and Terry departed. Surely, I went downstairs to say goodbye to her. To thank her again for the party and the alarm clock. It would have been rude not to. But my heart breaks a little when I think of my young self going through the motions with her, acting as if the world hadn't just come to a stop.

What I do know is this: It was an event whose trauma was too big for an 11-year-old boy to process all at once. I felt embarrassment, anger, shame.

"It's wrong," Terry had said. Something deep within me believed it was wrong, too. I'd seen it in the look on my mother's face the day I kissed Luke McCoy.

* * *

It was probably best we were moving. I wasn't sure I could face Terry again.

So, I didn't, not for a lot of years. After our move to Nashville, Mom and Dad let me invite other boys from Columbia to come up for an overnight visit. We'd ride the rides at the state fair or go ice skating at the Municipal Auditorium.

When my parents would return to Columbia occasionally, I'd visit other friends, but never Terry. As for the rest of the time, phone calls were out—it was long distance from Nashville to Columbia—but neither Terry nor I wrote to each other, not once through our junior high and high school years.

I don't know whether the sudden break puzzled my parents. If so, they never questioned me about it. They had other things on their minds, anyway. My sister Pat's diabetes was seriously out of control after our move to Nashville. Compared to her hospitalizations, the thrashing and bellowing of her nighttime seizures, the milder daytime episodes when the panicked scramble for orange juice brought everyday life to a halt, the loss of my best friend didn't seem worth mentioning.

He came to mind, though, every time I saw the clock on my bookcase headboard. Eventually, I tucked it away in a dresser drawer. I told Mom it was broken. I didn't need an alarm clock, anyway. Then my parents got a clock radio for their bedroom and gave me their old bedside clock as a hand-me-down. I put it in the exact spot where my going-away gift had been.

It was almost as if there had never been a Terry at all. But I knew better. I knew the feeling, a blue one around my heart, whenever I thought of him.

Chapter Three: Shy

My 10th-grade photo, pre-orthodontia, 1967-1968

I went through my junior high and high school years on the lower levels of the social hierarchy at my school in Nashville.

On the top were the football stars, cheerleaders and majorettes whose natural good looks contributed to their school success. Even the first chairs in the band, where I played second trumpet from the seventh through the 12th grades, mostly to avoid the agonizing experience of gym class, were good-looking, popular, active in the dating department. They managed to overcome the "band nerd" stereotype. I was not among them.

Senior year, I was nominated for "Most Dependable" in the election of class superlatives. It was a dubious honor, I thought. I was relieved when I didn't get it. With my photo in the yearbook along with the other superlatives, my high school loser-ship would have been preserved for all eternity. And I was puzzled why anyone would nominate me in the first place.

But then a friend from church told me she had done the deed because of my work on the prom the previous year. "You did such a great job," she said. "Everyone said so."

Actually, working on the prom was a project I enjoyed. At our school, it was the tradition for the junior class to decorate the gym as a sort of gift to the seniors before their graduation.

"Ebb Tide" was the theme that year. Yards and yards of cheesecloth were draped on wires strung wall to wall high above the bleachers on either side of the gym, the intended effect being that the dance floor was underwater. I volunteered to design, paint and help build the mural that would be erected as a backdrop for the queen and her court at one end of the gym.

My artist mom helped me sketch a prototype on paper and figure out the right balance and proportions, then I and another volunteer, a take-charge girl named Sandra who had an artistic flair, executed most of the painting on three big Masonite panels set up in her basement, where her father had a serious-looking workbench and power tools. He coordinated the construction of the two-by-four framework that supported the mural once we got the panels to the gym. He also had a serious-looking truck to help us with the transport.

The mural wasn't bad when assembled in its proper place. On a turquoise basecoat, we had painted underwater plants and boulders, orange and purple fish and an enormous, smiling sea turtle swooping in on the left-hand side of the piece.

With people posing in front of it, it looked as if the turtle were heading straight for them. I was afraid at first that it wouldn't work, that it would look silly having the turtle zooming toward the prom queen and her court. People did think it was funny, but funny in a good way.

The opinion of the prom's sponsor was the ultimate test. She was one of the most popular—and most outspoken—teachers we had. I had visions of her looking at our turtle and saying, "That's the dumbest thing I've ever seen." But it didn't happen that way.

"That's really cool," she said.

* * *

Then there was Miss Moore, another popular faculty member. Miss Moore was my Latin teacher. I studied the language from my freshman through my senior year in high school, with straight A's across the board. I liked it for several reasons.

First, my dad liked the idea that I had an interest in Latin. He had studied it and Greek at his high school in Buffalo.

Second, I loved reading and was discovering that I was good at writing, too. Latin helped me trace the origins of so many words we use in English. I figured it would help me be a better writer. (When I learned that *sinister* was the Latin word for *left* and a reflection of the world's bias against left-handed people, I was hooked.)

Third, I loved Miss Moore.

Today, students would call Miss Moore a rock star. With her auburn hair, porcelain complexion and delicately upturned nose, she was a striking young woman. She dressed to get noticed—a bright kelly green silk blouse tied with a big bow, a Chanel-style gray suit with a leopard-print scarf at the neck, furry ankle-high boots to match. Nothing shy about Miriam Moore.

She had a wicked sense of humor. She particularly relished the classic stories, the gorier the better. Prometheus getting his liver eaten by the eagle while he was nailed to the mountain in the Caucasus? Miss Moore described every detail. It seemed such a contrast to her elegant speech and demeanor. I loved it.

"Be that as it may," she would say to cut off a student's excuses for not completing an assignment on time. It was one of her favorite phrases.

"Mirabile dictu!" was another, the Latin for "wonderful to tell."

"Mirabile dictu! There is a new Chinese restaurant in Green Hills that you must try."

Or, "Mirabile dictu! Our fine principal has consented to letting us serve sparkling grape juice in plastic goblets for the Latin banquet this year."

She crooned the phrase, too, when I told her my parents had approved my going to the national Junior Classical League convention at the University of Arizona in Tucson in 1967, the summer after my freshman year.

"Mirabile dictu!" she said. "You will represent us well."

She said it again when I brought home a medal from Tucson for my recitation of one of Cicero's speeches, dressed in a thigh-length toga my mom had sewn for me. Mom had even stitched some trim with a Roman-looking design along the hemline. A pair of leather sandals completed my look—a young Jesus if he'd been cast as one of the Hullabaloo dancers on 1960s TV.

We went by bus—Latin students from my school and other high schools in Nashville, a few teachers as our chaperones. No parents accompanied us, which I feel certain would not be the case today. The two-week trip was a mix of new experiences for me. We saw New Orleans. The Grand Canyon. Our bus nearly floated away in a flash flood in the desert somewhere west of El Paso. All in all, it was a great adventure. I came home with gifts from our brief shopping stop in Juarez for everyone in my family, including a set of carved wooden bookends for my parents. I was proud of those. Mom and Dad seemed delighted with them.

The best experience of the trip? I made a new friend at the convention, a student from Tucson named Adam Patel. He had skin the color of coffee the way my mother liked it, with a splash of half and half. He had green eyes, dark eyebrows and lush eyelashes, an appealing pairing with his square jaw and solid body.

On the long bus ride home to Nashville from Tucson, I spent much of the time daydreaming about Adam, remembering the way he looked at me from the audience while I delivered my recitation that day, the way he applauded and gave me the OK sign when I finished.

I wondered if our group had stayed longer in Tucson, if there might have been a chance for Adam and me to be alone together, maybe to have a chance to touch. Something about the way he looked at me made it seem as if touching might have been possible, might have led to something far more pleasant than my disastrous attempt with Terry on the foot of my bed in Columbia. Mirabile dictu, indeed.

Maybe, I told myself. *Maybe*.

* * *

"She would have been a real beauty," I heard my parents and parents of Miss Moore's other students say, but I thought she was beautiful as she was. In fact, in an odd sort of way, the fact that she had had polio as a child made her even more beautiful to me.

Her mother brought her to school every morning, got her set up in an electric wheelchair with a wooden desktop across the metal armrests, where she spent the day in her classroom teaching Latin, German and, in later years, Russian. The dignity with which she held herself in that wheelchair impressed and inspired me. I was sad that the handicap prevented her from coming on the bus with us to Tucson.

I knew Miss Moore liked me. She called me "Mr. Coleman" sometimes in a half-teasing way that nevertheless made me feel honored. She was acknowledging my strength as one of her best students but cautioning me not to let it go to my head. There was a touch of irony in it. I also believe she noticed my "differentness" and made an extra effort to reach out to me. I like to think so, anyway. I felt a glow inside when I thought about her, when I realized she was my friend as well as my teacher.

When we studied the *Iliad,* when she mentioned a possible romance between Achilles and his comrade Patroclus, then went on to discuss the daring classical notion that male sexual relationships improved bravery and morale in the military, it was the first time I'd heard homosexuality mentioned without derision during my teen years. For that, I will always be grateful.

Miss Moore turned 28 while I was one of her students. She went on to become Dr. Moore, earning her doctorate in romance languages with a 4.0 average at Vanderbilt University, all while teaching high school week in and week out in an electric wheelchair. She continued her teaching career through the years and died at age 63 in 2005. I was pleased to read in her obituary that she had traveled extensively. Her mother, who looked so frail as she single-handedly got her daughter out of their big green Buick and into the school every morning, lived to 103.

I'd say she was a rock star, too.

* * *

I kept my humanities grades, at least, in the top tier. I qualified for AP English and AP History my senior year. Math was still my undoing, however, keeping me safely out of the realm of consideration for valedictorian.

It was a good thing. I had left my previous "ham" self, the one who loved performing, in Columbia. A Cicero recitation was one thing, but I would have been petrified to get up in front of all those students, parents and faculty to make a speech at graduation. That was a whole different ball game. The valedictorian was a role model, a leader, an example for everyone to follow. I was none of that.

It's difficult to say how much impact a bad childhood experience has as you approach adulthood, but I think it's a safe bet that Terry's rejection of me on my bed in Columbia dashed my confidence and self-esteem in my junior high and high school years. The ice had cracked under my feet that afternoon. I'd fallen into dark, icy water with no one around to give me a hand up. Terry had run from me. I had to pull myself out on my own.

Sometimes I wasn't sure I had. Sometimes it seemed as if I'd been exiled, forced to serve time away from my friends in Columbia because of what I'd tried to do with Terry. I knew these weren't the facts of the case, but it felt that way.

It wasn't just Terry's rejection that hurt. It was remembering what I dared to do. Along with playing second trumpet, declining Latin verbs and painting a mural for the prom, I had also learned the words *homosexual* and *queer*, and they did not have positive connotations.

I heard stories about a fellow named Vance, whose name was synonymous with queer at our school. He'd been caught providing oral sex to other male students in the boy's bathroom, was expelled and eventually institutionalized in Central State, a mental health hospital on the outskirts of Nashville. I couldn't imagine doing the things that Vance had done, but I worked to be sure I didn't communicate any body language to indicate I might. I knew my parents loved me but, sadly, I had no confidence that they wouldn't throw me in the looney bin, too, if they knew of my true leanings.

I had a few good friends in high school, guys from the band and from the youth group at the Presbyterian church we attended. Even though some of them had crush potential like Adam Patel, I kept my distance and held a stiff posture when we were together. I would never, ever, I told myself, lose another friend because I tried, or even was perceived as trying, to come on to him. I didn't want to be another Vance.

Still, as my high school years passed, I didn't forget my time with Adam in Tucson. A warm feeling uncurled inside me whenever I thought of him. I held that feeling tight within my secret self, like a candy Valentine heart in my pocket, small and sweet. That memory, not the medal from my Cicero oration, was the real treasure I brought home from Arizona.

* * *

In high school, I moved on from Mr. Brylcreem to the man in the Mennen Speed Stick deodorant ads. He was a well-built, 40ish, All-American guy posing as if he had just stepped out of the shower, a towel wrapped around his waist, another one draped over his shoulder. Something about the fact that the ad was in black and white when most magazines in the late 60s were saturated with color made it even more erotic to me. I couldn't take my eyes off it. I couldn't take my eyes off the latticework of hair on his chest.

Some Sunday mornings, I'd even feign a headache or a stomachache so I could stay home from church and have some alone time with Mr. Mennen. I could have disposed of the evidence more easily if I'd done it in the shower, but I wanted to have the image of Mr. Mennen in front of me while I whacked off. My emissions would usually end up in a T-shirt, but later I discovered they were better hidden in a sock. Even so, the sticky stuff dried as stiff as starch. I feel sure my mother encountered it when she did the weekly laundry, but she never mentioned it. I was grateful for that.

Maybe if I had been able to talk with someone about my feelings, it might have helped ease my anxiety, but that never happened. The closest Dad and I ever got to a sex talk was the time he told me about a health class in his Buffalo high school where the teacher showed the boys how to make a little hammock out of toilet paper to keep the tips of their penises from touching the rim of the toilet seat when they sat down to go to the bathroom—thus to avoid the gonorrhea or other nasty disease that might be lurking there. He encouraged me to develop the same practice.

Weird, I know. Hilarious, in retrospect. And not at all the kind of thing I wanted to talk with my dad about. Or did I? If we did attempt a sex talk, would it have led to topics I didn't want him to know about? Ultimately, I was relieved that we avoided it.

Still, it puzzles me why my usually responsible father shrugged off the responsibility of having a talk with his only son about sex. It's too easy to blame it on '60s tight-lipped mores before the sexual revolution came to town, but I have no other answer. Our church did offer a sex education series when I was in the seventh or eighth grade. The girls went to one room and the boys another for what was considered at the time to be a progressive thing for a youth program at a Presbyterian church—a sex talk.

Maybe my dad figured that was enough to cover it, to spare him an embarrassing conversation with his son. In those classes, we received counsel on dating, girls' menstrual cycles, how pregnancy happens, and tips and more tips on creative ways to abstain from premarital sex.

Of course, feelings like mine were never mentioned. I remember sitting through those sessions feeling isolated and alone as the other guys in the room shared their feelings about the opposite sex.

I kept silent.

My sisters were away from home and in college during most of my high school years. I wondered sometimes if having an older brother might have helped. I still wonder today. He and I would lie back in our beds and talk about anything and everything, all through the night.

Such were the dreams of a teenage gay boy in the 1960s.

Senior year, I took a date to the prom, a girl named Sarah Jane who was a friend from the youth group at our church. Openly acknowledging that we were just friends made for an enjoyable, pressure-free evening. We danced. We laughed. And we smartly avoided an awkward kiss at her front door when the evening was over.

My dating experience my first year in college was also notably free of romantic sparks. I took several young women to campus movies, football and basketball games, but I did it mainly to assure my parents that their son had a social life. My heart just wasn't in it.

Where my heart really was? Well, I didn't tell Mom and Dad about that.

Chapter Four: Friendship

My photo of the marquee at the Broadway revival of Boys in the Band *in 2018. The play has long been a part of our story.*

The first time I saw Blake, the Mormon Tabernacle Choir sang.

Seriously, I can say without doubt that he was the best-looking guy I had ever seen when he appeared in my dorm room my first quarter at the University of Tennessee (UT) in Knoxville in 1970.

I hadn't been very imaginative when it came to choosing colleges. My sisters had gone to UT, so I figured it was okay for me. (My parents put up no argument. They were pleased with the in-state tuition rate.)

Whatever, Blake made me feel that my choice was the right one.

He was 6'1".

He had thick, unruly blond hair that refused to stay in place no matter how carefully he wet-combed a left-side part in it.

Smoky blue eyes.

A killer smile.

And a complexion that was a Renoir blend of creams, golds, pinks—and bronzes in the summer.

His nose kept him from being pretty. The story was that he'd broken it as a kid, so the bridge, while straight, was broad and flat. It gave him a sturdy, prizefighter's face. All the better, I thought. If his nose had been perfect, the world wouldn't have been able to handle it. I know I wouldn't have.

My roommate that year was from Rochester, New York. Blake was from Long Island. The two of them had hit it off at a fraternity rush party they attended one evening at the beginning of the first quarter of the school year. Blake lived in the same dorm as we did. I'm not sure why he stopped by our room that night. I think my roommate had offered to give him contact information for other students on campus from New York who got together for social events and, most important, ridesharing between school and home.

Whatever the reason, I looked up from my history textbook to see Adonis standing at the foot of my bed in all his Technicolor glory. That's when the choir sang, "Alleluia!"

My roommate introduced us. He wasn't a bad-looking guy, but next to Blake he was a little brown mouse.

"Where you from?" Blake asked. He definitely was not from Tennessee.

"Nashville," I said.

"Home of WSM."

I was surprised. WSM was the leading radio station in my hometown; it carried the Grand Ole Opry. "How do you know that?"

"My dad's in broadcasting. I'm following in his footsteps, majoring in it."

I closed the book and put down the pencil. "What brought you to UT?" I asked. I frankly didn't care if I was leaving my roommate out of the conversation.

But he did interject. "What brings any of us here?" he said, hanging his jacket in the built-in closet and sliding the door shut with a thump. "It's affordable. And there's some decent financial aid if you know where to look."

"With me, it's about more than being affordable," Blake said, pushing his fingers through the bushy hair on his left temple. "I knew

UT's reputation as a party school. So, I checked it out and found it had other things going for it. They've made serious investments in the school of communications. It's a good program, so I thought, 'Why not go somewhere different?'" He shrugged. "Besides, New York winters are a bitch. When I came down last February to look at the place, it was 60 degrees. I walked around in a polo shirt all day. So, what's your major?"

I was glad he'd pitched the conversation back to me. "I'm not sure yet. Maybe psych, but I'm a pretty good writer. English might be—"

"What about journalism?" That little grin. Those eyes. There was something playful in them, as if he and I were the only two in the room. In the world, for that matter. *Why?* I wondered. *Why would this guy be interested in me?* My pulse drummed happily in my ears.

"I hadn't thought about it, but sure. I'm open."

"I'd be glad to take you to the communications college sometime. You could find out about the requirements."

"Okay," I said, and melted inside.

Say what you will about the folly of young lust, but having Blake guide me to the communications college the next day led me to a journalism major and a writing career that kept food on my table and a roof over my head for over 45 years. If not for him, I imagine myself living in a box under a bridge somewhere, with a master's in English. (I'm being facetious, but I do credit Blake for opening the door to a career I was ideally suited for—before I'd even considered it.)

* * *

Blake and I were taking classes together in the communications school the following quarter. I was on Cloud Nine. Even if nothing physical was happening between us, we were together so often that people suspected it was. With Blake, I didn't care what people thought. And frankly, I was so thrilled that this beautiful, articulate, New York-accented specimen wanted me as his friend that it was all I needed. I was happy simply sharing his golden aura.

But I hoped for more. And kept track of the signs that there might be.

With his deep, radio announcer's voice and confident stride, Blake had an effortless, polished masculinity. If the word *metrosexual* had been around in 1970, I don't think it would have quite fit him—he wasn't fussy, but he did have a certain urbanity that set him apart. Just when I'd convince myself that such sophistication didn't necessarily imply homosexuality, or at least a broader sexual horizon than the other guys I knew, along would come something that did.

He was the only guy I knew who was fascinated by Mart Crowley's *The Boys in the Band,* the daring play about a group of gay men in New York. A friend of his back home had given him a paperback copy of the play after its 1968 off-Broadway opening. Blake loved its bitchy humor. I wasn't sure how I felt about it, but I liked the lines when he quoted them. "Give me Librium or give me meth," he'd say, kicking off his cordovan weejuns and hitting the books for a big exam the following day.

He even organized a group of us guys to go see a campus production of the play. Like me, he was intrigued by the audience members at the performance we attended: students there for class credit, sure, but older guys we assumed were townies, some of them pretty effeminate looking, some not so much, some who could not take their eyes off Blake.

"Stay out of the men's room," he jokingly warned us before the play began, yet he was the first to go there at intermission. "I have to take a wicked piss," he said, adding, "They don't scare me."

Young women on campus and their admiring glances didn't scare him, either, though I didn't think he pursued the opportunities as avidly as he could have. His activities with little sisters from his fraternity and other members of the opposite sex seemed to spike after one of his phone calls with his father, who had been known to inquire if Blake was "getting some of that fine southern pussy" in Tennessee. I was grateful my father never asked questions like that. I had also noticed Blake's attraction to a good-looking suitemate we had one quarter, a fellow bound for medical school in Memphis. "That is one good-looking guy," Blake would say, and I'd feel a pinprick of jealousy. Still, I knew Blake and I had something solid, unshakeable—a bond we let no one else share. For a while there, we were an "us."

When we'd go to a movie, he'd insist on keeping an empty seat between us, but on Sunday nights when he'd attend the guitar mass at the John XXIII Catholic student center on campus, I'd go with him and we'd sit knee to knee. I liked the music, so different from the stodgy hymns at the Presbyterian church back home. But I liked sitting next to Blake even more. He always asked if I wanted to go with him. He generally didn't invite anyone else. Sunday evenings were ours.

Smoking Kent cigarettes (Blake's brand), we'd go for long walks after an evening of studying or when he'd return from a date, taking the same route no matter how cold it was, all the way across campus to Neyland Stadium and back, sometimes ending up side by side in his used red Mustang with the white racing stripe in the student parking lot near our dorm. I guess we weren't ready for sleep or were waiting for our roommates to zonk out so we wouldn't have to deal with them when we got back to our rooms. He never made a move on me. Maybe he was waiting to see if I would do something first. Whatever, nothing happened on those tattered bucket seats.

And just as he was the essence of the campus jock coming back to the dorm sweaty from a run on the track or a match with me on the tennis courts, Blake was donning a salmon-pink robe to wear to the weekly Tuesday-night viewing of *Marcus Welby, M.D.* Most all the guys in the dorm gathered in the TV room off the lobby to see the latest adventures of Dr. Marc. Granted, some wore pajamas and drab plaid bathrobes from Penney's or Sears to watch the show, but only Blake wore pink.

* * *

When freshman year ended, Blake went home to New York. I went home to Nashville. We planned to room together the following year.

I missed him that summer like crazy. We were a good match. I helped him with his English papers, including one on *The Great Gatsby* that he aced. He helped me with the horrid algebra course I had to take. We drank beer and smoked an occasional joint together. And we talked of a plan to drive to Florida for spring break the following year. He had a friend in school at Stetson in DeLand.

I missed his voice. I missed his asking, "A walk tonight, Mickey?" It was another reference to *The Boys in the Band,* whose lead character, Michael, states emphatically how anyone named Michael deplores the nickname. I didn't care for it either, but I put up with it because it was Blake. And I took to calling him Blakey occasionally as a kind of gentle retaliation.

I missed him so much that I spent part of my savings on a bottle of the pricey cologne he wore—Agua Brava, a cedar-like scent that made me feel as if I were standing next to a Christmas tree whenever he wore it. I kept it in my dresser at home and put a drop on my pillowcase a couple nights a week before bed. "You had it bad!" you say? I did. I bought a copy of his favorite album, *The Greatest Hits of Sergio Mendes and Brazil '66*, and played it at bedtime, too.

There were other things besides Blake on my mind that summer. I'd taken lifesaving and water safety instructor courses at UT my freshman year and got a job as a lifeguard and swim teacher at the Old Hickory Country Club outside Nashville.

Songs from Carole King's *Tapestry* album usually played from the jukebox over the loudspeaker system during those summer days at the club. But on August 5th, the day of the Vietnam War draft lottery for men born in 1952, the radio was tuned to the news.

Fortunately for me, the news was good on that long, agonizing day. My number was 348—well in the safety zone, since that year they only called men whose numbers were 95 and below. Blake got a high number, too. I knew his birthdate, of course.

The next day, I bought a touristy Music City postcard at the drugstore and wrote on the back of it, "I'm glad we'll live to be roomies next year!" I mailed it to him and said a silent thank you that I'd have the real Mr. Agua Brava in my room in the fall, not just a pillow that smelled like him.

* * *

I suppose there's nothing new about my Blake story. Crushes happen all the time. One might ask today why I didn't come out and tell Blake how I felt about him. The answer is easy. I liked his friendship. I didn't want to risk it or live through another scene like the one with Terry in my turquoise bedroom in Columbia. Anything but that.

Even a question I might ask like "Have you ever done anything with another guy?"—brought up casually during one of our late-night talks—seemed forbidden to me. Expressing my curiosity would have been tantamount to admission, as I saw it. I was nowhere near ready to accept "this gay thing" about myself.

Then there were our friends on our floor of the dorm. I was "one of the guys," which I considered a significant achievement for someone with a deep-down difference like mine. I'm passing, I told myself. Good for me.

Yet there might have been a crack or two in my veneer.

One Saturday night when Blake had gone to nearby Gatlinburg for a weekend in the Smoky Mountains with a blonde Kappa Delta from one of his classes, I blacked out on the floor of our dorm room in a puddle of pink puke after downing a bottle of Cold Duck, my drink of choice at the time. Our friends picked me up, cleaned me off, wiped up the mess on the floor with a bath towel from my dirty clothes basket, and tucked me into bed.

These guys were from small towns in Tennessee and Alabama. One had been a high school football star. Another had lettered in track and field. The third was a minister's son. I think it's accurate to say that all of them were straight. They had been engaging in the usual post-mortem in someone's room after returning from their own dates that evening when one of them inquired, "Where's Coleman?" After instigating a search and finding me sprawled on the floor of the room Blake and I shared, they sprang into action.

"Are you okay?" one of them asked gently. "What's the deal?"

Another one answered for me. "Blake's out again. With Kelly. They went to Gatlinburg for the weekend."

"Fucking Kelly," I said through the alcohol fog.

Hoots and laughter followed.

"I think he is, Mike," one of them said.

"Shhh. Don't rub it in," another answered.

They knew the source of my pain that night, though they didn't name it, at least not to me. They knew Blake's charm. They knew I had succumbed to it.

I felt awful the next day. Knowing that the guys had found me out, that I had revealed my feelings for Blake so… colorfully, shall we say, made the hangover even worse. But it didn't seem to matter to them. Things went on much as before. Sometimes that's the best thing you can do for someone who's done something off the charts: Go on as before.

Today, I look back at the experience and marvel at the things that were understood and not spoken of among us guys, especially in the early '70s at a state university in the South. They knew and still cared about me, still spoke to me the following day as if nothing had changed. It might have even been said that they liked me—no matter what they thought about my feelings for Blake. That was friendship. That was hope.

Cold Duck hangover and all, it's a memory that holds a special place in my heart in 2020.

* * *

DuPont had transferred my dad and mom again, this time from Nashville to a small Mississippi River town in Iowa, where the company had a Lucite paint plant. Iowa was too far away for me to go home for Thanksgiving. Blake wasn't going home, either. We were invited to Thanksgiving dinner with my cousin's family in Gatlinburg, where my dad's wavy-haired, imposing nephew, Dick, was pastor at the Lutheran church. My sister Pat, who was on a school project nearby, came, too.

It was good to see Pat. The middle child in our family, she and I were closer than I was with Marsha, who had gone to college while I was in grade school in Columbia. But then, I'd always felt closer to Pat. Hers was the bed I'd climb into while we watched the interminable hours pass until it was time to get up on Christmas morning to see what Santa had brought. On this Thanksgiving, I was eager to show off my new friend Blake.

"He's so good-looking!" Pat said. Blake had gone back to our room to get a wool scarf. It was a raw, gray day in Knoxville.

"Isn't he?" would have been my first response, followed by, "Hands off. He's mine." What I chose to say, however, was simply, "He's a lady-killer."

"He could slay me."

Once we were in the Mustang and on our way to Gatlinburg, about an hour away, I told Blake a little about our cousin and his family.

"They've invited a neighbor lady," I said.

"Groovy."

"She's a big donor to the church, so be nice."

"Have you ever known me to be otherwise?"

My cousin Dick had built a fire in the living room of the house in the hills above Gatlinburg, which in the early '70s was a sleepy resort town, most of its businesses locked and barred over Thanksgiving weekend. We gathered at 2:00 in the afternoon for the big meal. With Dick, his wife, Phyllis, their two young boys and the neighbor, we were eight around the table by the fireplace. Sleet tapped against the window while Dick said grace.

"I'm glad I don't have far to go to get home," the neighbor said.

"I'm glad we got food on the table before the power goes out," said Phyllis.

"New York only has rain today." Blake spooned mashed potatoes on his plate. I felt a rush of affection for him, for how easily he joined the conversation, how nicely he'd dressed for the meal with my family. He looked extra glorious in an open-collared white shirt and the sky-blue V-neck sweater that brought out the blue of his eyes. "Odd world we live in."

"Where do your folks live on Long Island?" Dick asked.

"The North Shore. Manhasset."

"Isn't that the Gold Coast? Great Gatsby territory?" Dick took a sip of the sweet red wine he had poured.

"It is. Ah, Gatsby." Blake gave a wicked grin. "He's one of my role models."

Dick laughed. "Do you… have a Daisy?"

"Not yet." Blake nodded toward me. "Although this guy here might be it. I don't know. I haven't seen him in a dress."

My heart froze. Maybe he was settling in a little too easily with my family. "Meet my friend Blake," I said, passing cranberry sauce to Phyllis, trying to act nonchalant. "He likes to say crazy things to make sure everyone is paying attention."

"Are you two…?" The neighbor wagged her finger between us.

The mantel clock ticked over the fireplace. I started to deny her suggestion—this was my family, after all—but Blake was one step ahead of me. "When I came to UT, I was this lonely guy from New York, a fish out of water," he said. "But your cousin here made me feel right at home. I've never felt so comfortable with… well, anyone." He leveled his eyes with mine for a moment, then turned to the neighbor. "If that makes us homosexuals, so be it."

Pat raised her eyebrows. My cheeks went hot. I was grateful the boys weren't paying attention. The younger one held up a piece of turkey skin to the other, who was busy making a design in the gravy on his plate.

"How refreshing," the neighbor said. "Two young men who care about each other. There's so much fighting in the news these days."

"Hear, hear," said Dick.

Blake raised his glass. "So, here's to my friend Michael. And thank you, Dick and Phyllis, for welcoming me into your lovely home."

In nearly 50 years of family and social dinner gatherings since that Thanksgiving in Gatlinburg, I've never seen anyone charm a table so quickly, so completely. Blake was devastating. He'd said the word *homosexual,* and the house hadn't exploded. Even more impressive, he'd answered the question about us without really answering it. That was the story of our relationship, wasn't it, keeping everyone guessing, including my sister, including me? Proud of my friend, so different from the other guys I knew at school, I lifted my glass. He never ceased to make life interesting.

"Of course, the real reason I wanted to room with Mike is to have first dibs on those cookies his mom sends." Blake set down his glass. I was relieved he was bringing the conversation around to more comfortable territory.

"Auntie Boo's cowboy cookies?" Phyllis wiped one of the boys' hands with her napkin.

"Auntie Boo!" the other crowed.

My mom's name was Beulah. Dick and Phyllis' family called her Auntie Boo. This was the first Thanksgiving Pat and I had spent away from our parents. I felt a little homesick, but being with Blake was a fine substitute.

"What are cowboy cookies?" the neighbor asked.

"I can't eat them. I'm diabetic," Pat said.

"They're chocolate chip," I answered, "but Mom adds oatmeal so they're sturdier for shipping in a shoebox. I… we… get one every month or so."

"Oatmeal and walnuts. God's gift," said Blake.

"You can't visit again unless you bring some of those cookies." Phyllis folded the napkin and returned it to her lap.

"Now Phyl," Dick scolded. He looked at Blake and me. "You two can visit anytime you like." He paused. "You, too, Pat, of course."

* * *

The roads were icy, so we stayed over. Dick threw another log on the fire. Pat took the guest room, dashing the opportunity for Blake and me to sleep together in a double bed. Phyllis put sheets, a pillow and blanket on the living room sofa for Blake. Then she spread a sleeping bag by the hearth for me.

"You were great today," I said to Blake once we were settled in. "Everyone loves you."

"Even the neighbor lady?"

"You charmed her silly. She'll probably give a million bucks to the church. You realize, though, that you called us homosexuals, right there in front of God and a Lutheran pastor… and my sister."

He laughed his high-pitched little laugh. I knew what it meant. It meant he was delighted to have stirred things up. It meant he hadn't meant a thing. "Mickey, Mickey, Mickey," he said. "Kelly wants me to come to Memphis to visit her and her family at Christmas."

After helping clear the dishes from the table, Blake had asked Dick if he could call Kelly collect in Memphis, her hometown. Dick had insisted he not reverse the charges. "As long as you don't talk all afternoon," he teased.

"Do you think I should go?" Blake asked me.

"It's up to you," I said.

"It would be a good excuse not to spend the whole break with my parents. Things are a little tense up there these days."

"You need more of a reason than that, don't you? It's a big step, meeting her family."

"I guess so. She wants to meet you, by the way."

"You've told her about—?"

"Of course."

"I'd like to meet her, too." I propped my head on my hand. "Look, I'd have to talk to Mom and Dad about it, but I think you'd be more than welcome to come home to Iowa with me."

"That sounds good." I could hear him rubbing the hair on his stomach, the soft, whispery sound I had become so accustomed to when we talked late into the night, he in his bed on one side of the room, I in mine on the other. It meant he was thinking it over. "I think I'll go to Memphis, though. But thanks," he said.

Done and done. I'd been expecting, "I'll sleep on it," at least.

"Hey." He reached across the coffee table and grabbed my hand in an arm-wrestling grip. "Thanks for the great Thanksgiving. I love you, man."

"I love you, too."

So, there it was. *I love you.* Why did it feel like goodbye? Because I knew no matter how many times Blake quoted from *Boys in the Band,* no matter how many times he called us homosexual, there'd be no holding each other naked in front of a roaring fire the way I imagined Achilles and Patroclus closed out their evenings. Not tonight. Probably not ever. Still… it was something. Blake had said over our turkey dinner that he felt more comfortable with me than anyone else. I felt that way about him, too. I'd never told anyone I loved them before, not even my parents. Yes, that was *something*.

I released his grip, pinched his chin between my thumb and forefinger. His day's growth of beard, rusty in the firelight, felt rusty, too, but evenly so, like fine sandpaper, rough and smooth at the same time.

He gave a quick laugh. Just as quickly, I let go.

"Let's get some sleep now," I said. I turned over so my back was to him, punched the skimpy pillow with my fist, the feel of him lingering on my fingertips.

Chapter Five: A Boy Like That

Ted in Illinois, August 1960

In Nashville six years later, the smell of cigarette smoke and stale beer struck me as soon as I opened the door to the Other Side that Mother's Day evening in 1977. Not a surprise. I had been there before. I'd been to other gay bars, too. They pretty much all smelled alike in those days, when smoking and cheap beer were part of the package when you went looking for men.

Because it was Sunday and still early—the bars didn't get cranked up until 10 or so—there were empty stools on the long side of the L-shaped bar. I sat down and ordered a beer. I shouldn't be here, I thought. I didn't see anyone who interested me among the few other patrons, and it appeared they felt the same about me. Just as well. I decided to have my one beer and leave.

It didn't help when an older fellow with a bad dye job, shiny white dress shoes and a shirt with an alligator logo sat down a few seats away from me. He nodded at me. I nodded back. It only sharpened my urge to head home as soon as my beer was empty.

Then a guy closer to my age took a seat on the short side of the bar and gave me a smile. My spirits suddenly lifted. Where had he come from?

He had amazing, swimming-pool-blue eyes with dark eyelashes and eyebrows. He was husky, with broad shoulders, thick wrists. His bushy dark hair had a slightly wild look that was balanced by the sweetness of his smile, the dimpled cheeks. Often, smiles weren't that open at the Other Side. I'd seen some that were more like snarls expressing their owners' disinterest in me. Or maybe they were as nervous as I. But no… this guy was different. He didn't seem afraid to be here at all.

After he got his beer, he stood and approached the empty stool next to mine. Unlike me in the dress shirt and slacks I'd worn to church with my parents that morning, he was in jeans and a polo shirt with wide blue and white horizontal stripes. The buttons were open on the V-neck collar, revealing a hairless chest. An unbuttoned collar on a great-looking guy, hairy-chested or smooth, had always made me feel a little weak.

"Mind if I join you?"

"Sure," I said, happy he'd be blocking Mr. White Shoes' view.

He settled on the stool. "You look like you've had a long day."

"Yeah, Mother's Day, you know." There was a dark freckle slightly off-center on the bridge of his nose. Like a beauty mark. Made sense to me. He was beautiful.

"Sunday with Mom?" he asked.

"Sunday with Mom," I said, wiping sweat off the beer bottle. He had a clean, just-out-of-the-shower smell, not drenched in cologne like some guys I'd met here. I appreciated, too, the fact that he wasn't pressing his knee next to mine right after sitting down, the way some guys did.

"My mom's in South Carolina. I miss her."

"Is that where you're from?"

He nodded. "I'm in grad school here. Vanderbilt. Poli Sci."

That was a good sign, I thought, a promise of more interesting conversation than the last fellow I'd met here, a Levi's store manager who talked mostly about his pet chihuahuas.

"I'm Ted," he said, holding out his hand to me.

I shook it. "I'm Mike." His fingers were cold from the beer, his grip firm, unhurried, a playful light in his eyes. I was the first to let go.

"Do you… come here often?" I asked, wrapping my fingers around the neck of the beer bottle, as if returning to the safety of home plate. It was a trite question, but the best I could come up with at the moment. The handshake had thrown me a little. It was a clear indication he was interested in me. Or maybe just toying with me. A tease.

"Every once in a while. I was here a few weeks ago when the place got robbed."

"You're kidding." Anxiety churned in my stomach. What if something similar happened tonight? Or worse? I imagined gunfire, fatalities, my name on the list of those killed in tomorrow's paper.

He swallowed some beer. "I was dancing, and the next thing I knew the police were here, making us all lie down on the floor. It turned out the guy next to me was the robber. A cop held a gun to his neck while the rest of us cleared the building."

"That must have been pretty scary."

"I guess so. It all happened so fast."

White Shoes got up and walked toward the small crowd gathered around the pool table.

"He was lusting after you," Ted said.

"Thanks for, you know, sitting there," I said. "He was creeping me out."

"You're welcome," he said, smiling.

I relaxed a little. Nothing bad could happen in the light of that smile, could it? "I was in a bar in Montgomery, Alabama, a few years ago when the police came through." I told him about my one visit to a place called the Rainbow. It was the first time I had seen a black guy and a white guy dance together. "Montgomery's not exactly known as a beacon of equality. I sat there thinking, 'This is cool.' Anyway, at midnight the police came through with flashlights waving. They did it regularly, apparently. They checked IDs, shined their flashlights in people's faces. I knew the guy who checked me out. He was on the vice squad. I saw him a couple times a week at the Montgomery police station. I covered the police beat for the local paper."

"Did they do anything?"

"Just tried to intimidate everybody. I could tell the next day at the station everybody knew. They didn't say anything, but I could sense raised eyebrows, whispers behind my back."

"Those must have been the closet cases."

"Probably so." I laughed. With my thumbnail, I gouged a vertical line through the soggy label on the beer bottle. "I'm glad to be away from there."

"So, you're a reporter?" Ted asked.

"I work for the *Banner* now."

"I read the *Tennessean*."

"Doesn't everyone?" It was common knowledge the *Banner* was the second-string paper in town.

He laughed. "The *Banner* looks better. Not as gray."

"Thanks." It was nice of him to compliment the paper.

"What kind of stories do you write?"

"A little bit of everything. I covered the Melisha Gibson case."

He grimaced. "That was horrible."

"I know." A four-year-old girl had been beaten and tortured to death by her mother and stepfather, Wanda and Ronald Maddux. Child abuse was nothing new, of course, but the circumstances of the case and the method by which the abuse was carried out made it an international story. The Madduxes had been convicted of second degree murder after a highly publicized trial earlier in the year in Athens, Tennessee. "There were reporters there from all over. It was—"

"A circus?"

"You could call it that." What I'd wanted to say was that, even with the awful subject matter, covering a story that garnered so much attention had been heady and exciting. I'd won commendation from Gannett for my work and more high fives in the newsroom than I could count.

Donna Summer's "Love to Love You Baby" started playing. A couple took to the dance floor. "Party's getting started," Ted said.

"It's not a party without Donna."

The music was loud. He leaned closer. Now the knee touched mine. I felt a stirring in my groin, pressed my knee a little tighter against his.

"So… are you out?"

"No… I have a girlfriend."

He nodded, as if it were an old familiar story.

"She knows. About this." I spread my hands to indicate not the room, specifically, but *the whole gay thing*. "Sort of. After graduation, she moved to Montgomery with me. I was going to put it all behind me. I didn't. She moved here. Now I'm trying to put it all behind me again."

"I've been there. I came out to my family a year ago, and—"

The bartender pointed at our nearly empty bottles.

Ted looked at me. "Do you want another one?"

I took a chance, stepped out on the ice. "Would you like to have one at my place? Where it's quieter?"

The ice didn't crack. He smiled. "Sure."

* * *

It was always a risk, doing things like this, taking someone home, or going with someone to their "place." I'd read *Looking for Mr. Goodbar,* Judith Rossner's novel based on the true story of a New York City schoolteacher who spent her nights cruising bars and ended up murdered. Practically everyone had read the book in those days. And though I felt comfortable with Ted, it touched me that he showed me his Vanderbilt student ID in the light from the open door of my Toyota before we got in our cars.

"Just so you know I'm not an ax murderer," he said.

"Thank you. And I'm not an undercover cop." I pointed to the two-way radio the *Banner* had installed under my dashboard. "All the reporters get these. So be careful. I can call for help at any time." *Like I'd use it for that,* I thought.

He laughed. "I'll follow you."

I'd heard those three words or spoken them myself a few times over the past year; they held an erotic connotation for me. They meant the green light had been given. They meant *this is really going to happen.* But with this guy, they seemed even more promising somehow. I liked him, and the realization set off a warning in my head.

This is just for tonight, I said to myself as I pulled the Toyota to the parking lot's exit, then waited for the headlights of his car to appear in my rearview mirror. *Just tonight.*

* * *

My calico cat greeted us when we entered my apartment.

"She's beautiful." Ted stroked her back as she wove around his brown loafers.

"She's my buddy," I said from the kitchen. There were four beers in the refrigerator. I took out two of them.

"What's her name?"

"Copy."

"Perfect name for a reporter's cat. You live alone?"

"Just the two of us." I handed him a beer.

"I have a kitty, too. Olivia. We call her the Big O. She's a hoot." He looked at one of the unfinished chairs around the small table in the dining room. "Your next do-it-yourself project?"

"I might tackle them tomorrow. I've got the day off. I need to buy a smaller brush, though, to get between the slats."

"They are tight. I might have one you can use."

"Okay," I said, flattered by his suggestion that our acquaintance might extend beyond tonight, apprehensive about it, too. *Just tonight*, I told myself again.

"You're a reader, I see." He stepped over to the bookshelf, my makeshift assembly of concrete blocks and unfinished shelving. "Dos Passos." He pulled out my paperback copy of *U.S.A.* "I've always wanted to read this. He was a journalist like you, wasn't he?"

I liked his putting me in the company of John Dos Passos. "He was. His writing is so… clean. Uncluttered. It's a great trilogy." I paused. I was obligated to repay his kindness about the paintbrush, wasn't I? "You can borrow it if you like."

"Thanks." He set it on the coffee table. "So I don't forget it."

What am I getting into here? I wondered. Brushes and books. Ties and entanglements.

"This your girlfriend?" He eyed the acrylic photo cube on the bookcase, the picture of Maggie and me in a tango pose, facing the camera cheek-to-cheek.

"It is."

"She looks like Ali MacGraw."

"Lots of people say that. I'm a lucky guy, they say."

"Where does she live?"

"Across town. She has an apartment with a high school friend." Enough about Maggie, I thought. "Have a seat. And for the record, this lovely early American sofa and chair aren't mine. They came with the apartment."

"I'm happy to know that."

"My mom says the upholstery is a bilious green."

"That's perfect." He laughed and sat down in the chair, his knees spread wide. "What about the bookcase? Was it here?"

"No, that's mine, I confess. I had to have something."

"I think I'd tell people it came with the apartment, too." There was that playful look again, as if there were no other way to feel about cinder block bookshelves.

"Maybe I'll stain the shelves while I'm at it tomorrow," I said. "It probably won't help. Do you like John Prine?"

"Sure."

I set my beer on one of the shelves, took Prine's first album from my small collection and put it on the turntable. The truth was I wasn't crazy about his music, at least not then. But if you had the slightest ambition to be a cool 20-something in Nashville in 1977, you had to say you liked John Prine. I set the volume low.

"This is an interesting painting." He gestured toward the dark oil over the sofa.

"My mom did it back in the '60s for a church workshop. Gave it to me when I moved here. It's a collage. The big PEACE behind the homeless guy is the headline from the *Buffalo News* the day after we dropped the bomb on Hiroshima. See the subhead? It says, 'Our Bomb Clinched It.'"

He cocked his head. "Those were different times."

"I know, but—"

"The painting… the collage… doesn't celebrate it. The bomb, I mean. That's why I like it."

I was pleased we thought along the same lines. I was impressed, too, that he pulled a coaster from the set my mom had given me and put it under his beer, even though the battered coffee table hardly needed protection.

"Did your parents live in Buffalo?" he asked.

"I was born there."

"I'm a Yankee, too. Muskegon, Michigan. My parents moved south when I was a kid."

"We have similar stories. Mine did, too."

Copy jumped in my lap and curled up as soon as I sat on the sofa.

"She loves you. How old is she?"

"Next month it will be three years since I got her from the shelter. She was just a kitten."

"The shelter here?"

"In Montgomery." I rubbed Copy's silky head. "When I moved

there after graduation, I didn't have a car yet, but I met a girl who had one. She lived at the YWCA down the street from my apartment."

"Uh-huh," Ted said suspiciously.

"She was just a friend. They had an indoor pool at the Y. I used to swim there a couple times a week. Anyway, she insisted that a single guy living alone should have a cat. So, she drove me to the shelter. When I went to the cage where all the kittens were, Copy ran up to the wire and looked at me with her big green eyes like, 'Where have you been? I've been waiting all this time!' She cost three dollars. Best three dollars I ever spent, wasn't it, Cop?"

"Aw." Ted reached over and scratched Copy's ears. "Her purr is so loud!" He leaned back in the chair, shaped an imaginary frame with his hands. "That's a good picture—a boy and his cat."

"A cat and her boy, more like it." The beer was cheap but cold and tasted good. "Was it hard coming out to your family?"

"My mom and dad were upset at first. They're adjusting."

"Do you have any brothers?"

He looked taken aback. "Why do you ask? Because my last name is Brothers?"

I'd seen the name on his ID. "No… I was wondering if it made coming out easier, knowing there were others to carry on the family name."

This seemed like a strange concept to him. "Not really. I have one brother, yes. He's not married, but he probably will be one day. My dad has five brothers and some of them have sons, so I'd say the Brothers family name is safe for another generation or two. And my sister has twin boys, so my parents have their grandchildren." He looked at me. "Is this the reason for the girlfriend? You feel obligated to carry on your family name?"

"It's one of them."

"Isn't that kind of… archaic?"

"Maybe to some, but to me… I don't know. I'm the only male in this generation of Colemans. It's all on me."

"Do you have sisters?"

"Two."

He raised one finger in the air, as if to say, *Eureka!* "When they marry, they can have hyphenated last names. There'd be dozens of little half-Colemans running around."

I laughed. I liked that he was funny. "I guess it is kind of ridiculous, isn't it?" I said, though I wasn't sure I fully agreed.

"I don't mean to make light of your situation. I had a laundry list of reasons why I shouldn't come out to my family… and the woman I was engaged to."

"You were engaged?" I asked.

He nodded. "Her name was Lynn. I realized all my reasons were excuses. I was doing what other people expected of me. Or what I thought other people expected of me. It was time to be true to myself."

"Regardless of how many people you hurt in the process?"

"You can be grim about it. Or you can view it as an opportunity."

"I guess so." I turned the can of beer on my knee, glanced at the bookcase, the photo of Maggie and me. Next to it stood the sturdy hardbound copy of Alexander Solzhenitsyn's *Gulag Archipelago*, the one Maggie's parents had given me for my birthday. Photos. Books. Paintings. Coasters. I am surrounded by family love and kindness, I thought. Yet here I am, with a Sunday night trick.

Ted slapped his thighs. "Okay," he said, standing. He sounded final, as if he'd made up his mind about me, as if he'd had enough.

"See. I don't blame you."

"For what?"

"For leaving. That's what you're doing, isn't it? I could see it once I asked about your family. You're probably going to tell your friends how you went out to get laid and ended up with this closet case—"

"I didn't come here just to get laid." He took my face in his hands. "And I'm not leaving. I'm going to kiss you. You look like you need to be kissed."

He tasted faintly of cigarettes, which surprised me. He hadn't smoked at the bar. Maybe he'd had a cigarette in his car on the drive here. I didn't mind. I thought it was sexy.

He sat next to me on the sofa, one hand on my knee. Copy jumped to the floor, then up to the chair where Ted had been sitting. She likes him, I thought.

"You have so much pain on your face," he said softly.

"It shows?"

"I want to kiss it away." He kissed my forehead, both cheeks.

They were light kisses. They tickled. I grinned.

"There's that smile. The smile you get when you talk about Copy."

"I tell her everything. She hasn't walked out on me yet."

"You can tell me everything. I want to hear all of it."

I put my hands around his neck, buried my fingers in the tangled hair on the back of his head. John Prine was singing his song called "Paradise." He was sounding better right along.

"This feels so good," I said.

I rested my forehead against his. I took a long breath and exhaled slowly. It felt like the first time I had breathed all day.

Chapter Six: The Road You Didn't Take

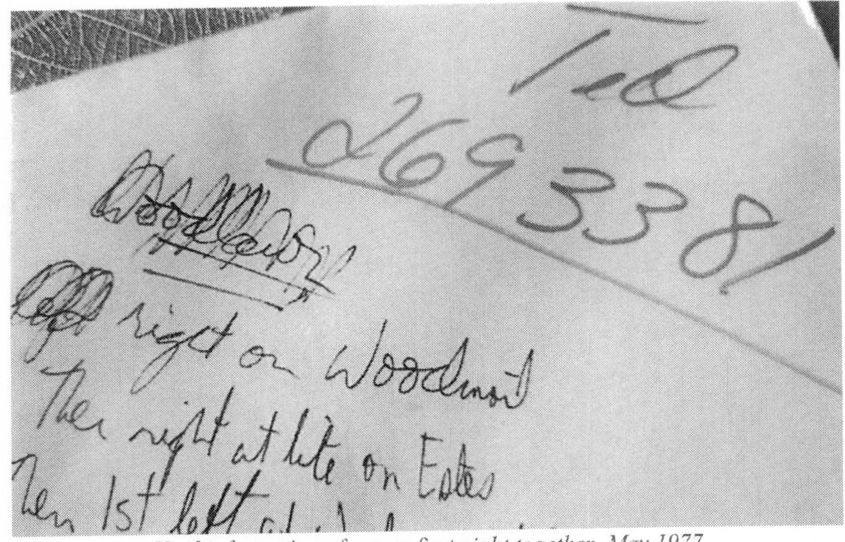

Vital information after our first night together, May 1977

The next day, I didn't call Ted as I'd promised—a fact he still rubs in my face to this very day. I needed time to think. Although the precision with which I had written down his contact information makes me laugh. It certainly reveals an enthusiasm Ted needn't have questioned.

I spent a usual day off doing laundry, going to the grocery, pretending the night before and the morning—when I woke up to the light of those blue eyes—hadn't happened. Yet I had made sure he took the copy of the Dos Passos book on his way out that morning. And I didn't stain the chairs because I was counting on a brush from Ted. Ties and entanglements. There was no denying I wanted some with him. The question was where to put them. How would they fit into my life?

I talked with Maggie and arranged dinner with her the following night, Tuesday. That was our routine. Dinner together one night during the week, weekends together at either her apartment or mine. The arrangement was my choice, not hers. As I'd told Ted, she shared an apartment with a high school friend in a suburb on the other side of Nashville. I told her I needed to live closer to town in case the newspaper needed me. It was a flimsy excuse, getting flimsier. I needed to make a choice, and soon.

At work the next day, I wanted to call Ted. But in an open newsroom with my editor and two other state desk reporters just beyond arm's reach around me, I didn't have the guts to phone him and risk conveying a different sort of emotion than two guys typically convey over the phone. In short, I was afraid my lust would show.

So, I waited until lunchtime and called him from the payphone in the downstairs lobby, the employee entrance to the building. There was generally a security guard there, but fortunately, he was away from his desk.

I put a dime in the slot and dialed Ted's number. He had written it on an envelope at my place. I'd carried it in my pocket all morning.

"Hello?"

"Ted, it's Mike."

"How nice you got around to calling me." There was a definite jab in his voice.

"I'm sorry about that. I just got busy yesterday. Look, I've been thinking things over—"

"And?"

"And I couldn't find any reason not to see you again." I was trying to be funny, keep things light, but his silence worried me. Maybe the call was going to be a dead end. I tried a more direct approach. "Can we get together tonight?"

"Look, I don't want to cause you any trouble."

"Trouble is exactly what I want from you."

He laughed. "You're on. I'll fix us some dinner."

My heart fluttered in my chest. Something farther down was happy, too.

* * *

Later that afternoon, I drove to the red brick duplex on Woodmont Circle where Ted lived. It was only 5:00 p.m. That was one of the good things about working for an afternoon paper. You'd start work early in the morning and could clear out of the office by 3 o'clock or so.

Another thing I liked about it was that I got to catch a glimpse of Ted working in the yard. He had told me keeping up the lawn was part of the deal with the landlord to knock some dollars off the monthly rent.

In a white tank top and light blue shorts, he waved at me. His well-muscled thighs and calves tapered down to an old pair of Adidas, no socks. I thought he looked amazing. In the spring humidity, his dark hair was bushy, wild-looking. He looked like Mr. Brylcreem after the ladies got hold of him.

I parked in the driveway. He walked up to me smiling, a pair of hedge clippers in one hand.

"Need some help?" I asked.

"Look at you in your nice shirt and jeans. I wouldn't want to mess you up." The grin was wicked. "I'm done anyway. Come on in."

"I brought some wine."

"Great." I followed him into a sparsely furnished living room with bare wood floors, a table and chairs and a spool daybed functioning as a sofa by the window. "Why don't you open the wine while I jump in the shower?"

A chubby tortoise-shell cat greeted us.

"Meet the Big O," Ted said.

"Hi Big O," I said to her. Then to Ted, "She is… round." She was already rubbing up against my leg. "What a sweetie."

"She likes you." He gave me a quick, salty kiss. "I'll just be a flash."

I decided to wait to open the wine when Ted was out of the shower. I placed it in the refrigerator, where a cut-up chicken marinated in a bowl with barbecue sauce. Then the front screen door opened. A young man and woman came in. I stood at the threshold between the kitchen and living room.

"Hi," I said.

"Hi," said the fellow. "I'm Ted's roommate."

"I'm Mike. Ted's in the shower."

"Oh no!" The young woman pounded on the bathroom door. "Ted, my back teeth are floating. Can I please use the toilet? I'll be quick."

He laughed. "If you promise not to look."

"If you promise not to look at me!"

She entered the bathroom, slammed the door behind her.

"My girlfriend," the roommate said, rolling his eyes.

"Are you going to be with us for dinner?" I asked.

"No, we've got a thing to go to tonight. I need to change clothes and we're outta here."

I was happy to hear they wouldn't be joining us. He went to what I assumed was his room across from a bedroom I assumed was Ted's. He closed the door. I sat on the daybed and scratched Big O's head.

"Ted is a prince," the girlfriend said when she was finished in the bathroom. She introduced herself. "Are you the new boyfriend?"

Her openness threw me. "I'm not sure."

She laughed.

It was true. I wasn't sure. I liked the idea of being Ted's boyfriend, yet was intimidated by it, too. What would it mean if we were boyfriends? Some sort of regular thing? Was I ready for that?

What I was sure of was that I liked being here. A breeze through the front door felt cool and soft on my skin, and the spicy smell of Ted's soap or shampoo wafted in from the bathroom, giving me about the 50th hard-on I'd had that day. I had called Maggie after my phone call with Ted. Told her I thought I might be coming down with something and it would be best to cancel our dinner plans. I'd cut one tether. I was temporarily free again. That felt good, too.

"Ready!" In slacks and a dress shirt, the roommate emerged from the bedroom. He and his girlfriend made their goodbyes and off they went. Then the bathroom door opened.

"Coast clear?" Ted asked, his skin pink, a skimpy white towel around his waist.

"It is."

He came toward me. "It's so nice to see you in my living room."

Another kiss and the towel was off.

* * *

In college, I liked the silkiness of women. I understood the heterosexual male's appreciation of a nice pair of breasts. And the things that happened down below. The natural lubrication, so surprising at first to my exploring fingertips. So right. For a while there, I found myself agreeing with the sex book I'd read in high school that male and female bodies are designed to fit together, synchronized to function most expeditiously during intercourse.

But the programming left me wanting more. Feeling I was missing something.

I had long conceived of a male lover, dreamed of what it would be like with Terry. Adam Patel. Blake. The design of two men having sex might seem awkward to some. But I had discovered in my limited experience with other guys that it wasn't… not when the heart finds what it wants. When that happens, the body follows. The body explores, adapts. Unlike what I heard in the Presbyterian sex class when I was in junior high school, there is more than one way to have a good time. Spit is a natural lubricant. Other manufactured types are available at any drugstore in town.

My body's desires were clearer than ever with Ted that evening. It liked the touch of silky skin against mine, but accented by a leathery hand, sandpaper cheeks. Hairy limbs, calloused feet, a tight-muscled chest. Instead of the sweet taste of cherry lip gloss, saltiness, the metallic bitterness of come, like a penny on your tongue. The nose had its preferences, too. Not perfume any longer, not Maggie's Chanel No. 5, but the way Ted smelled when he greeted me in the yard that afternoon: new-mown grass, sun-warmed fabric softener on his T-shirt, sweat, the hint of the lawnmower's gas and oil on his fingertips, stinky work shoes on his feet. This was what the coming summer would smell like. Summer and life. I wanted all of it.

I wanted all of him.

* * *

After we dressed, I poured the wine. Ted had taken his contact lenses out—we were still wearing hard contacts in those days—and donned a pair of round gold wireframes that gave him an intellectual look.

"Carlo Rossi," he said, eyeing the label.

"Hope it's okay."

"It's fine. Dan drank so much of it I thought I should buy stock in the company."

I handed him a glass. "Who's Dan?"

"This guy I was seeing. An actor. He was in a musical at the Barn." The Barn was a dinner theater outside town. "He was weird. Fun but weird."

"Does he live in Nashville?"

"Philadelphia. He went home last month when the play closed."

I was relieved to hear that, though I wasn't sure if any other suitors waited in the wings for Ted. Was I feeling possessive over someone I hadn't even spent a day with? An inner voice cautioned me to slow down.

Ted clinked his glass against mine. "That was really nice. Thank you."

"Thank you," I said. "I liked drifting off to sleep like that afterward. With you next to me." What I started to add was, *I never feel that relaxed with her.* Or maybe the word was content.

"Me, too. Now, let me light the fire or it'll be midnight before we eat." He took a box of matches and a can of lighter fluid from the counter, went to the concrete porch off the kitchen, where he opened a bag of charcoal, poured it into a small grill and lit it. It was past 7 p.m. The sun was low, a pastel orange ball behind the hackberry trees that lined the backyard.

"Now to make the salad," he said, closing the screen door behind him.

"Could I help with anything?"

"Do you mind feeding Big O?" He took a head of romaine from the refrigerator. "We're late for her dinner time."

"Not at all." The cat scurried in as soon as she heard the rustle of the dry food bag. "She doesn't talk as much as Copy."

"She has a high little voice that she uses sometimes, when she has something important to say."

I filled her bowl and set it next to the water dish by the back door. She proceeded to chow down.

"Thank you," Ted said.

"You're welcome." I felt a rush of warmth inside me. Maybe it was the wine. Or maybe a moment of pure happiness. I'd enjoyed what Ted and I had done in the bedroom, but I liked being in the kitchen with him, too, sharing the chores with my lawn-mowing, intellectual new friend. Could I live a life doing this? *Maybe*, I thought. *Slow down. Slow down.*

With the romaine rinsed, Ted tore the leaves into bite-sized pieces on sheets of paper towel. "Could I ask you something?"

"Shoot." I leaned against the refrigerator.

"I'm not your first guy, am I?"

"You mean to have sex with?" I wondered what answer he was looking for, what might delight or repel him, if I said I'd been a virgin or had a stash of spicy, salacious tales from the time I was 12. I went for the truth, which lay somewhere in between. "There have been a few."

"I want specifics."

"I had a crush on my roommate sophomore year."

He rolled his eyes. "Everyone has a crush on their roommate sophomore year."

I laughed. I told him a little about Blake, how, despite my fervor, we had never made it in the sack together.

"That's the saddest thing I've ever heard," Ted said.

"I know." I felt a case of the Blakes creep in. I still missed him. I supposed I always would, no matter how many hot guys like Ted came along. The last I'd heard from Blake was the previous fall, just before I'd left Montgomery. He had called late one night to tell me he and Kelly had divorced. He was working for a radio station in Miami. And losing his hair, he had said. *You cannot sound so beaten down,* I had wanted to say to him. *You're my Blake. My Achilles.* Since that call, I'd considered there might be hope for the two of us getting together, then pushed the idea from my mind. It had become a reflex action after all this time. *Get over it. There will never be any future for you and Blake.*

"Tell me a happy gay sex story about you," Ted said, pulling me from my blue thoughts.

There was really only one, a fellow who, unlike Blake, opened his arms to me. "His name was Griff," I said. "We had a… sort of a thing at the end of my sophomore year. I stayed in Knoxville for summer school to get some courses out of the way because I was spending so much time on the school paper… and because of Griff."

"Ah, a summer romance." Ted's voice had a lilt to it. "Was this before Maggie?"

"It was. She and I didn't start dating till senior year." I decided to share more with Ted about Griff. I didn't want him to think my sex life had been a total desert. "Griff was Canadian. His family lived outside Toronto, near Niagara Falls. He was the polar opposite of Blake, kind of hippyish, with long brown hair and a mustache. I saw him playing Frisbee shirtless in the quad in front of the communications building one day and thought, 'Hmmm.' Then I met him at a meeting of gay and lesbian students on campus."

He raised his eyebrows. "You were that 'out' in college?"

"No way. I was covering the meeting for the paper. Griff was one of the organizers."

"Hiding behind the guise of fine journalism," Ted said. "I get it."

I laughed. "He and I talked after the meeting. He asked me back to his place for a drink or some coffee. I said no thanks. I was afraid someone at the paper might find out. He had described himself as 'proudly bisexual' at the meeting. But then he called me a few days later to thank me for the story I wrote. He invited me over again. That time I said yes. He was just so… I don't know… irresistible." I still had a soft spot in my heart for Griff. "Like you," I tossed out.

Ted grinned. "You were just cultivating sources."

"Right. No, I was more than ready for some physical contact with someone—anyone. Griff and I had some wine at his apartment, smoked a little grass. Then he looked at me and said, 'You know, I always consider it my patriotic duty to kiss a fellow Canadian.' I said, 'What's stopping you?' Things went on from there."

"Wait, you're Canadian?"

"My mom was born in Moose Jaw, Saskatchewan. So yeah, that makes me technically a Canadian citizen."

"What was she doing in Saskatchewan?"

"My grandfather was a manager at a flour mill there."

"Remind me to kiss your Canadian side after dinner. You are full of surprises." He turned back to the counter, chopped a tomato and celery on a wooden cutting board. "What happened to Mr. Frisbee?"

"He graduated and went back to Canada. He was two years older than me. We both knew he'd be leaving. There was never any talk of commitment between us. He was a nice guy, though." I laughed at a memory. "Griff came to our dorm room one day with a bouquet of primroses he'd picked on the walk from his apartment. Blake was there. I was at the library." I whistled. "Blake was not pleased."

"He was jealous?"

"I don't think so. Blake was very careful about his frat-man image. I don't think he wanted to be associated with somebody so… open."

"The flowers were sweet."

"Griff was sweet. And patient. Whenever we'd try something new in bed, he'd say, 'Is this okay? Is this okay? You're sure?'"

"So, I have Griff to thank for your finely-honed skills?" Ted put the salad ingredients in a blue ceramic bowl, then rinsed the knife and cutting board under the faucet.

"He's the one." It was either the wine or being with Ted, or both, but I was talking much more than usual. "Tell me one of your happy gay sex stories."

"How much time do you have?"

"That many, eh?" I felt a surge of something. Was it a protective impulse because I didn't like the thought of anyone else touching him? Or was there something else, too? Envy that he'd had more conquests? Jealousy? A feeling that I had been missing out?

"The first one that comes to mind is meeting you." A red dishtowel in his hands, he stepped closer and kissed me. Then he tossed the towel on the counter and slid his hands into the back pockets of my jeans. "Is this okay?"

"More than," I said. If I were a cat, I'd have purred.

* * *

Ted put Boz Scaggs on the stereo in the living room, lit a candle on the dinner table. Through the kitchen window, I could see a bright moon rising.

"You did a good job on the chicken," Ted said. He sliced into a drumstick.

"Thanks. Grilling was always my job at home. I like doing it."

As we ate, I told him about Marie, my German step-grandmother. A wonderful cook, she insisted food was best when cooked "mit love."

"Well, we've been 'mit love' all evening, I'd say," Ted said. "I like being with you."

"I like being with you, too."

Quickly, as if he didn't want the mood to get too serious, he said, "I've been meaning to ask if you knew a guy at UT named Bud Rose."

I set my fork down. *Bud Rose.* A name that followed me no matter where I went, it seemed. Even here. I swallowed. "What's your connection to Bud?"

Ted shrugged. "I just think he has a great name. But no… the last guy I was seeing worked with him at one of the banks downtown."

I knew through Maggie that Bud had taken a job in Nashville.

"Actually, more than seeing," Ted said. "Ryan lived with me here for a while. After he and his wife separated."

That was new information. Living with a married man. No doubt he was far more experienced in this scene than I was.

"I think Ryan had a crush on Bud. I never got the whole story."

I sat back in my chair. "This is really bizarre."

"How so? Did Bud bring you primroses, too?"

"No. He and Maggie…" I looked down at my plate, then met Ted's eyes. I'd had a feeling the evening had been going too well. Now came the black cloud. Bud Rose. My greatest shame. "Maggie left Bud for me," I said.

He drew his head back. "Wow. That is bizarre." The Boz Scaggs song ended on the stereo. We sat in silence for a few moments. I could tell Ted was reading the grim feelings pulsing through me. "I think we need some more wine."

I pushed my glass forward. Ted poured.

* * *

The wine gone, we got ice waters after dinner, took them out to the porch, where we sat on the edge, our feet on the grass. The moon was full and high.

"Bud and Maggie were an item since their early days at UT," I told Ted. I knew this wasn't going to be pleasant. But I liked Ted so much. Liked talking with him. I felt we were building trust with each other. I owed him the truth. The whole ugly story. "Bud was a business major. Maggie was in one of my writing classes. We hit it off. We were just friends at first, but then senior year, I thought, 'Why not? Maybe it's time to put the gay stuff away.'"

"Never a good idea," Ted said.

"I was so… stoked that she was attracted to me, Ted. I was editor of the paper that year, too. I felt like… I don't know, like I was putting a future together."

"A career and a wife?"

"Something like that." I felt the old guilt rise like a fist in my chest. I also felt a new distance between Ted and me, as if he thought I was an object of curiosity now that he knew about my history with Bud Rose.

He asked, "How did all this start? With you and Maggie, I mean. And Bud."

Living alone the past few years, I'd had lots of time to figure out how it started. And why. All the major turning points. But I'd never shared it with anyone. Now it appeared I had no choice.

"It's a long story," I said.

"Go ahead," he said. "I told you I want to hear everything."

I swallowed some water. *Here goes.*

* * *

The only place to start was the beginning. My beginning. Or my false start. Camp Sunup.

"My junior year, after Griff went back to Canada, I threw myself into my work at the student paper. I got one of the paid positions on the staff. It was pretty much my life that year—that and keeping my grades up."

"Where was Blake?"

"He'd moved into the frat house. I shared an apartment with some guys I wasn't crazy about, friends of a girlfriend from high school. Toward the end of the year, I looked for something different to do in the summer. My parents were in Iowa on the assignment DuPont gave Dad a few years before his retirement. I didn't want to spend the summer there, and I didn't want to stay in Knoxville like I had the summer before to carry on with Griff. So, I got a job with a YMCA camp on the coast of North Carolina."

"The YMCA? Did you pack your Bible?" he teased.

"There were plenty of Bibles there already. It was my summer to be a straight arrow."

"How did you get the job?"

"Every spring, the directors go around to colleges in the Southeast to hire instructors and counselors. They came to UT, placed ads in our paper about it. Camp Sunup is mainly a place where rich people send their boys to learn how to sail, but they have a big swim program, too. I interviewed and got a job as a lifeguard and swimming teacher, so off to the coast of North Carolina I went."

"Did you like it?"

"I loved it." I knew I couldn't put it into words for Ted now, but there had been something about the sharp scent of those sun-warmed pines towering over the cabins at Camp Sunup that made me happy. Inhaling that air as the summer mornings began, I'd felt clean, bright, fully alive.

"Any crushes on the other lifeguards or sailors?" Ted asked.

"One or two. But there was no hanky-panky at Camp Sunup, at least none that I knew about. Besides, after Griff, I thought maybe I was through with hanky-panky. The gay kind, at least. I was a junior counselor for the first six-week session. For the second six weeks when a new batch of kids came in, I got promoted to senior counselor. I had a cabin of a dozen 12-year-old boys assigned to me. I was their father, mother, big brother for six weeks. I led devotionals every night, or rap sessions where we'd talk about guy stuff. 'You're a fine role model for these boys,' the camp's crusty old director told me one afternoon. I was... proving something to myself, I guess."

"Proving what?"

I swatted a gnat away from my face. I wasn't sure I was ready to tell the next part to Ted, wasn't sure he was ready to hear it. I had never told it to anyone. "You probably didn't have the same experience, but I was kind of a... well... a sissy growing up. I never wanted to play Little League. It scared me to death. I hated Boy Scouts." I gave a quick laugh. "I even overheard my mother talking to a friend's mom one day about how I wasn't all boy."

"Ouch. How did that come up?"

"Another friend and I—not my best friend, Terry, but another friend who wasn't all boy either—had been carping about the war games we had to play at scout meetings. 'Kill the Krauts! Kill the Japs!' All that. Mom and my friend's mom were discussing why scouts couldn't have more activities for boys that weren't all boy. I don't think she said it to be mean. It's just the way things were. And then later, high school sports were beyond me."

"I think you're all boy." He chucked me under the chin. "That's why I like you."

"Thank you." That same warm feeling bubbled near my heart. Maybe I'd only imagined a distance between Ted and me earlier. I hoped so. Or maybe my confession was drawing him closer again.

"When Sunup came along... okay, it wasn't exactly boot camp, but it was a totally different experience for me, something I wasn't sure I'd be able to do. At the end of the summer when I got back to Knoxville, I felt like a new person. More confident. I had a nice chunk of money in the bank. The pay was okay at Camp Sunup. But then at the end of each session, we got cash tips from most of the parents of the kids in our cabins. It seemed they tried to outdo each other. I nearly doubled the amount Sunup paid me for the whole summer. Nice surprise. And tax-free, to boot."

I paused, looked at his handsome face, shadowed in the pale glow from the porch light. "I know you're wondering what all this has to do with Maggie and Bud Rose. I'm getting there."

He shut his eyes for a moment, then looked at me. "I have total confidence."

I had never revealed this much to another person, ever. Not even Blake. It felt good and a little scary. "I had another surprise at the end of that summer. At Sunup, for 12 weeks I was outdoors almost all the time, got a killer tan, ate three square meals a day, got eight hours of sleep every night and drank practically zero alcohol, except on counselors' nights off once in a while. When I got back to Knoxville, I was in the best shape I'd ever been in. All of a sudden, people were looking at me. I mean, really looking at me. Guys and girls. Jumping me, in some cases. There was the older sister of a friend's girlfriend who'd come to Knoxville for a ball game one weekend. I rode with them to pick her up at the airport that Friday night. She'd had some drinks on the plane. She tried to ravish me in the backseat on the way back to campus. I mean—" I lowered my voice. "She had her hand on my dick."

"Who can blame her?" Ted said.

"Yeah, yeah. Then there was this clerk at a record store off campus. Good grief! He propositioned me even before I'd paid for the Elton John album I went in to buy. Those kinds of things had never happened to me before. Not like that. I mean… I'd been such a dork in high school. It was all very… different."

He grinned, but I saw a trace of sadness in it. It wasn't as bright as his smiles had been before dinner. "Was Maggie one of the ones who jumped you?"

"No, but she noticed the change in me. We had another class together fall quarter senior year. It wasn't just that I was looking good, with my George Hamilton tan and my skinny waist and buffed-up shoulders. I was… coming into myself, or the version of myself I thought I wanted to be."

"The straight arrow?"

"Exactly. So, we started dating. I told myself I could either waste all the attention by hopping in the sack with someone new every night, or I could make it work for something. Something that meant something. And in some weird way I thought since I had done such a good job changing the external me that summer at Sunup, I could change the internal me, too."

"Wow." He sat very still. "What about the sex?"

"It was fun. For a while. But it's just not…" I started to say, "It's not like it is with you," but decided against it.

"Like it is with guys?"

I nodded.

"What about Griff? Didn't that give you some clue?"

There was that distance again. As if he were having doubts about me. "Griff was part of the old me. And we'd had such a nice experience that I told myself it was enough to last me… while I went on with real life. I was still telling myself the gay thing was something I could switch on and off."

His laugh was sharp, full of ridicule. "I bet you wanted to make your parents proud of you, too. Being with Maggie, I mean. Their little Mike was all boy after all."

"Yes." It sounded awful, I knew, using Maggie to prove myself to my parents, but I supposed it was the truth, no matter how much I thought I loved her.

"How did Bud feel about all this?"

I sipped some more water, turned the glass in the palm of my hand. Now came the hardest part. "He didn't take it well. He called my apartment one night when Maggie was with me. Asked to speak to her. He was hysterical. Sobbing. Begging her to come over so they could talk. It was awful."

"Ah, what a tangled web," he said. "She didn't go back to him, did she?"

"No. He left school on account of it. Had some sort of breakdown. He'd been in an honors program in the college of business. Star student. It shocked everyone there, apparently." I looked up at the moon shining through the dark, intertwining tree branches. Tangled web indeed. "I should have insisted she go back that night. It wasn't right to let her stay—"

"It was her choice, wasn't it?"

I nodded. "But I could have stopped it right then and there." I rubbed the back of my neck with one hand, kneading the tight muscle under the skin. It's a horrible thing, I thought, the sound of a young man begging.

I might have been building a future for myself, sure, but I was wrecking the futures of others. And yet part of me had been proud that night. Proud that Maggie had chosen me over Bud. I had liked the idea that I was playing a starring role in a juicy campus scandal. Me, the boy who wasn't all boy. The memory stirred a grim mix of dark feelings, like a bad hangover. But there was one thing I could do to keep the story from ending in total disaster.

"Now you see why it is that I've got to marry Maggie." I avoided his eyes, looked straight ahead into the dark trees. Shame lowered the pitch and volume of my voice. "It's the only way the story makes any sense. Otherwise, it's a train wreck… a total waste."

A ladybug climbed a blade of grass between my feet. The sweet innocence of it made me want to cry.

"Would Maggie go back to Bud? If you left her?" Ted asked.

"I can't imagine her going back. Can't imagine him taking her back."

"Well…" Ted stood. "I'm not going to be your counselor about Maggie."

His clipped words surprised me. I had been hoping for a different response, his hand on my shoulder, perhaps. My gut tingled with dread. *What next?* I wondered.

"I need a smoke," he said, heading for the kitchen door. He did not sound happy.

* * *

My fingers clasped behind my head, I lay back so my shoulders rested on the concrete porch, my eyes taking in the moonlit sky above me. I felt ragged, my spirit frayed. I'd worked from 6 that morning to 3 in the afternoon, had two orgasms a few hours later, grilled chicken, drunk half a bottle of wine and spilled my figurative guts over Ted's newly mown backyard. No wonder I was worn out.

He returned with a lighter and box of Benson & Hedges cigarettes, sat down again—a few inches farther from me, I noticed. He slapped his box of cigarettes on the concrete.

I sat up. He was angry. Even without the noise the box made, I could tell something was up because he didn't remark about seeing me flat on my back. Any other time, I would have bet he'd make a joke about it.

One of his light, pithy comments. Maybe I shouldn't have told him so much.

"I've been involved in a triangle before," Ted said. "With Ryan." He lit a cigarette, took a long drag. I'd never pictured him being so proficient at smoking. I felt an odd sense of disappointment. Maybe it wasn't the only thing about him I'd misjudged.

"You guys were serious?" I softened my voice, did my best to show I cared for him.

"Briefly. Before he went back to his wife and little boy. You wouldn't believe the drama this house has seen. Jesus. I like being gay. I'd like to find somebody who likes being gay with me." He flicked cigarette ash into the yard. "It shouldn't be so fucking difficult. And I'll tell you something else. I was a sissy boy, too."

His tone was so aggressive, I decided a compliment might lighten things up. "I would have pegged you as the star linebacker type."

"Are you kidding? Knocking heads with a bunch of guys on Friday nights? No thank you." He looked hard into my eyes, as if there were one message and one message only he wanted to get through to me. "Mike, we don't have to prove anything to anybody. All we need to do is be who we are. If you don't have the guts to do that, then…"

I knew what he meant but hadn't said—*then I want nothing more to do with you.*

"I'm sorry. I'm not there yet about the gay thing. I mean, accepting it as final. Deciding to… live that way and that way only. It's like jumping off a cliff."

"You sound just like him." He shook his head. "I like you, Mike, but with all due respect, you are one fucked-up puppy."

Anger flashed through me. It was one thing to know what a mess I was. It was another to have him agree.

"I know you think it's honorable and all to be living your life for your parents and Maggie and Bud Fucking Rose. But have you ever really listened to yourself? Have you ever considered for a minute that maybe nobody gives a shit what you do?"

I was tired of all the criticism. I hit back. "Look, you knew going into this—"

"This is hardly a 'this.' This is two fucks and dinner. And don't tell me I don't know what it's like. Lynn and I were going to be married, for God's sake. I loved her. That's why I let her go."

That's it, I thought. *I'm outta here.* I stood. I'd packed my shaving kit and toothbrush in the car, just in case. The image of it on the front seat made me feel sad and silly. *Great expectations*, I thought. *So much for that. You tried to run away but it all caught up with you, didn't it?*

"I'll be right back. Excuse me," I said.

I set my empty glass on the kitchen counter, went to the bathroom, peed, avoided looking at myself in the mirror as I washed my hands. I switched off the light, wishing we could start the whole evening over. Then I walked to the kitchen, hoping Ted would be there. Ted, the guy I'd been mooning over for two days. In the brighter light, the mood might shift. Tempers might cool. We could talk. I could tell him how I felt about him.

But he was still on the porch, cigarette in hand. This was going to play out just as I'd left it a few minutes ago. A disaster. Another chapter in the sad story of Mike and Maggie and Bud Rose. Another one-nighter that, like the others I'd had since moving to Nashville, ended with nothing but guilty feelings and a promise never to do it again.

"Look—" My voice sounded as tired as I felt. "I better be going. Dinner and everything… were great. Thank you."

He kept his eyes downcast. "You can take the Dos Passos. It's on the dresser in my room."

My heart sank. "So, this is it?"

When he looked up at me, his eyes were wet. "I can't go through it again, Mike. I am not the gay ride at Disneyworld." He spoke like a carnival barker. "Send your men to me, ladies. I'll have 'em running back to you in no time." He looked down. "Once was enough, thank you."

I swallowed over the tightness in my throat. We had come to a serious pass here, hadn't we? And so quickly. "What if things change?" I said. "Between Maggie and me?"

"If you leave her?" He removed the gold-rimmed specs, wiped his eyes with his thumb knuckle. "I might not hang up if you called. But I will not…"

I moved a step closer to him. He held up his hand. "Please."

Message received. I stepped toward the door, reached for the handle, then turned to him.

"Just for the record, this was more than two fucks and dinner to me. We held each other all night the other night. I liked that."

"So did I." He flicked another ash into the yard.

I couldn't resist one more hit. "I guess you didn't mean it when you said you wanted to hear everything. Thanks a lot."

I went through the house, turned on the overhead light in his room and got the Dos Passos, glanced at the bedsheets we had made such a fine mess of a few hours before. Then I went to the living room, where Big O was curled on the daybed. I put my hand on her little round head.

"Bye, kitty," I said.

I got my keys from the table and walked out the door to my car.

Chapter Seven: This Had Better Come to a Stop

Senior year at UT, 1974
Photo courtesy of Tim Dalstrom

The next day at work, I tried to put the whole disaster of the night before out of my mind. But when I got home… that's when the soul-searching began.

Looking back on the things I had told Ted on his back porch, I realized I hadn't once said, "I'm in love with Maggie." My story was all about how she boosted my ego, how she had been part of the new me I tried to be, how I had to marry her because "it's the only way the story makes any sense." But I never said I loved her. Even if I didn't see Ted again, I'd be forever grateful to him for helping me discover that truth. I had told myself I loved her, over and over, until I'd convinced myself it was fact.

Of course, I had feelings for Maggie, but not in the way I knew love was supposed to feel. There was always a shadow inside me when I was with her. Something dark and secret and sad. Ted lit me up so bright inside that all the shadows were gone.

Sure, Maggie was fun to be with. I liked her laugh, her sense of humor, her interest in politics, theater, books and movies. The older the movie, the better. I liked her adventurous spirit. One Saturday our senior year, we drove to Gatlinburg with friends, waded through the shimmering cold of the Little Pigeon River and spent the afternoon sunning ourselves on a massive flat-topped boulder mid-stream, while the radio played Jackson Brown and Linda Ronstadt. I liked the way other guys looked at her that day, too, her cutoffs and halter top showing off her long tan legs and slim, shapely figure. But besides being an attractive young woman, she was also a kind, sharp, caring person who had shown me far more love and patience than I deserved.

Especially during some scary days in Montgomery.

* * *

Like the leaders of Camp Sunup, newspaper editors from around the southeastern U.S. came to UT looking to hire young talent. The managing editor of the paper in Montgomery was one of them. (I learned later he had a girlfriend in Knoxville and arranged interviews at UT so he could expense a few days' visit with her.) It was the time of Nixon and the Watergate scandal, when newspaper work was the place to be and competition for jobs was fierce among journalism grads. I wasn't thrilled about going deeper south to Montgomery, but it was my best offer.

When I moved there after graduation in 1974 and settled into the apartment on Perry Street next to the big Baptist church downtown, I learned there had been a murder in my building a few months before. A fellow named Jack Doane, the sports editor of the *Montgomery Advertiser,* the city's morning counterpart to the afternoon *Alabama Journal,* where I worked, was accused of killing his estranged wife in a first-floor apartment below mine.

Jack allegedly barged into her unit one night while she was entertaining a gentleman friend. The fellow escaped, his pants around his ankles, so the story went, while Jack pulled a butcher knife from a kitchen drawer and stabbed Kitty Doane to death.

When I'd come home from work in the late afternoons, Jack would be sitting in the open window of the apartment where the murder had occurred, beer in one hand, one leg inside the building, the other hanging outside, a tasseled loafer dangling from his bare toes. I didn't know the story the first time I saw him, but his florid complexion, gray T-shirt and ample gut signaled a troubled soul. I found out a few weeks later just how troubled he was.

What was he doing out of jail? He was free on bail, of course. He might not have been part of Montgomery's good-old-boy power structure, but he had entertained that power structure for years as sportswriter and editor for the morning paper. People knew him and liked him. He was part of their breakfast, their morning coffee, their lunchtime and happy hour conversations. "Did you see Jack Doane's column today?" No one was going to keep him in jail while he awaited trial. So, there in the window he sat, marking the days until his eventual conviction for first-degree manslaughter and sentence to five years in prison at age 39.

Sitting in that window as I walked below him, he never made eye contact with me. I figured he was too busy staring into the past.

It freaked me out. With the stress of a new job and a new city to learn and an accused murderer hanging out in my apartment building, I was a stranger in a strange land. When Maggie moved to Montgomery a few weeks later, took the apartment across the hall from mine and quickly found a job, I felt safe, like a little bit of home had returned.

Sure, I still lusted for men. My latest crush was on a bright young banker who lived in our building, but I still believed I could keep those feelings at bay with Maggie by my side. So, we both made friends with the young banker with the sexy cleft chin, drank with him, played cards with him, enjoyed his anecdotes about adjusting to Montgomery after his upbringing in the wealthy suburbs of Washington, D.C. I told myself that's what adult life was all about—abstinence for the greater good.

* * *

I had other scary experiences in Montgomery, especially after Maggie left the city and moved back to Nashville, her hometown. We had had our first big break-up. Even with a decent job, she wasn't happy in Montgomery, and I was feeling increasingly stifled having her there. It was a relief to have her gone… at first.

As the *Alabama Journal's* police reporter, I made daily visits to Montgomery's public safety building, which housed the police department, the city jail and Municipal Court. I frequently saw Sonny Kyle Livingston, a local bail bondsman who worked for the bonding company across the street. If you were arrested, the company charged you a fee to post your bail—a guarantee to the authorities that you would show up for your court hearing. Part of Livingston's job was to come after you if you didn't keep your side of the bargain.

Sexy in a hard-edged, polyester-suit-and-boots sort of way, he strode through the halls of the public safety building as if he owned the place. I didn't like the feelings he sparked in me. While I usually tried to build some sort of working relationship with everyone I encountered on my beat, his swagger cautioned me to keep my distance. Something about him spelled trouble.

My instincts were correct.

From my colleagues at the paper, I learned that Livingston had been part of the mob that assaulted the Freedom Riders when they rode through Montgomery in 1961. A few years before that, when he was only 19, he was tried for dynamiting a black church that supported the Montgomery bus boycott. Though he had confessed to the bombing in a statement to detectives, young Livingston walked free when the all-male, all-white jury quickly delivered a not-guilty verdict for him and his co-defendant. In the newspaper's "morgue," or library, I saw a 1957 black-and-white photo showing a jubilant crowd gathered around Livingston on a Montgomery sidewalk after the verdict was announced. To some, he was a local hero.

Now he was in his late 30s, and whether I liked it or not, it seemed that Livingston was determined to enter my life in 1976, my second year at the *Alabama Journal.* In January that year, I wrote my first story about him. Headlined "Six Armed Policemen Coax City Bondsman Into Talk Solution," the front-page story told how officers armed with rifles surrounded the bonding company where Livingston worked.

They were responding to reports that he had been drinking and had "gone crazy" after his pursuit of a man who jumped bail. Livingston holed up in a back office after the failed capture. Knowing Livingston went armed to pick up bail-jumpers, the officers stopped a tractor-trailer truck at the intersection by the bonding company to serve as a barrier in case gunfire was exchanged. (No doubt Livingston scared them, too.) They eventually calmed him down, leaving him with a warning about drinking on the job. No charges were filed.

After the story was published, I received a midnight phone call at my apartment from someone who sounded like an angry Livingston.

"I saw your Mickey-Mouse face out there with the police," the caller said, sending a chill through me. "You think you're a real hotshot, don't you?"

I phoned Maggie the next night at the apartment she shared with a girlfriend in Nashville. Still shaken, I told her about the call. I tried to keep the mood light.

"The guy is nuts," I said.

"I wish you'd get your butt up here."

"Tell the *Tennessean* to hire me, then." I had interviewed unsuccessfully at Nashville's reputable morning newspaper toward the end of my senior year in college.

"There's always the *Banner*." The *Banner* was Nashville's afternoon paper.

"The *Tennessean* is better."

"I know." Her voice softened. "I worry about you, is all."

So, the old feelings were still there, on both sides, even after our breakup. Neither of us was willing to abandon the idea of a future together. The story we told family and friends was that Maggie had left Montgomery because she hated the Deep South—not that she needed a break from me—and that I stayed to log at least two years at the *Journal* before I could be a credible applicant for jobs at bigger, better papers. That part was true. What I hadn't told Maggie was that I had already sent inquiries to papers in Tampa, Clearwater, St. Petersburg. Part of me dreamed of starting a new life in a new place—with a good newspaper, yes, a beach nearby, and no more strings with Maggie.

With no offers on the horizon, however, I continued my job as police reporter in Montgomery—and continued to lean on Maggie. Through the first half of 1976, I wrote so many stories about Sonny Kyle Livingston that my colleagues teased me about it.

"How's life on the Sonny Kyle beat?" they asked.

The most shocking story came in February 1976, when Alabama's attorney general revived the 19-year-old murder case of Willie Edwards Jr., a young black Winn-Dixie truck driver allegedly forced by a group of Klansmen to jump from a bridge into the Alabama River one winter night in 1957. Along with the bombings of black churches and businesses, it was one of the acts of white rage in the violent weeks after the city's buses were integrated in December 1956. Livingston was one of three men charged in the case.

Liberal folks I was getting to know in Montgomery were overjoyed. They viewed the Edwards case as a step forward in lifting the city out of the shadows of its racist past.

A few days after Livingston's arrest, the story about his release on $25,000 bond ran under my byline. In that story, I quoted District Attorney Jimmy Evans' argument for denying bail. "Livingston's propensity to violence in this community is well-known," he said. A few days later, I covered an explosive preliminary hearing where horrible details emerged about the night Willie Edwards jumped off that bridge.

Indeed, it appeared the noose was tightening for Livingston and his co-defendants. But two months later, the rope broke. In April 1976, State Circuit Judge Frank Embry dismissed the indictments on technical grounds that they failed to specify the cause of Edwards' death. The case unraveled further when a key witness recanted his story that Livingston was among the men who abducted Edwards. Livingston himself passed a lie detector test that established he wasn't involved in the crime.

"There was so much going on at that time," Alabama Attorney General Bill Baxley said about the weeks after Montgomery's buses were integrated. He was acknowledging he had more work to do in the Edwards case. "They were riding the streets every night, beating people. He (the witness) thought Livingston was there (when Edwards was abducted), but he admitted he was wrong and it was someone else."

So, Livingston was free and out of the headlines… temporarily. As Montgomery's sweltering summer began, I wrote another story about him—and got a taste of his "propensity to violence" firsthand.

The story involved a woman whose husband had jumped bail. Livingston claimed Jean West scratched him when he went to her home in pursuit of the man. Mrs. West claimed he slapped her and knocked her down. The story was he-said/she-said, although Mrs. West maintained she did what any woman would do when Livingston failed to show proper identification and began roughing her up: She fought back.

Livingston met me at the Municipal Court clerk's office after both he and Mrs. West filed assault charges in the incident. He asked if I was going to write a story about it.

"It's my job," I said.

"All I expect of you is the truth and to spell my name right," he said in his nasal twang. "Or you know what would happen."

His threat ruffled me, but energized me, too. As a reporter, I'd been feeling my oats, especially since I'd landed the story about the alleged wrongful police shooting of a young black man named Bernard Whitehurst, and the accusations in a federal lawsuit that officers had planted a gun on his body to cover their mistake. The attorney representing Whitehurst's family turned to me when there were new developments in the case. I'd write another above-the-fold, page-one story. This latest news with Livingston was small fry in comparison. He couldn't threaten me, I thought.

Headlined "Livingston Is Charged With Assault, Battery," my story was published on an inside page of the paper on Thursday, June 24, 1976.

The next morning, Livingston stood at the steps that led to the glass-door entry to Municipal Court. Overhead on the flagpole, the Stars and Stripes hung limp in the humid air. In a brown suit, his hair slicked down, a little smirk on his face, Livingston watched as I approached the building from the parking lot to make my rounds for news.

Fear sizzled through me. What was he up to? Still, this wasn't some dark alley, I told myself. It was broad daylight at the city's law-and-order headquarters. Livingston wasn't going to try anything here. I walked resolutely toward him, anticipating the good story that might flow from whatever he had to say to me.

"Good morning, Sonny," I said cheerfully.

Wham! He socked me in the jaw. For a moment, the lights went out in Alabama.

I fell backward on the sidewalk. My glasses flew onto the grass nearby. The next thing I knew, Livingston was standing over me. The acrid scent of his aftershave filled my nostrils.

"What'd I tell you about that story?" he snarled. "If you didn't get it right?"

I started to say something, then decided against it. I wasn't going to win any argument flat on my back.

He puffed out a laugh, kicked the sole of my loafer with the toe of his boot. "Go run to the cops now. And your mama." He turned and walked away.

I brushed sidewalk grit off my hands, ran my fingers over my cheek. No blood, thank goodness. I stood, gathered my notebook and glasses and went inside the building, where I made a beeline, albeit slowly and painfully, to the office of the police chief to tell him what had transpired on his turf.

At the direction of my editors at the *Alabama Journal,* I filed a second charge of assault against Livingston. (My colleagues at the paper appreciated the irony that Livingston had responded to an assault accusation with another assault.) After I signed the warrant, he was jailed for about 30 minutes before his release on bail.

In a Municipal Court hearing the following week, Livingston told Judge Matthis Piel that my story had provoked him. He claimed he no longer worked for the bonding company I had identified as his employer, the one where he'd staged the standoff. This was true, an oversight on my part. Additionally, I had relied on city jail records, which showed Livingston was incarcerated a few hours before Mrs. West. From this information, I concluded that her charge against Livingston was filed first, when in fact it was the other way around. The point enabled Livingston to claim that Mrs. West filed her charge as retaliation for the one he filed against her.

Okay, my story was not journalism's finest. In my rush to make my noon deadline that day, I hadn't confirmed some key facts. I was 23—young, green, a handy scapegoat for Livingston's grievances against the press.

At the hearing, Livingston made an impassioned statement about his reputation's abuse at the hands of reporters. He said he had been "crucified in the newspapers." He said the headlines about his exoneration in the Willie Edwards case were played nowhere near as prominently as the ones that announced his earlier indictment. I could understand Livingston's feelings on that score. I think the judge did, too.

Piel fined Livingston $200 and gave him a ten-day suspended jail sentence. Later, he dropped Mrs. West's charge against Livingston when she failed to prosecute. (Because she didn't appear in court, I never learned much about her, whether she was black or white, or why she dropped her case.) The judge fined her $25. Once again, Livingston was a free man.

Yes, it was a harrowing experience, though I chalked it up to the risk and adventure of reporting. Part of me was proud of the assault, proud that I had completed another course in the school of hard knocks on my way to being a successful journalist. I'd fortunately suffered nothing more than a sore tailbone and a broken frame on my glasses.

Still, I knew I had to get out of Montgomery for the weekend after Livingston's assault. The small apartment where I'd moved after Maggie left town had an exposed entrance at the back of an old house amid the moss-draped trees along Court Street—a vulnerable location, I thought, when someone with "a propensity to violence" is on your case. Granted, Livingston was no longer an accused murderer, but he still scared me.

I remembered his armed standoff with police.

The midnight phone call.

The grim satisfaction on his face when he hit me.

My colleagues kindly offered to let me bunk with them for the weekend, but Maggie was the one I turned to.

It was a reconciliation of sorts. She met me halfway… or thereabouts. When we agreed to meet in Birmingham—a few hours' drive south from Nashville, an hour's drive north from Montgomery—I sprang for a room at a nice downtown hotel. We had a weekend of movies and good meals and a return to romance.

"Come here," she said when we met that Friday afternoon.

I buried my face in her shiny, Clairol Herbal Essence-scented hair.

I was safe. I was home.

* * *

Another incident sent me back to Maggie for what I thought would be a permanent stay.

It was the vice squad raid at the Montgomery gay bar I had told Ted about. Sure, it was a stirring thing to see a black man and a white man dance together in a town known for its racist history, but I hadn't told Ted how much the police tromping through the place had unnerved me. I'd been chatting with a student from one of the local colleges, but the raid doused any thoughts of tricking; I settled my tab after the police left and drove home alone.

A few nights after that experience, I phoned Maggie and told her I was tired of life without her. I told her I was going to apply for a job at the *Banner* in Nashville. It didn't matter that it was the second-string paper in town, or that its conservative editorial slant didn't jibe with our view of the world. I'd make a phone call to their managing editor in the morning. And my starring role in Montgomery's developing Bernard Whitehurst story? I'd let it go. I told her it was time for us to be together for good. She knew about my fling with Griff in college, my "occasional interest" in other men; I told her all that was over.

I got the job. I moved to Nashville.

I was home. I was safe.

But I was learning that love and safety aren't the same thing.

I kept coming back to the words Ted had said to me on the porch after dinner at his place: "I like being gay. I'd like to find somebody who likes being gay with me."

I wasn't sure I could like being gay yet. But I could stop keeping Maggie in limbo. Stop using her as my crutch.

It was time for her to start life without me.

And it was time for me to start living, period. To stop thinking that being gay was something I could turn on and off. Or had to. It was time to be free, whether Ted was with me or not.

* * *

I did it by phone that evening, Wednesday, the evening after I'd had dinner at Ted's apartment. There was no use procrastinating any longer. Unsettling though it was, my conversation with Ted had triggered something in me. I needed to act before the feeling waned.

"I can't do this anymore," I said to Maggie.

"What?"

"I'm sorry. I've led you on long enough."

After a long silence, she said, "It's not like I haven't seen it coming. When you called yesterday, I—"

"I know."

A few more beats of silence. "What's his name?"

"What do you mean?"

"You've met someone, haven't you?"

I swallowed. She knew me well enough to know I wasn't going to make the leap on my own. I needed a push. "His name is Ted. I'm not sure we have a future together. But… he's helped me see things more clearly."

I could hear the tears starting. "I kept hoping you'd change," she said.

"Me too. Once."

I remembered the gold necklace I had given Maggie after we graduated. It was a dime-sized medallion that had her initials engraved on one side, mine on the other. It was a stalling tactic, something to keep our relationship going without the full commitment of an engagement ring. A symbol of the fault line on which our relationship was built. No wonder the necklace ended up on the floorboard of my Toyota one night. She ripped it off her neck after yet another "I'm not ready to get married" discussion. We had driven from Montgomery to Birmingham one Saturday for the Alabama-Tennessee football game and dinner afterward. It had been a hot, unhappy day.

No more.

Maggie was sobbing. "We could have had such beautiful children, Mike."

"You'll find someone, Maggie. Someone who loves you the right way. It's just not me." It felt awful, dashing those tender dreams. There was a time I wanted children, too. I could see us being good parents. But there were things I wanted more.

"Take care of yourself."

She gasped, as if I'd said the most horrible thing in the world to her. Then the line went dead.

* * *

I couldn't eat dinner that night. I'd been right the night before when I'd said accepting being gay was like jumping off a cliff. It's exactly how it felt.

But I knew jumping was the right thing to do.

I went to bed early. I said a prayer to whomever or whatever was up there watching. A prayer for peace for Maggie. A prayer that she'd move on. A prayer for forgiveness for me. And a prayer that Ted might still want to see me. Then I fell into a heavy, dreamless sleep, Copy curled at my feet.

* * *

Over the next two days, I put off calling Ted. I told myself it was time to be a grown-up, live on my own without the safety net of Maggie or anyone else. I also thought I needed to put more space between the last time I saw him and any possible reunion. I thought my news of breaking up with Maggie would have more credibility if I gave it a little time, even though I was bursting to tell him.

It was more than telling him I had extricated myself from Maggie. It was telling him I knew who—and what—I was.

One night while we were in Montgomery, I had asked Maggie if she'd consider an arrangement, if she'd let me see men occasionally. (I think the young banker down the hall was on my mind.) Other people did it, I told her. Smart, sophisticated people. Leonard Bernstein. Laurence Olivier. Men and women of that generation had made it work. Why couldn't we? Griff had had a girlfriend while he and I were seeing each other. She seemed perfectly fine with his varied interests.

Of course, I had known what Maggie's answer would be. And since there wasn't a Blake or other man waiting in the wings, only vague dreams of some sort of involvement with the young banker, I didn't push the issue.

Now, however, I knew I didn't want that kind of arrangement. The switching back and forth might even seem exciting to some, but it wasn't for me. I wanted to be in love with another man. I wanted a relationship that went deep. Not a weekend thing. Not a month-every-summer-with-my-fishing-buddy thing. A forever thing. Maybe Ted was that guy. Maybe someone like him. It was just that simple. It had always been that simple.

* * *

On Friday, my dad came over for dinner. My mom was attending a Presbyterian women's retreat in North Carolina.

Dad arrived in his trademark plaid Bermuda shorts, tan socks and slip-on canvas shoes, the leather holder for his reading glasses clipped into the pocket of his crew-neck T-shirt. It was an outfit my sisters had kidded him about through the years, though the gibes hadn't altered his fashion choices.

I grilled hamburgers on the hibachi, doctored up some barbecue beans with chopped onion and Worcestershire sauce, the way he liked them. I thought the best time to tell him that I had broken up with Maggie was while we ate. Somehow it wouldn't seem so serious that way.

"I'm just not ready to get married, Dad," I said.

He swallowed a bite of burger, wiped his lips with a paper napkin. "Your mother's not going to be happy."

He sounded unfazed by the news. I was relieved about that. "That's why I wanted to tell you first."

"Is there… some sort of problem?"

I wasn't ready to come out to my father. The thought of it filled me with dread. I'd seen his temper flare a time or two through the years, but it was over little things—bad TV reception no matter how he adjusted the antenna, my mother's undercooked turkey one Thanksgiving, our beagle Scout's horrible gas some evenings—but I didn't think he'd lose his temper if he learned I was gay. I pictured a deep, quiet, disturbing disappointment.

"Maggie wants children and… I don't know, my job takes so much time and focus. I want to be good at it. I'm not ready to put it in the background and start a family. Yet."

He put his hand on my forearm. "Whatever you think is right, Mike. We're fine with whatever you do."

"Thanks." *That wasn't so bad now, was it?*

"Are you happy?"

"I think so. I love my job. I'm glad I moved back from Montgomery."

"Then that's all that matters." His words eased my dread, although I heard an implication that my choice came at some cost to him and Mom. I knew she loved Maggie. I also knew she'd have more questions as to the reasons for the breakup. Her response was not going to be pleasant, but at least I didn't have to face it tonight.

"Anyway, I wanted to tell you. I know Mom and Maggie talk to each other. I didn't want you to be surprised."

"That's the way to do it," he said.

As if to put an end to any more talk about Maggie, Copy jumped into my father's lap. She was, without doubt, the best friend I had ever had.

* * *

Finally, I couldn't stand it any longer. Not even a week had passed since Ted and I had met at the Other Side on Mother's Day, but the change was monumental. I was a new person. I wanted him to know.

I picked up the phone and called him the Saturday afternoon after the Friday dinner with my father.

"Hello?"

"It's Mike," I said. "The fucked-up puppy."

He was silent for five beats of my heart. "Hello," he said. His voice was flat. The lightly hopeful sound I heard in his first hello—when he didn't know who was calling—was gone. I knew the guard was up.

"How've you been?" I asked.

"Fine." I waited for him to say more. He didn't.

"I just wanted you to know I broke things off with Maggie. It's over. It's permanently over."

More silence.

"And I want to thank you. Maybe I'm not quite so fucked up anymore."

"You're welcome." Did I hear a slight thaw in his tone?

"I wanted to say I've missed you, too."

"Missed me?" he asked.

"Yes."

He let out a long breath. "That's nice of you to say."

He was warming up. I gathered my courage. "I was thinking maybe we could get together and talk this afternoon."

"Well… not today. Let me think about it, okay?"

"Sure," I said, feeling grim. "If you'd—"

"Olivia!" He sounded fierce.

"What's the matter?"

"She's got the cord from the blinds wrapped around her neck. How did you do that, you crazy cat? She's swinging from the cord! Look, I've got to go. Could we plan to talk next week, maybe?"

"Okay," I said. "I'll call you."

"Olivia!"

It wasn't at all the joyous reunion I'd hoped for. But rushing into each other's arms after what had transpired between us? It would have been too fast. Too easy. "It will happen if it's meant to happen," I said to Copy. "Keep your paws crossed."

I got busy to take my mind off my disappointment. Saturday chores. I vacuumed. Cleaned the litter box. Went to the hardware store for the small brush and other supplies I needed to stain the chairs for the kitchen table. Ted had said he had a brush to loan me, but after the tone of today's call, there was every likelihood I'd never see it. At least not anytime soon.

I went to the grocery, picked up some things for dinner—frozen chicken pot pies, coffee, milk and cereal for the following week. I imagined what I'd buy if Ted had said he'd come over today. One of those fancy pecan coffee cakes. Strawberries. Cantaloupe. It would be breakfast after another great night together. *Dream on*, I thought. *Dream on.* Instead, I bought some treats for Copy. She and I would have breakfast together tomorrow. A boy and his cat. A cat and her boy.

I drove gloomily home. I was free tonight—single and free in Nashville. I could go out and do whatever I wanted. Maybe even hit the Other Side again. Funny, all I could think of was Ted.

I put the groceries away, turned on the TV just to have something on, considered starting on the chairs before dinner. I got some newspapers to spread on the carpet to catch any drips from the stain, then decided it would be better to stain the chairs outside. It wasn't even 5 p.m. yet. Plenty of daylight left for my project. But who was I fooling? I didn't feel like refinishing any chairs. I put the supplies away, decided to open a beer and hit the pool. It was just a few doors down from my apartment. A crowd had gathered there. I could hear the Bee Gees singing. Who knew? I might get lucky with one of my neighbors during poolside happy hour.

But I didn't want one of the neighbors. I wanted the guy I met last Sunday night. We fit together somehow. *We clicked.*

I was back in the kitchen when a knock came at the door. Maybe it was the manager, I thought, finally getting around to fixing the drip in the bathroom faucet. Or collecting the rent? No, I'd paid for the month. I hadn't been late since I'd had the apartment. Maybe someone inviting me down to the pool?

I went to the living room and opened the door.

There stood Ted. Husky, blue-eyed Ted.

"Hi," he said.

"Hi." I couldn't read him, didn't know whether to be overjoyed or to brace myself for the news that he never wanted to hear from me again.

"Does the invitation still stand?"

"To talk?"

"To talk," he said. There was that smile, those dimples. A good sign, indeed.

And then the oddest thought crossed my mind. The yellow polo shirt he was wearing wasn't right for him. It made his skin look sallow, brought out a tiredness under his eyes. Or maybe it wasn't the shirt. Maybe he'd lost sleep, too. Maybe he'd missed me as much as I missed him.

I opened the door wide and let him in.

Chapter Eight: Something to Believe In

Ted at the Detroit Zoo, August 1977

We didn't get much talking done that afternoon or evening, but I do remember a few things that were said.

Ted: Big O survived trying to hang herself.

Me: I'm glad.

Ted: And *I'm* glad you did what you did.

Me: It is scary. Jumping off the cliff.

Ted: Don't worry. I've got you.

* * *

Our relationship moved at a fast clip through the rest of May and the month of June 1977. I spent a lot of nights at his place; he at mine. We had good reason for such devotion: A deadline approached.

A solid grounding in statistics was essential to the political science graduate degree Ted was pursuing, and the level of statistics courses he needed wasn't offered at the time at Vanderbilt. He and a fellow student had been accepted into a program at the University of Michigan from late June to mid-August, with Vanderbilt covering most of the expenses for their time away.

Facing an upcoming six-week separation, Ted and I were determined to make each other impossible to forget—no matter what temptations came along in Nashville and Ann Arbor that summer of 1977. And we made sure the memory lingered with the letters we wrote to each other once Ted got to Michigan.

There are 35 letters from that summer. Ted wrote 24 of them. (Some days he wrote two!) I wrote 11. I have to hand it to him. He was speedier than I, but I don't think any more romantic.

Copy and Olivia also wrote to each other occasionally. And Ted sent two postcards. On one of them he wrote: "I still love you more and more. I wish I were there with you. I miss you. Take care of yourself. Soon. T." The nine-cent postcard is not dated and—curiously—not postmarked, either, but I know it came from Ted while he was in Ann Arbor because it's addressed to the apartment on Rosewood Avenue, where I lived that summer.

Most of Ted's letters are on lined notepaper in blue or black ink, his handwriting as difficult to decipher even then as it still is now. Some days he used notebook paper; others, sheets of graph paper, and once, a sheet of old-school computer paper with holes punched in perforated strips along either side of the page. My letters are on long sheets from the yellow legal pads the *Banner* provided us reporters, though at work I preferred the skinnier pads bound with a metal coil at the top. For the letters, I used the black felt-tip pens the paper also provided. I was nothing if not thrifty in my choice of letter-writing materials.

Ted has the first and the last word in the letters, which total over 16,000 words of text. That's the length of a short novella. We had lots to say.

In the first letter on June 28th, 1977, Ted wrote after lunch while he and his friend Greg, the other Vanderbilt student attending the program, waited to move into their apartment in Ann Arbor: "Dear Mike, How long has it been since you received a letter on notebook paper—that's what happens when you fall in love with an academic."

In the last letter, dated August 15th, as Ted was preparing to leave Ann Arbor, he wrote of the likelihood of his being able to work at the library of the *Tennessean*, where a friend had a part-time job, to help us pay our expenses and travel "sometimes perhaps." (We had agreed early on to move in together when he returned from Michigan.) I don't think we had talked much about money up to this point, but I liked the idea that Ted was thinking ahead, preparing for the day his scholarship funds ran out. Still, I wasn't worried. Living with him would be the first time I had shared rent with anyone since college. Financially, we would be fine.

In between Ted's first and last, the letters are full of declarations of love that almost shock me today. We were so sure of ourselves!

And downright gushy. The letters overflow with "angels," "darlings" and "sweethearts," words we haven't used with each other, except sarcastically, in decades.

The letters beg the question: When did you guys first tell each other, "I love you?" The short answer is I don't remember. Neither does Ted. The long answer: I think our not remembering says a lot about how we felt about each other. Sometime rather quickly after we met, we knew we loved each other, so the moment we put it into words seems redundant, hardly worth noting. Neither of us wondered, "Should I tell him I love him today?" or "What if he tells me he loves me today? What will I say?" The subject wasn't up for debate; it simply was what it was. And no, I don't remember the exact moment I realized I was in love with Ted. But I knew something serious was up after our first night together. Maybe after our first kiss. Maybe that's "love at first sight." It's close enough for me.

* * *

Reading the letters now, I see the outlines of how our relationship would take shape once Ted returned to Nashville in mid-August.

On August 4th, I wrote:

"I finished Don Clark's *Loving Someone Gay* today. Parts of it were very good, only it just barely touched on sustained relationships and ways to make them work. However, one paragraph especially reminded me of us. Clark writes how copying a heterosexual marriage doesn't work for most gay people, and he counsels gay partners to build a relationship that fits their own needs, not someone else's.

I want you, Angel, and I want to keep our relationship growing. You are the center of my life right now and I want to keep it that way. It's so right between us—I can feel the way you care for me and I hope you feel my love and trust for you. I want this to work."

On August 11th, Ted replied:

"I've been thinking a lot about the passage from *Loving Someone Gay* concerning homosexual relationships. I agree that we have to be wary of not patterning it after a heterosexual marriage. That would destroy us. It does, however, leave us with no real pattern to follow, which means we have to create our own norms. But I don't think there are as yet any real prescriptions for behavior which can be given. Obviously, there must be a great deal of respect and mutual understanding. But those qualities also entail honesty—about feelings and desires on each of our parts. There will obviously be some sacrifices each of us will have to make, we just need to be careful in order to assure that we don't compromise our self-respect, although I don't believe that could ever happen with us.

Perhaps most importantly, what we need to keep in mind is a respect for what we have together—a love that is special and wonderful. When small things come along—annoyances or temptations—we only have to remember what it is we want in the long run, each other's love. What could be more important?

Olivia just stuck her nose in my yogurt. She loves cherry vanilla flavor."

Today, I'm not sure why we singled out "heterosexual marriage" as a model that "would destroy us." Perhaps we were keeping the door open to have sex with other people, an "open marriage" as it was described at the time. I'm not sure.

But then I remind myself that in 1977, though the women's movement was making important strides, we still thought of heterosexual marriage as a Rob and Laura Petrie arrangement from *The Dick Van Dyke Show* of the '60s, where the male was the breadwinner and the "little woman" the homemaker. When I was in college in 1971, my mother sent me a clipping from the *Des Moines Register* about Michael McConnell and Jack Baker, the Minnesota gay male couple that applied for a marriage license (and who were still together when NBC news did a story on their marriage on March 7th, 2019). Blake and I were rooming together when my mom's clipping arrived. Mom had penned a little comment at the top of it, something like "Can you believe this?" I showed it to Blake, who proceeded to expound on the daily routine of a gay male couple he knew about on Long Island.

"One of the guys goes to work in the mornings and the other one stays home and vacuums," Blake had said. Oh, he had it all figured out.

Perhaps Ted and I were struggling against such a vision of our own life together. Neither of us wanted to be the one who stayed home and vacuumed. I believe the women's movement, in its work over the years to resist traditional gender norms and create a broader vision of women's choices, has made it easier for gay and lesbian couples to thrive today without people wondering "who is the man and who is the woman." But, in the 1970s, we were still bumping against the old stereotypes.

(The irony here is that, much as we carped about heterosexual models in our youth, Ted and I agree today that our parents' sturdy marriages were—and still are—the models for ours.)

* * *

In the letters, we also discussed things more concrete than models for our relationship.

"Find an apartment for us, Angel, a place where we can be alone with each other when we wish, to share our love," Ted wrote on July 19th.

I went looking and found one in the complex where I was already living, a larger, two-bedroom unit that I sketched out in my July 22nd letter to Ted. It was nice, but not perfect.

"Well, the apartment is ours as of Sept. 1st," I wrote. "I think you'll like it, even though the kitchen appliances are avocado green."

In another letter, Ted drew on graph paper a detailed plan of an A-frame house he thought would be perfect for us and the cats one day. It was done to scale, with precise arrangements of furniture, including a sectional sofa in front of the fireplace, and a careful rendering of how the kitchen would be laid out.

It was so detailed. I loved looking at it, and yet its message scared me a little. I asked myself: *Are you ready for this?* I thought my answer was yes. Of course, it was. This guy wanted to have an "us" with me. How could I argue? He was the greatest.

* * *

The letters substantiate what I already knew about Ted: He was smart. That's what shone behind those amazing blue eyes: Intelligence. Wit. (His July 6th letter notes in deadpan style that, while my letters were beautiful, my two previous missives began the same way: "I just opened a beer and…")

And then there was his aptitude for math, a skill that had eluded me all my life. The statistics program was another language to me.

"Did you know that B^=(X'X-)X'Y or Beta hat equals x transpose times x, inversed, times x transpose times y?" he wrote in his July 19 letter. "Aren't you excited? If you are, I'll send more equations later. You would be thrilled, I know."

In another letter, he not only took a fellow student to task, but also made a stunning analogy to explain the student's error in terms I'd understand.

"In four weeks, we are going to learn matrix algebra, calculus and trigonometry," he wrote. "It may be a challenge. I felt more confident, however, after some idiot asked the instructor (who is cute as hell and teaches in tennis shorts) why you didn't just add all the numbers up in a matrix and have only one number. If you aren't familiar with matrix algebra, the question was equivalent to asking why newspapers don't combine all their individual stories each day into one big story."

If not on a par with Ted mathematically, I showed an eagerness in the letters to share my knowledge of and interest in literature and the arts. I wrote that I had been enthralled by an excerpt from Philip Roth's new novel, *The Professor of Desire,* in the new issue of *Harper's*. With references to *Anna Karenina,* the book gave me the opportunity to mention that I had read Tolstoy's huge novel in AP English in high school. (I was shameless!) But I did return to the subject of our relationship when I closed the letter.

"With other men I've been with I've usually felt a deep-down dislike for myself, as though I'd hate to be watching what we were doing while making love. But with you, I feel even more manly when I make love with you. I feel the love we share is something beautiful and a response to our most basic feelings as men. You have helped me come to terms with my homosexuality in ways I never imagined possible.

I want us to let people know we're gay and I want us to have gay friends, many of them. Just because I'm happy with you doesn't mean I want to shut ourselves off from the rest of the world. We have a responsibility not to do that. We must be gay at all times if possible, not just when we close our apartment door, turn down the lights and make love.

Ted, I'm sure most of this is stuff you already know, but for me it's a breakthrough. I too feel ashamed when I deny your existence and your love to people who ask if I'm seeing anyone. I love you and I can't deny it. I don't like hiding it. You are the most beautiful person I've ever known."

Ted waxed romantic, too. A few weeks before my scheduled visit to Ann Arbor, he wrote:

"Only 17 more days and you will be here in my arms. I can't wait. It's amazing that we don't really know what it is we are looking for or how it will make us feel, but when we find it we suddenly realize we never want to lose it again. Before I met you, I was relatively happy or at least content with the way things were, but now I could never go back. You have made me need something which I never knew existed before, and I'm glad you did. And I believe that only you can give it to me and I hope I can to you."

Such declarations of love! "I love you and I can't deny it. You are the most beautiful person I have ever known." And such finality! "I was relatively happy or at least content with the way things were, but now I could never go back."

Indeed, it was a magical summer. Not bad for two guys who'd met in a sleazy bar on Mother's Day.

* * *

A newspaper clipping I enclosed in one letter to Ted paints a picture of the world in which he and I fell in love. It's the June 27th, 1977, *Nashville*

Banner article about the city's first gay pride event. It wasn't even a parade. It was a picnic in Centennial Park, but still the police had to come show who was boss. They forced the approximately 40 attendees to remove their signs, which bore harmless messages about being out and proud, about Jesus saying gay was okay.

The story—one of the few I sent Ted that I didn't write—has an odd, "this whole gay thing is new to us" tone. But then, the *Banner* was the city's Republican paper. It wouldn't have been seemly to display too much familiarity with such topics as homosexuals and gay rights in Nashville. The story's headline: "Nashville Gay 'Picnickers' Charge Metro Harassment" gave away the newspaper's view that the participants were just a bunch of pussies and troublemakers, anyway.

* * *

After a month without him, I planned to fly to Michigan to visit Ted for a long weekend in late July.

The day before I left, a curious thing happened.

I had been assigned to interview the Amazing Kreskin, the mentalist who had made quite a name for himself on appearances with Johnny Carson on *The Tonight Show* and elsewhere. He was in town to do a show.

Accompanied by his publicist, I met Kreskin in his hotel room by the Nashville airport. Wearing slacks and a dress shirt with the sleeves rolled up, he looked more casual than his besuited appearances on TV. His enormous horn-rimmed glasses were gone. He was more attractive without them, I noticed, the face beneath his neatly combed brown hair younger and more handsome than it appeared on TV.

We talked for about 30 minutes about his upcoming show. As I was leaving, I told him I was going out of town and was sorry to miss his performance.

He looked at me and said, "You're taking a trip with someone named Ted." He had a twinkle in his eye.

I was, understandably, floored. I wasn't sure I believed in Kreskin's special gift. I thought that, like any good magician, there was nuts-and-bolts craft behind what he did, science behind the hocus pocus. I figured I must have had Ted's name written with my travel plans on one of the pages of the notebook I used during the interview. So, when I got back to the city room, I searched each page. No mention of Ted. Had I somehow let his name slip out during our conversation? At that time, I didn't record my interviews, so there was no way to confirm it, but I knew I would not have let that happen. I was concerned about anyone getting the wrong (which, of course, would have been the right) idea about my vacation with Ted, so no… I wouldn't have said his name.

Nonetheless, being a good reporter, I knew the story I wrote about my visit with Kreskin had to include what he said about Ted. My editor loved it. I continued to maintain the fiction that Ted and I were just good buddies who liked to hang out together, but perhaps my visit with Kreskin was the moment I began to see the futility of keeping what Ted and I had a secret from the rest of the world. It also revealed how desperate I was to hide it.

On Friday morning, July 29th, I boarded the plane bound for Detroit. As we reached cruising altitude, I remembered Kreskin's face when he mentioned Ted's name, the glint of something—was it recognition?—in his eyes. I realized I had another secret, one that embarrassed, scared and thrilled me all at the same time:

Kreskin knows everything about us. Kreskin sees all.

* * *

I swooned when I saw Ted waiting for me at the gate in the Detroit airport. He looked even better than I remembered, though we didn't touch until we got in his '65 Chevy Impala in the parking lot, where we had a long and proper make-out session—with me looking around to be sure no one was nearby to see us, of course.

I was bursting to tell him the story about Kreskin, so I shared the details on the hour's drive to Ann Arbor. Ted didn't give the incident quite as much weight as I did. He thought I must have had his name written somewhere in my notebook and I overlooked it. But his skepticism was okay by me. I liked the idea of Kreskin and me sharing our own little secret. And if I'd had the feeling early on in my relationship with Ted that we were meant to be, Kreskin's insight was a little more evidence that I was right.

We had a beautiful time in Ann Arbor. My heart had never been so full, so happy. Every day was Christmas. It didn't matter that the windows in Ted's basement bedroom looked out on the chrome grilles of the cars in the parking lot above. It was Shangri-La. And when we weren't in the bedroom, Ted came up with all kinds of creative ways to show me a good time. We drove into Detroit and spent the day at the zoo. We danced by candlelight in his living room to Boz Scaggs' *Harbor Lights*. We had dinner at a Mediterranean-style restaurant (exotic for us at the time) in Detroit and saw a first-class production of Jack Heifner's clever play *Vanities* at the Ford Theater. We felt like any other couple out on a date. Nobody gave us any trouble.

Until my last evening in Ann Arbor.

Ted and I walked from his apartment to a movie theater downtown to see a new flick we'd been reading about, *New York, New York*, with Liza Minnelli and Robert DeNiro. It was dark when the theater let out. We walked along the sidewalk in the cool summer air to find a place to have a beer. Ted took my hand. It was a new experience for me, holding hands with a guy in public. It felt good. As we walked, I mentioned how Blake had insisted whenever we went to a movie at UT that we keep an empty seat between us lest anyone get the idea that we were a couple out on a date. I laughed, held Ted's hand tighter and appreciated this thing we had all the more.

Ted faced me as we walked. "So, what happened to—"

"Faggots!" a husky voice called from a car behind us.

I let go of Ted's hand.

"Hey, you fucking faggots!" came another voice from the same direction.

"Queers!"

The traffic light turned green. The car crossed the intersection, its red taillights merging with the lights of the traffic up ahead. Ted tried to take my hand again, but I resisted, my fingers stuffed in the front pockets of my jeans. The spell had been broken. I felt naked out there on the sidewalk, people all around us. What had we been thinking?

"I didn't think that kind of stuff was supposed to happen here," I said, trying to make light of it, but my stomach still clenched.

"It happens everywhere, Mike," Ted said. "We're going to have to get used to it. We're going to have to be strong."

I wasn't sure I could do it. Maybe I wasn't strong enough to be gay, strong enough to be with a guy who wanted us to show it off. Ted was the one who had taken my hand, I reminded myself, not the other way around. I was angry with him. He should have known better. We should have known better. Fuck!

We nixed the idea of stopping for a beer. We went on to Ted's apartment, where he told his roommate what had happened.

"Jerks," Greg said, straightening his thick, wire-framed glasses on his nose. "Jesus. Where did they come from? Kalamazoo?"

"Some sort of zoo." Ted got two beers from the refrigerator. "Mike's more freaked about it than I am."

"Don't let it get you down, Mike," Greg said. "Assholes will be assholes."

My temper rose. "You weren't out there on the sidewalk getting yelled at, Greg. Has anything like that ever happened to you and Cynthia?" Cynthia was Greg's wife.

"Mike," Ted cautioned. "Take it easy."

I wasn't finished yet. "Isn't Ann Arbor supposed to be one of the most liberal towns in the country? What's going to happen when we get back to little ol' Nashville?"

Ted gave me a quick kiss. "We'll be fine."

I wasn't sure. It was as if the rosy glow of our time together had turned bright red. *Warning: Danger ahead.* But we could handle it, couldn't we?

When Ted and I got in bed that night, I put my arms around him, held him tight, let my love for him and his strength wash away my fears.

Yes, I said to myself. *Together, we can handle it... I think.*

Chapter Nine: I Am Changing

A date with Anita Bryant, late 1970s
Photo reprinted by permission of Nashville Public Library, The Nashville Room

The night of the hecklers in Ann Arbor showed me that life with Ted would have its challenges—once we began living in our own apartment in Nashville. Who knew what awaited us?

I was certain of one thing.

It was increasingly apparent that I had found a soulmate. I hesitated to use the word. It seemed too fast, like a rubber stamp of approval on something that had barely been road-tested. Still, we clearly had something.

For example, Ted and I agreed on most of the big issues: Church was a waste of time. The Vietnam War had been a mistake. A strong centralized government was essential to democracy. We had both voted for Jimmy Carter in the 1976 election.

We were in alignment on little things, too. Neither of us had ever eaten a Pop-Tart and didn't intend to. People who drank Bloody Marys at night were weird. Football was as big a waste of time as church. We laughed when we discovered we'd both had crushes on the Mennen Speed Stick guy when we were in high school.

Ted had also been a fan of *Mad* magazine when he was a kid. He remembered the Tipsy Headrinse spoof of *The Birds*—although it would be years before I told him about the role it played in the loss of my childhood friend Terry. I thought I was over the hurt of it, but in my early days with Ted I was still downright embarrassed by it. And I feared if I told him about it, he might have a similar story in which his Terry counterpart willingly returned his kiss. I didn't want to hear about that. He had enough one-ups on me already in the sexual exploration department.

The fact that I was only eight months older than Ted further substantiated my thinking that we were a good match. For four months each year—my birthday is in August, Ted's in April—we are the same age.

I even fell for his last name. Brothers. It felt solid, masculine. Perhaps it hinted at a brother-ship, this thing that Ted and I had, although I quickly steered my thoughts to other topics when they hovered over the idea that Ted was perhaps the brother I never had. The love between us was an entirely different animal, wasn't it? I knew I liked being with him in an open, brotherly sort of way as much as the sexual things we did together. I also knew my longing for each of those varieties of male-to-male bonding was equally strong. Unlike Blake, this new guy Ted, whom I had known for only three months, checked all the boxes.

That was thrilling. And unsettling. Had it all happened too fast? Should we be a little more cautious?

No, I told myself. *You have a good thing here. Go with it.*

* * *

Ted came home in mid-August. In September, we moved into the larger, two-bedroom apartment on Rosewood Avenue. Our summer of love letters was over. It was time to start the serious business of sharing our lives together. It was easier at first than I'd thought.

I suppose it's the same today, but in 1977, it was common for two guys in their 20s to share an apartment without suspicion of being gay. Even the interior of our apartment wasn't a dead giveaway that we were lovers. One of the bedrooms had a double bed with two bedside tables on either side and a lamp on each. The other bedroom had a twin bed tucked against one wall.

If one was more comfortable in assuming that one of us slept in that room—even though it was also where we kept the litter box for Copy and the Big O—one was certainly welcome to do so, although I remember my father's puzzled look when he toured the apartment for the first time. "The talk" with my parents about my sexual orientation and the exact nature of my relationship with Ted was several years in the future. My parents knew I had ended things with Maggie, but I hadn't been able to summon the courage to tell them the exact reason why. I knew it would be horrible. (I was right.) So, I let things slide.

My parents liked Ted. They enjoyed his company. Ted and I went to dinner at their apartment; once they came to ours. Ted prepared veal saltimbocca, a complicated dish he and I had shared on our first on-the-cheap trip together to New York City (where we paid what we thought was an exorbitant $34 for two orchestra tickets to *A Chorus Line).* We were all playing a form of charades, I guess, avoiding the dreaded word "homosexual" as long as we could.

Meanwhile, life with Ted was good. We chopped down a cedar tree on the Hillsboro Road property of friends of Ted's, now friends of mine, too, and decorated it for our first Christmas together. Early Christmas morning, I got out of bed to turn the lights on the tree and make coffee, only to find that the lights were already on. Certain we had turned them off before going to bed, we concluded that one of the cats had done it—likely Big O, who was more prone to mischievous behavior than Copy. Still, it was hard to imagine either cat jumping high enough to flip the wall switch that controlled the outlet the lights were plugged into. Had we had a small Christmas miracle? Was it the universe's way of endorsing our relationship? I liked to think so.

One day, I had a bad cold and stayed home from work. While I lay under a blanket on the daybed in the living room, Big O sauntered out from the kitchen after one of her mid-morning snacks. She was a round, hefty cat, with a belly that hung much closer to the ground than trim, ladylike Copy's. I watched as Big O used her left hind foot to push her belly to the side. At the top of its swing to her right, she quickly lay on her left side for a little snooze.

I called Ted at work at the *Tennessean* library.

"You won't believe what your daughter just did," I said.

"Nothing would surprise me."

I told him about the neat trick she had performed in the living room. "She kicked her belly out of the way to make it easier to lie down on her side. Unbelievable."

"She's a talented girl."

There were no smartphones or camcorders in those days, but I wish I had a video of Big O's cool move.

She made another move that wasn't so cool. We were having a party to celebrate my birthday. Ted had invited four friends over for dinner. We had moved the table out of our small kitchen and into the living room to give everyone more space while we ate.

During dinner, Big O jumped to the top of a low bookshelf against one wall. Annoyingly, she made figure eights on the surface, weaving in and out among the items on the bookcase. I started to get up and shoo her off, but I was hemmed in between our guests so let it go.

One of the items on the bookcase was a wooden candleholder with holes for three candles. Ted had lit all of them before we sat down to dinner. The next time I looked over at Big O, I counted four flames.

Four?

Then I realized: There was a flame on the tip of Big O's tail, perfectly matching the flames on the three candles.

With the wail of a banshee, Big O leapt from the top of the bookcase to the middle of the dinner table. Guests screamed. Plates clattered. Wine glasses toppled. I grabbed Big O and snuffed out the flame with one of the blue cloth napkins Ted had bought for the occasion.

The cat was fine. Once she calmed down in Ted's arms, we could see that her tail wasn't burned, but the fur on the tip was singed. I wet the napkin under the kitchen faucet and gently rubbed Big O down with a cool cloth. She ambled off to our bedroom and curled up on our bed, where well-mannered Copy had wisely settled when the guests arrived.

Meanwhile, the apartment smelled like burned tires. Ted turned the air conditioning on high and opened all the windows and the front door to air the place out, but with no ceiling fans it took a while.

Even so, it was a great party. We finished dinner and had cake and champagne. Around midnight, we said goodbye to our guests, happy that we were sending them home not only wined and dined, but also with a good story.

"I love Thurber's *The Night the Bed Fell In,*" one of our writer friends said on her way out the door. "But I think you've topped it with The Night the Cat Caught on Fire. Thanks for a memorable party."

* * *

I look at pictures of Ted and Big O now and laugh. I realize one of the reasons I loved him was because he loved that crazy mutt of a cat. She could knock over a 20-pound bag of cat food when she was hungry, which was all the time. And there was the famous cord-hanging episode. In short, Big O was a mess. But she was more than that. To me, she was a symbol that Ted had not only brought love into my life, but also life into my life—lively, messy, fun.

My previously staid, get-to-bed early Sunday nights were replaced by beer and bowling with Ted's friends from grad school. Ted and I would come home after 11:00 and, quite often, rip each other's clothes off.

"Undressing you is my most favorite thing," I'd say.

"You're drunk," he'd answer, tickling my ribs.

We took pleasure in domesticity, too. I'd left the concrete block bookcase at the old apartment. Ted and I bought flea market furniture and refinished it—a real bookcase for the living room, a bentwood rocker with someone's initials, WJD, carved in one arm, a table for all the plants Ted was growing from cuttings his friends had given him—jade, spider plants, peace lilies.

I was cordial to our neighbors, two ladies who lived next door, but Ted went a step further and invited them to dinner one night. They told us their story—they were ex-nuns who'd fallen in love in a convent in Pittsburgh, left the order and moved to Nashville to start a new life. We told them our story, too.

"To ex-nuns," I said, raising my glass.

"To ex-straight boys," one of them replied.

One semester, Ted had a temporary, well-paying job with a state-funded project analyzing criminal justice patterns in Tennessee counties. Greg, Ted's roommate in Ann Arbor, worked with him. They traveled across the state together.

Greg's wife, Cynthia, and I once joked that her husband and my boyfriend were spending the weekend together in Paris—Paris,

Tennessee. Ted tells a funny story about his and Greg's meeting the leader of the project in the fellow's hotel room there one evening. According to Ted, the fellow was the epitome of 1970s male sexiness, with dark curly hair, a mustache, an open-collared shirt and a jacket with wide lapels.

"Was he hot?" Greg asked Ted when they got in the car after the visit.

"Incredibly hot," Ted said.

"Yeah, I thought so," said Greg.

I was enjoying being out to friends of Ted's and making new friends among our neighbors who knew Ted and I were lovers. I wasn't ready to take Ted to a formal *Banner* gathering like the office Christmas party, but we did go together to a party my friend Frank and his roommate threw for the younger-tier reporters and editors at the paper.

At one point in the evening, the rear legs of Ted's chair sank between the unmortared bricks of the backyard patio. Ted did a slow-motion backward tilt and landed flat on his back on the bricks, ankles in the air. Like Big O setting her tail on fire, it was a party act everyone remembered. As for me, it just made me love him more.

* * *

Not long after Ted and I started living together, we did something we considered quite daring: We went to see Anita Bryant. A singer and runner-up in the 1959 Miss America pageant, the former Miss Oklahoma was a familiar face to America, what with her TV appearances and the orange juice commercials she did in the 1970s for the Florida Citrus Commission. She also drew considerable attention by speaking out against gay rights.

One weekend, she brought her national campaign against homosexuals to Tennessee, staging a rally in Cleveland, a good half-day's drive east of Nashville. It was technically my state desk territory, so I took the assignment. Ted and I made a weekend of it. He came to the rally and stayed with me in the motel room I had rented for the night, on the *Banner*'s dime. I figured they couldn't object to my taking a friend along on a Saturday assignment so far away.

My story ran the following Monday.

Anita Bryant Gets Warm 'Bible Belt' Welcome

By MIKE COLEMAN
Banner Staff Writer

Cleveland, Tenn.—Proudly calling itself "the buckle of the Bible Belt," this Bradley County town greeted controversial singer Anita Bryant Saturday without a hint of protest.

Granted, police said they received a few telephoned bomb threats before Miss Bryant's arrival, but the 6,000 persons who paid $4 each to see her concert proved the anti-gay rights advocate was indeed in friendly territory.

"God's gonna hold us accountable for what we've let happen so far in America," said the Florida Citrus Commission spokeswoman, who sources said was paid $7,500 for her two-hour concert. "We have no business being apathetic or ignorant."

And the crowd, decked out in church-going finery, gave her a standing ovation when she vowed to heed God's call for her "to put prayer back in public schools."

After the concert, which was a combination of popular tunes, patriotic speeches and show business shtick, Miss Bryant said it was "quite refreshing" to entertain where there were no hecklers or demonstrators.

That surprised police officers and officials of the YMCA, which co-sponsored the event with the Church of God of Prophecy, whose international headquarters are in Cleveland.

"We didn't have any incidents at all," said Police Chief Bernard Snyder. "But I didn't anticipate anyone in Cleveland doing anything. If there had been trouble, it would have come from out of town."

Security was practically airtight at the concert, with 12 uniformed guards and eight plainclothes officers stationed at auditorium entrances. When the concert began, the officers surrounded the in-the-round stage and halted any would-be photographers from entering the aisles.

Miss Bryant, who led the successful fight in Miami earlier this year to repeal an ordinance prohibiting housing discrimination against homosexuals, said she liked "all the signs" which marked Cleveland's business district with messages of "Welcome, Anita" and "the buckle of the Bible Belt supports you."

Never actually mentioning the terms "gay" or "homosexual," Miss Bryant, once a runner-up in the Miss America pageant, nevertheless made her message clear when she called for "more guidelines" and the need to be "right and decent."

It apparently was a message the people of Cleveland wanted to hear.

According to YMCA President Harlan White, attendance at Saturday's concert was "nearly double" the attendance when Miss Bryant appeared here in 1975.

"This is the first year we haven't lost money" on our annual Christmas program, said White. "We hope we've made enough to replenish what we've lost in past years."

* * *

After Anita's concert, Ted and I went back to our motel room and had some of the best sex we had ever had. I moaned so loud I was sure the guests on either side of our room—and possibly beyond—had heard me.

"That was a revelation," I said afterward. "A religious experience."

"I bet you woke the neighbors," he said.

"Maybe Anita's next door. Anita and her husband."

"God, I hope so." He laughed. "Are you ready to go to sleep?"

"Are you kidding?" I asked. "Lie back. I'm going to do to you exactly what you did to me."

I suppose it was our own form of protest after being subjected to an evening of her flag-waving rhetoric. Whatever… we slept a long and peaceful sleep that night, content in the knowledge that, for these two young gay men, at least, attending an Anita Bryant rally was an incredible aphrodisiac.

* * *

Back home, I sprang for a print of one of my favorite watercolors, Paul Jenkins' *Phenomena: Sun Over the Hourglass*, framed it in clear acrylic and hung it over our bed. It was a celebration, a big splash of color, a symbol of what Ted had brought into my life.

I loved our budget dinners at the International Market on Belmont Boulevard not far from our apartment, where you could get a plateful of glass noodle beef, fried rice and a monster-size egg roll for $3.02. Loved scrounging up enough change between us for a cheap six-pack of "Hudy"—Hudepohl beer—on summer evenings. Loved being able to make love and sleep together without one of us having to get up and go home the next morning. We were home. That was good.

To top it all off, Ted had quit smoking!

Things were still good on the work front, too, although in the letters I wrote to Ted while he was in Ann Arbor, there are hints of a growing dissatisfaction with reporting. Why I turned down the opportunity to cover the multiple-fatality Columbia jail fire—Ted had sent me a clip of a *New York Times* story on the young man accused of setting the fire, as if to underscore what I'd lost by letting the story go—is still beyond me. I think it suggests a weariness and realization that, with Ted in my life, there were more important things than the next big story or byline on the front page of the newspaper.

Still, newspaper work was important. In the days before the Internet, you'd see a folded paper in nearly every driveway each morning, rain or shine. Print journalism was an exciting place to be; there was nothing quite like the adrenaline rush it gave me. It wasn't until the afternoon of Friday, February 24th, 1978, that I seriously reconsidered my career choice.

Chapter Ten: With So Little to Be Sure Of

For Try At $800 Jackpot

Nashville Banner

NASHVILLE, TENN., SATURDAY AFTERNOON, FEBRUARY 25, 1978.

24 PAGES

Waverly Death Toll
5 Missing, Scores H

was compiled by
riters Mike Cole-
gan, David Lyons,
Brittingham and

persons were
st 18 were miss-
as 200 were
ailed L&N tank
gallons of
as exploded

Editorial, "The Waverly Tragedy And Its Aftermath," Page 4.

As the death and injury toll climbed, weary and cautious workers laid plans today for transferring gas from an adjoining tanker to another train car for transport to Nashville by rail.

Many of those injured were treated at first aid stations, but 50 persons were confined to nine area hospitals — many in critical condition — as a result of the Friday afternoon explosion.

The devastating blast occurred at 2:58 p.m. and rocked this small Humphreys County town, hurling burning bodies into the air and blowing a path of destruction throughout a two-block downtown area.

Ambulances from across the Midstate converged on the area, as rescue efforts continued far into the night.

President Jimmy Carter called Mayor Jimmy Powers to offer federal assistance and also authorized the use of an Air Force plane to transport a burns team from New Jersey to the scene.

Civil Defense authorities today began evacuating about 500 city residents within a three-quarter

See EXPLOSION

List Of Known

Authorities said today at least nine persons were killed in the Waverly explosion and fire. Six of them were identified as:

1. Waverly Fire Chief Wilbur York, 65, who died in Vanderbilt Hospital early

Banner front page, February 25, 1978

Reprinted by permission of Nashville Public Library, The Nashville Room

On that cold Friday morning, there wasn't much going on. The only story of interest to the state desk was the clean-up of a derailment of an L&N train in Waverly, Tennessee, a small town in Humphreys County 77 miles southwest of Nashville. What made it newsworthy was that two of the derailed cars held thousands of gallons of liquid propane, making the clean-up a delicate operation.

The state desk reporter whose coverage area included Waverly had the day off, so my editor asked if I would take the assignment. With nothing else on my To-Do list, I said yes.

My first-person account on the front page of the next day's paper tells the rest of the story:

Banner Reporter Skips Assignment With Death

By MIKE COLEMAN
Banner Staff Writer

Waverly—If I had stayed here an extra 15 minutes Friday, my name could be on the explosion casualty list instead of as a byline on this story.

Luckily, I left this small Humphreys County town in the nick of time. But one worker I talked with wasn't so lucky.

Before the explosion that sent flames and smoke hundreds of feet in the air, I interviewed workers at the train wreck site. One of them is dead today.

In fact, I stood within three feet of the deadly propane tank.

And about three hours before the disaster, I photographed Rex Gaut, a smiling young construction worker from Alabama, as he smoked a cigarette less than 10 feet from the tank.

Today, he is dead. But when I photographed him, he joked about sending his picture to girls back home, along with his phone number.

I was here on assignment to write a story about the second day of evacuations in one area of Waverly as transfer of the propane began.

The townspeople seemed nonchalant about it Friday morning. Some even brought their children to the site to watch the debris from Wednesday night's derailment be cleared away.

Granted, at least one woman said she moved temporarily out of her home within a few blocks of the wreck site to her daughter's house because she was "scared."

But one worker at Meriwether Lewis Electric Cooperative seemed to sum up the town's atmosphere pretty well. "We don't get too excited about things around here," she said.

That was about two hours before the explosion.

I first went to the wreck site about 11 a.m. Crews were using cranes to move mangled cars from the track in preparation for the afternoon's transfer of the liquid propane.

I talked with Ron Collins, state Civil Defense official

from Jackson, who was giving orders to other workers to begin evacuating residents of the small white homes across the tracks and downwind of the wreck site.

Everything seemed to be going smoothly in preparation for the pumping, so about 1:45 p.m. I left the site to call my editor to dictate a "featurey story" about the cleanup operations.

I drove to a nearby shopping center, drank a Coke, assembled my story and called Nashville. By about 2:30 p.m., I had finished my dictation. I loaded my notebooks and camera in the car and drove through town.

From traffic-slowed U.S. 70 through Waverly's business district, I considered making another visit to the wreck site.

But it was close to 2:45 p.m. and, I confess, I had decided the story wasn't worth another stop.

As I approached McEwen, a small community about 10 miles east of Waverly, three ambulances heading toward Waverly rushed past me.

I pulled my car into a convenience store parking lot and ran for the telephone. A clerk sped by me, hollering, "There's a wreck somewhere. I'm going to see if I can hear about it on the CB."

And after a check with my editor, I left the store and saw a strange, mushrooming cloud on the horizon, ominous in the way it completely dominated the rolling landscape.

Approaching Waverly, it seemed every resident along the highway and every business worker was outside, standing by the road and watching the cloud rise.

Waverly was chaos. Regular traffic was practically at a stand-still as ambulances and fire engines from neighboring communities weaved between cars.

Telephones were out of order. The sidewalks were packed with people, some crying, some yelling. Shattered glass from windows blown out by the force of the blast littered the street.

It had all seemed so easygoing earlier—construction workers operating cranes at the wreck had smoked cigarettes near the tanker as they joked during a work break.

And those same men, the ones who were killed or injured in Waverly's most horrible tragedy Friday, just a few hours earlier were drinking soft drinks and talking about their weekend plans.

I parked my car and, breathing a word of thanks, pulled my notebook and camera from the front seat and walked toward the disaster site.

* * *

Sixteen people died as a result of the Waverly explosion, including Rex Gaut and the town's fire chief and police chief. Forty-three were hospitalized with burns and other injuries.

Though phones were knocked out, one payphone—oddly enough—was still working when I got downtown. I called my editor again to let her know I had made it back to Waverly. She told me there was a crew of *Banner* reporters and photographers on their way from Nashville to take over for me in the evening. An aerial photography team, too.

I told her about the photos I'd taken of the worker smoking and drinking a Dr Pepper by one of the tanks. Then I asked her to call my parents, let them know I was okay and request they call "my roommate Ted." (It heartened me that Ted and my parents functioned together so well that day, sharing their relief that I had escaped the blast. It led me to think that when I did come out to Mom and Dad, it might not be as difficult as I'd imagined.)

After my call, I drove to the hospital to gather details about the injured. I interviewed other townspeople who had witnessed the blast, which had hurled burning bodies into the air and blown a path of destruction across two downtown blocks.

I carefully spooled the roll of film that had Rex's photo on it, checking and double-checking to be sure it had rewound completely before opening the back of the camera. (In the days before digital photography, the risk of accidentally exposing a roll of photos made for some tense moments.) Then I loaded fresh film, walked around town to get more pictures and returned to the hospital.

I must have bought something to eat from the vending machines in the facility. I don't remember what. It seemed as if time froze. When I looked up from my notepad to see a member of the *Banner* relief crew walking through the front doors of the hospital, it was nearly 8 p.m.

I gave him a download of where I'd been and what I'd learned.

"You guys okay if I head back to Nashville? I want to get these pictures in."

"We'll take it from here. I hear you got a shot of a guy smoking down there?"

"I did. I hope it turns out."

He squeezed my shoulder. "Glad you're okay, man."

"Thanks," I said. "Me, too."

* * *

It was past 10:00 p.m. when I returned to the *Banner* city room.

"There's the man!" said the editor in charge that night. "Got your pretty pictures?"

"Plenty," I said. I handed him the four rolls of film I had shot. While he called the photo department to let the photographer on duty know they were here and ready for processing, I took off my tan corduroy jacket, slung it on the chair at the desk next to mine and got to work.

The editor asked me to write a first-person account of my day at the scene, beginning with my early visit to the wreck site and my narrow miss of the explosion. I was touched that one of the gruffest guys in the newsroom treated me as tenderly as if I were his wife delivering their first baby. I was fried and he knew it. I'd reported to work at 6 that morning and had been running on adrenaline and caffeine most of the day. He was determined to get the story out of me before I crashed.

He walked across Broadway to McDonald's and bought me a hamburger and fries for a late-night supper. (There was a cafeteria in the building the *Banner* shared with the *Tennessean*, but it was closed at this hour.) As I thumbed through my notepad and clicked away on my IBM Selectric, he stood behind me and massaged my neck and shoulders. His hands even moved down to my lower back just above my belt, where he rubbed hard.

"This is where it gets me, doesn't it you? Being on your feet so long?"

"Yes," I said. "Driving, too."

"Driving is the worst."

He brought me fresh coffee.

"Sugar?" he asked.

"No thanks."

"I'll put some in anyway. You need it."

When the contact sheet of my pictures came up from the photo department, there was a full-sized proof of the money shot. My editor held it in both hands while he studied it, then looked to the fluorescent lights on the ceiling. "Thank you, Jesus," he said.

My photo of Rex Gaut was clear and well-composed. You could see the cigarette between the index and middle finger of his right hand. You could read the logo on the can of Dr Pepper beside him. About half of the metal frame around the valve on the top of the propane tank showed to the right of Rex's head, so there was no question what the long white object was behind him. The entire story in one shot. Perfect.

The editor clapped me on the back. "This will go around the world tomorrow," he said.

And so it did.

* * *

I got home after 1:00 a.m.

Ted met me at the door with a cold beer, but I set it down. I wanted one thing and one thing only.

I fell into his strong arms and wept.

Chapter Eleven: My Shot

Ted and the Big O, late 1970s

Waverly did a number on me.

There was career success. Picked up by the wire services, my first-person account ran in papers across the country. I've kept clips from the *Houston Post* and the *Galveston Daily News*, along with the stub of a check from Scottish Television for use of the photo. The *Banner*'s chief editor scrawled a note to me across the top of the day's edition: "Congratulations on a fine piece and the great distribution it got. It still scares me, as I know it does you, to think about it. Thanks."

The crowning glory? The *New York Times* mentioned me and quoted a few lines from my story in its coverage of the disaster. I was riding high. But to experience such success at the cost of such tragedy? It didn't feel right.

Sure, Rex had been smoking while taking his break by tank car #83013 (it was indeed the one that blew), but we all had been assured by the leaders of the clean-up that both tanks had been thoroughly checked and were not leaking. Though I'd thought it foolish of him to smoke so blatantly, I had gone right along with him, bantering about girlfriends and phone numbers, maybe even flirting a little, thinking how he very nearly resembled a blue-collar version of my friend Blake from my college days. I had so eagerly captured that grin of his on film. It perfectly reflected the relaxed atmosphere I witnessed at the derailment site that morning.

Now, the world suspected he was the one who caused the explosion. There was no proof, but it didn't matter. The image was proof enough for most of the media-consuming public.

Rex's family threatened to sue the *Banner* for the damage they said my photo had done to his reputation, but nothing came of it. We'd done nothing illegal. I'd had every right to be at the clean-up site that day with my camera and my notebook, and the paper had every right to print what I'd secured there. Still, I could only imagine how my photo had compounded their grief.

I rested Saturday and drove back to Waverly on Sunday for a week of follow-up stories. Late Sunday night, my last stop of the day was the local funeral home to pick up a list of service arrangements for the deceased.

"It'll just be a minute before we're finished typing them up," said the director. "Have a seat in the parlor here. Next to your buddy." He nodded toward a shiny closed coffin on a table in the middle of the maroon-carpeted room.

"My buddy?" I asked.

"Rex Gaut. The fellow you took the picture of. We're sending him back to his hometown in Alabama first thing in the morning."

A chill passed through me. I wanted to run, but then the director left the parlor and I steeled myself to take a seat in the wingback chair by the coffin. I wondered if, at some new level of existence, Rex could see me now, could hear my thoughts. I mentally ran through the apologies that had welled in me since the disaster: *I'm sorry for what happened. I'm sorry I made it out of here alive on Friday and you didn't. And yes, I'm sorry for the photo. I'm sorry it went so… public.*

The director returned to the parlor and handed me the list. I stood, shook his hand, thanked him. Then he said goodnight and returned to his office, leaving me alone again with Rex. I started to put my hand on the coffin, but something stopped me. It just didn't seem right, touching it, leaving my fingerprints on the polished wood. It seemed presumptuous somehow. An intrusion. I figured he would have scoffed at my apologies, too. I was probably the last person he'd want near him now, if given the choice.

I folded the list, tucked it into my notebook and headed back to the motel. When I got to my room, I opened the half-pint of Jack Daniel's I had packed for the week. I poured a stiff one. No doubt about it, I'd covered some grim stories in my time as a newspaper reporter, but sitting by the remains of smiling young Rex—he had only been 21, so the local authorities said—was the grimmest experience of all.

It was an eye-opener, too. I hadn't forgotten Sonny Kyle Livingston's punch in the face at the Montgomery police station a few years earlier. Now, after a brush with death, here I was making a name for myself off the tragedy of Rex Gaut and others. Was this any way to earn a living? What else would I do? Newspaper work was what I knew. Still, considering the way I felt after the Waverly disaster, even waiting tables sounded good.

The week after the explosion, there were stories about what investigators had found and dramatic features about some of the people killed and injured in the blast. Few of them were mine; the *Tennessean* and other competitors got the best ones. The following week, when I was back in the newsroom at the *Banner,* there was another note from the chief editor to my editor on the state desk. The gist was: "I don't know what happened, but you guys really dropped the ball last week."

I accepted full blame. I couldn't get the image of Rex's coffin out of my mind.

* * *

The bright spot in the tragedy was Ted.

What I hadn't reported in my first-person account was the real reason I didn't stop at the wreck site on my way home from Waverly. Ted and I had plans that evening. I wanted to get home to him, get our weekend started.

If not for Ted, if I were still a single guy devoting all my energy to "the story," I think it's highly likely I would have turned off the highway to visit the wreck site again. "One more time before I go" and all that.

Maybe I would have tracked Rex down and had another chat with him. Notebook in hand, maybe I would have been flirting with him again when the world blew up.

But that's not how it happened.

The ice beneath my feet on that frozen pond in Columbia had held one more time.

I went home to Ted.

* * *

My Waverly success teed me up for a promotion. It didn't hurt that I had recently won an Associated Press investigative reporting award for a series I had written. It dealt with the misuse of low-interest federal disaster loans in two rural counties whose landscaping nurseries, an economic mainstay in the area, had been ravaged by a harsh winter.

It was time to move off the state desk, my training ground for the past year and a half.

In March 1978, I was offered the city-side court beat, meaning I would cover all the trial courts in Nashville's consolidated city/county system. Instead of working in the newsroom at the *Banner* office, I'd work out of the *Banner*'s pressroom in the courthouse downtown. Though the pressroom was little bigger than a coat closet and sometimes housed three other *Banner* reporters who covered other aspects of county government, it was considered a plum place to work.

The offer was a flattering one. Daunting, too. Kirk Loggins, my counterpart at the *Tennessean,* was older than I and had more experience covering the beat. But, as the saying goes, it was an offer I couldn't refuse. My coverage of the Maddux trial and another big out-of-town case—a $6 million libel suit filed in Winchester, Tennessee, by an Alabama woman who claimed she had been wrongly portrayed as a whore in an NBC-TV movie about the Scottsboro boys—had given *Banner* management confidence that I could handle the new court-focused assignment.

So, I set aside my post-Waverly disillusionment and viewed the new opportunity as a breath of fresh air, something to rekindle my interest in my chosen career. I told myself it would be safer, too. In the courthouse, I'd run less chance of encountering exploding propane tanks and other disasters the *Banner* state-side reporters frequently had to cover.

Nevertheless, it was an assignment destined for failure. The folder of clippings I've kept from my days at the *Banner* tells the tale: All the clips are from my work on the state desk. Nothing from my not-so-grand and glorious days in the Nashville courthouse.

Nashville government and its system of elected judges were heavily Democratic in those days, and the *Tennessean* was the city's left-leaning paper. Kirk Loggins had a network of sources in the courthouse who turned to him whenever a big story was brewing. Why should they talk to this new guy from the city's "Republican rag?"

A story in the *Nashville Scene* when Kirk retired from the *Tennessean* in 2002 gives a good picture of what I was up against. It describes Kirk as "the peephole into Nashville's courtrooms for nearly a generation" with the friendly manner, the contacts and the expertise to make "the messy details of the court system" an interesting read.

If Kirk was the peephole, I was the blindfold. The Davidson County court system was a complex maze that I couldn't even find the door to. I dug and dug and did my best to establish relationships with the judges and clerks in the courthouse, but it was a gargantuan task.

"You need to start screwing some secretaries," said one of my editors.

It was not the kind of advice I needed to hear.

To make matters worse, the *Banner* pressroom at the courthouse was a testosterone hot spot. The guys who shared the room with me were either talking football or grousing about their wives when the subject moved away from metro government. Looking back on it, if I'd been honest with them about my relationship with Ted, they probably would have been okay with it. They were sharp guys who weren't naïve about the ways of the world. I just didn't have the courage. As a result, I stayed quiet whenever the conversation turned to personal matters. I sensed that my silence kept me from being fully accepted as one of the boys.

One morning as I got in my car to drive to the courthouse, I threw up the cranberry juice I had downed on my way out of the apartment. Our ex-nun neighbors' living room window faced the parking lot. I hoped they hadn't seen me; I didn't want anyone to witness my bout of morning anxiety. It wasn't the last.

A pattern soon developed. Kirk would break a story in the morning paper. I'd be tasked with doing a follow-up piece. Everyone saw it. Everyone noticed. In the daily news business, especially when you're a beat reporter, there's no way to hide your struggles. Your job is to break stories, not ride on the competition's coattails.

My timing was off, too. During my time covering Davidson County courts, there were no high-profile cases to fall in my lap as they had when I was on the state desk. No Scottsboro Boys. No Madduxes. I was left with stories about the "messy details" of the court system—details Kirk was so good at covering. Maybe if I'd had a stronger interest in those details, I would have fought harder, but it seemed like a hopeless struggle for something that, in the end, was not of much interest to me.

The final blow came in August. One of my responsibilities was to check the filings in the state Supreme Court to see what stories were "cooking" there. One Friday afternoon, late in the day, I quickly scanned the filings and didn't see anything of earth-shattering importance. While wanting to get home to Ted had saved my ass in Waverly, the same urge fried it this time.

What I dismissed as nonsense turned out to be a big story. As I recall, it was an early "hot coffee" case brought by a woman who claimed she was burned at a fast-food restaurant. The *Tennessean* grabbed the story and ran with it.

(The big "hot coffee" case, the one that became a national flashpoint for tort reform after a New Mexico woman was awarded nearly $3 million in punitive damages for the burns she suffered from a cup of McDonald's coffee, didn't happen until the early '90s. I can't find any record of a similar case in Tennessee, so my memory might be failing me here. It's likely, though, that if the Tennessee Supreme Court threw out the case, it wouldn't have received the national attention the Stella Liebeck case did. Still, I'm puzzled that I came up empty-handed in my research. Whether or not scalding takeout coffee was the subject of the case, my point is that I overlooked a good story and my editor, the massage therapist, was not pleased.)

"Why did you miss this?" he asked on Monday afternoon. I'd been summoned from the courthouse to the *Banner* office for "a talk."

"I didn't think it was important. I'm sorry."

"It was a lapse in news judgment, that's for sure. There's nothing to be done about it now."

He leaned back in his chair, cupped his fingers over his mouth and pinched his lips together till they puckered. Then he dropped his hand. "You've been at the courthouse for what, six months now? What do you think about going on the features desk? You're a fine reporter, but I think you'll agree that you're not in the right place."

"I don't know. Let me think about it, okay?"

"We'll talk in the morning."

* * *

"I quit," I said to Ted after work the following day.

"You what?"

"I quit. I'm tired of being compared to Kirk Loggins every day. I'm tired of being told I need to start screwing secretaries—"

"You should have talked with me about it."

"It's my career, Ted. I can do what I want with it." Whoa. I knew that didn't sound good.

He was quiet for a moment, his eyes dark. "It affects me, too."

"I know."

"It's our life together. We're supposed…" He threw up his hands. "We're supposed to talk about these things."

"I have some money saved up. We'll be fine until I find—"

"That's not the point." I'd never heard his voice so sharp, so cold.

"What do you want me to do… beg for my job back? It's a little late for that." I faked a laugh. "They took the two-way radio out of the car this afternoon." That had been a sad business, had made my abrupt end at the *Banner* real. I had hated that radio, but now that it was gone, I missed it.

"You don't get it, do you?" Ted asked.

He turned back to the kitchen sink, took the peeler and savagely attacked the carrot for our dinner salad.

Miserable, I went to the bedroom to change clothes.

Copy followed. She looked up at me, her green eyes bright.

"Don't tell me," I said. "I should have talked to you, too."

* * *

The offer of moving to the features desk was a generous one. A smart one, too. I might not have had it in me to handle the court beat for the *Banner*, but I could write features till the cows came home. I probably would have enjoyed the assignment. The schedule would have been calmer. I could have moved out of the courthouse pressroom and returned to the newsroom at the *Banner* office—a noisy, lively venue I liked.

I might have stopped puking up my cranberry juice in the mornings.

But to my young self, it was a demotion. How could I look my colleagues in the eye with that spot on my record, especially after my high-flying days covering big stories out of town?

Impulsive? Very. I'd never been sure I'd spend my entire career in newspaper work, but I hadn't expected the leaving to come this fast. Or be this clumsy. If you were young, talented and on fire, you could rise quickly in daily newspapers… at least in the 1970s. At 28, the *Banner*'s managing editor who hired me was one of the youngest people to hold an ME post at a U.S. newspaper. He was a fast-rising star, and his success held promise for all of us. I'd nipped that promise in the bud for my future in newspapers—in the Gannett system, anyway.

Several of my colleagues at the *Banner* showed unbelievable support. Thanks to their generosity, I had an easy landing. One city desk editor who respected my work knew the executive director of a healthcare lobbying group that was looking for someone to manage its communications. I called him, set up an interview and got the job. I was trying to be positive about it, although inside, the truth rankled. I was leaving the world of newspapers to become that thing most reviled by reporters: a hack. I was going into *public relations.* Egad.

"The money's good," I told Ted that evening while I grilled burgers on the hibachi in the breezeway outside our apartment. "Better than the *Banner.*"

"Good." He was still a little chilly since our previous disagreement.

"See, everything's worked out okay."

"And what if it hadn't?"

Spatula in hand, I shrugged. "I told you I was sorry."

"But sorry isn't…" He shook his head. "You really think you'll like it?"

I could hear the skepticism in his voice. "Sure. It'll be a nice change."

"Mike, please talk to me."

"We're talking."

"But there's stuff you're not telling me."

That annoyed me, too. I had failed, okay? Why did we need to belabor it? I wasn't up to it tonight. It wasn't just a failure in my chosen career of journalism. The sting went deeper. I'd been sent from the state desk to play with the big boys on the city beat in that testosterone-filled pressroom and hadn't made the cut. It was a failure of manhood, plain and simple. Proof, yet again, that I wasn't all boy.

"This year has rattled me a little," I said finally. "I haven't been happy for a long time. With work, that is. I didn't want to bother you with it. I'm fine."

Ted nodded toward the grill, where flame engulfed one of the burgers. "Isn't it time to turn those?" he asked.

My anger flared like the fire. He was not going to tell me how to cook the burgers, too. "I'll turn them when I'm fucking ready."

"Jesus." He went inside the apartment, closing the door quietly behind him. *Why not slam it?* I thought. *Why not let's have a proper fight?*

"Bastard," I whispered. I shoved the spatula under the burning burger, lifted it a few inches while the flame died down, turned it over onto a cooler part of the grill. Then I spoke to the door Ted had shut between us. "Are we happy now?"

Chapter Twelve: It's Hot Up Here

In association business attire at one of my mother's art shows

With my troubles at the *Banner* came troubles on the home front. Trouble in paradise? I guess you could call it that. It was my trouble, but it eventually became Ted's, as well. *Our trouble.* Sure, I gave our relationship credit for saving my life that day in Waverly, but beneath that glorious statement were things about us that bothered me—irritations that grew after I left the *Banner*. The problem? As we entered the second year of our life together, I was feeling overshadowed by Ted.

When does it happen? When does the beloved one shift from being a comrade to being a competitor? I know exactly when it began for Ted and me. Though there are hints in the letters we wrote to each other in the summer of 1977, the trouble didn't fully show its face until a few months later.

When it did, it startled and baffled me. I'd never experienced it in any other relationships I'd had as a maturing adult.

With Blake, with his otherworldly beauty, quick wit and sharp New York accent slicing through the sea of southern drawls at UT, he'd won any contest between us long before we'd even met. It didn't bother me that he was usually the brightest light in the room. I was his best friend and roommate and maybe something more. That was good enough for me.

With Griff, he and I rarely appeared in public as a couple, spending most of our time together at his place. There weren't many opportunities for others to make side-by-side comparisons between us. When we were together, I welcomed his greater experience in matters of sex. He was two years older than I, after all. And sometimes I was the one being deferred to. I always sensed a bit of mischievous pride on his part over the fact that I, this guy with a publicly straight persona, was in his arms or in his bed, reading the Sunday paper, my legs entwined with his. If the Canadian saw me as his southern boy conquest, I didn't mind.

With Maggie, too, I never felt her looks or accomplishments upstaged mine. *Horribile dictu*, Miss Moore might have said, Maggie was my trophy. Her glow only amplified mine. We were male and female; any comparison between us was apples to oranges, wasn't it? That's how I saw it as I considered a prime difference between the heterosexual relationship I had left with Maggie for the homosexual one I had embarked on with Ted in 1977: Because Ted and I were American male and American male, any comparison between us was apples to apples. And more and more frequently, it seemed that Ted was the bigger, shinier McIntosh in the bowl.

As the only son and the youngest child in my family, I had grown up never having to share the spotlight with anyone. And then in college, I relished the attention I received as editor of the paper and as Maggie's beau. In the years that followed, I loved seeing my name in all caps at the top of a story in the newspapers I worked for.

Things were different now in my new, post-newspaper life. My job at the healthcare association didn't have the glamor I thought journalism had had. And being cast in the role of sidekick to Ted was something I just wasn't used to. What surprised me was how angry it made me.

* * *

The first time these feelings registered was our first Halloween together in 1977, when the managers of the Rosewood Avenue apartment complex where we lived in Nashville threw a party with a costume contest.

I thought dressing up was silly, so I put together the lowest common denominator costume, my London Fog raincoat over a pair of gym shorts and nothing else. I was a flasher.

Ted, on the other hand, spent time on his costume. He used the old sewing machine his mother had handed down to him to shorten a pair of brown polyester pants, so the cuffs were a few inches above his ankles, revealing white crew socks with red stripes at the top. He found a loud, orange and brown striped polyester shirt and a worn denim jacket. A misshapen straw hat and camera with shoulder strap completed the ensemble: He was a Nashville tourist.

When the crowd voted at midnight, Ted placed second after an elementary school teacher who had designed and created an elaborate witch costume with an enormous black hat and scary makeup. My flasher, sadly, was overlooked in the competition.

"You should have won," said one of our neighbors to Ted after the contest. She was dressed as Peter Pan. "You make an adorable hick."

Others agreed. Ted got kisses and kudos from Count Dracula, Dorothy Hamill and our friend John, who applied red and white paint to a cardboard box, fit it around his torso and came as a box of Colonel Sanders fried chicken. I thought he should have won, or at least come in second after the witch.

The fact that Ted edged him out was an uncomfortable one for me. I rolled it around in my head and came up with the reason why: Ted had a charm, a charisma that made him a winner, even with a costume that wasn't as funny or clever or crafty as the fried chicken box. Heck, Ted probably would have placed even if he'd worn my flasher costume, I reasoned. He would have carried it off, whereas I hadn't been able to.

It sounds silly now, being jealous over a Halloween costume contest, going into such mental contortions over it, but it was something more to me. It was the moment I discovered a hairline crack in this thing I had with Ted, the flipside of what had been a terrific original record. I tried to ignore it at first, but there were reminders of its presence in the months that followed.

"You have the most amazing blue eyes," people would say to Ted when he and I went somewhere together—a party, say, or a restaurant. Ted would accept the compliment gracefully while I stood by in silence, thinking, *What am I? Chopped liver?*

There were occasional gibes about how Ted, with his blue-ribbon academic career—undergrad at Furman, grad school at Vanderbilt—deigned to be involved with someone with a considerably less-than-blue-ribbon bachelor's degree from UT.

"Go Big Orange!" someone invariably joked, or asked me, "Will you sing 'Rocky Top' tonight?"

A more secure person might have let these comments slide, but they got to me. Underscoring my resentment was the galling truth that Ted didn't view me as a competitor at all. At least, he didn't appear to.

Ted's having already come out to his parents, while I kept delaying telling mine the news, was another way in which I felt Ted was several steps ahead of me. And his wider sexual experience was a sore spot. Ted had told me of several other men he'd had affairs with since moving to Nashville. Besides Dan, the dinner theater performer, and Ryan, the married guy, there was also a brief fling with a well-known local TV personality who had the smooth good looks of a Harry Belafonte. My gay history was tame in comparison, downright boring, come to think of it, much of it dominated by a passionate love affair that had never come to fruition. Griff was the one halfway interesting story—and even that was a stretch.

Was it twisted to feel this way? I wondered. Did it happen with other gay couples, this lopsided rivalry? I didn't know anyone to ask. There was Mark, an ex-boyfriend of Ted's, and his new boyfriend, Andy, whom we saw occasionally. They were getting serious with one another, talking about their dream of getting rich by flipping houses until one day they could buy into Nashville's most prestigious zip code, 37205. They seemed like such a cohesive team. How would I ever broach the topic with them? I would have been embarrassed to bring it up.

And the straight friends who knew about us? Leslie, Ted's friend from Vanderbilt. Greg, his roommate in Ann Arbor and his wife, Cynthia. John, he of the Colonel Sanders chicken costume, and his soon-to-be wife, Eleanor. Frank, my copyeditor friend at the *Banner,* the only person other than my sister Pat in whom I had confided about my relationship with Ted. How would I even begin to talk with them about this problem, this bug in the new software release that was Mike and Ted?

So, I kept silent. But I began to look for methods to deal with my feelings, to even the score between Ted and me… in my own private way. In the year immediately following my departure from the *Banner*, when my ego was at its most fragile and my professional future anyone's guess, I put some of those methods into action.

* * *

My job with the healthcare association was not challenging. I wrote a newsletter that went out every other Friday to the facilities that were members of the group. I wrote occasional op-ed pieces for the executive director, and letters from him to the membership. I edited the new membership directory, a tedious proofreading task.

I learned quickly that I was addicted to headlines and deadlines. After four years of working for afternoon dailies in Montgomery and Nashville, I had grown accustomed to an adrenaline rush around 11 o'clock in the morning. It fueled me through the nerve-jangling hour while I cranked out my stories to meet the noon deadline that both the *Banner* and the *Alabama Journal* had for their first editions of the afternoon.

Now, I was like Pavlov's dog. In my quiet office at the association's headquarters, the adrenaline flowed with nowhere to go. Some days I'd want to jump on my desk and shout, "Get me out of here!"

I knew taking the job wasn't the best choice. But then, had I done anything right since the day I drove out of Waverly?

My new colleagues were nice, but I resented their lunch invitations to get to know me. I didn't want to sit at the local meat-and-three or barbecue joint and make pleasant conversation. I wanted to get in my car and drive somewhere, anywhere.

One of the places I drove to at lunchtime was the apartment of a young man I had met in a swim program at a high school's indoor pool near my office. (I'd pretty much abandoned any regular exercise when I worked at the *Banner*. I'd made a commitment to change that.) While we walked to our cars in the chilly fall air after our workout one night, the fellow invited me back to his place. There was something impetuous, teasing about the invitation, so I had little doubt about his intentions.

I declined, but I kept the fast-food receipt on which he'd written his phone number. Over the next few days, questions tumbled through my head:

Should I call him? Why do I want to? What harm could it do?

I stuffed the receipt in my sock drawer and tried to forget about it until a few days later, when Ted attended a lecture at Vanderbilt and came home around 11 p.m.

"That was a long lecture," I said to him. I had watched Johnny Carson's monologue on *The Tonight Show* and was getting ready for bed.

"A bunch of us went over to Marty's afterward. We had a heated discussion about Hannah Arendt," he said.

I rinsed my toothbrush, put it in the holder by the sink. "She wrote about totalitarianism, right?"

He stood at the bedroom door across from the bathroom, unbuttoning the pale pink and white pinstriped Oxford cloth shirt, the one that looked so good on him. "How do you know about Hannah Arendt?"

His emphasis on *you* irritated me, as if I couldn't possibly have known about one of the key political thinkers of the 20th century. "AP history in high school got me into a great world history class freshman year at UT. We did a whole section on Nazi Germany."

"Good for you."

I walked past him into the bedroom. "UT was nice. We had books and everything."

"Michael…" he cautioned.

"While I was there, they even got rid of the Sears catalogs and put toilet paper in the restrooms."

He came toward me, kissed my temple. "Don't be defensive."

I called my swim buddy the next day.

Since moving in together, Ted and I had never made vows of fidelity to one another. Were we supposed to be monogamous? I didn't know and wasn't about to bring up the subject. I simply decided to take advantage of the ambiguity. Besides, I had no guarantees that Ted wasn't doing the same thing during those long afternoons when he said he was at the Vanderbilt library, or after those grad school softball league games when they'd gather for beer with the opposing team. As long as we weren't getting serious with anyone, what difference did it make?

I had no intention of getting serious with the guy from the swim program. His name was Michael, too. I don't remember much else about him. He was blandly good-looking. I think he was a nurse of some sort. It was the reason he had some days off during the week. There weren't dazzling sparks of passion between us, but he had one important feature:

For the times we were together, he gave me his undivided attention. With no requests to sing "Rocky Top." No comments about Hannah Arendt.

* * *

Another place I visited at lunchtime was a hair salon within a mile of the association's office. I had first gone there to get my hair cut late one afternoon. With his heavily product-treated mullet (was it mousse, gel, hairspray?), pierced ear, colorful wardrobe—yellow shirts, baby blue slacks—and penchant for rings and bracelets, the owner was clearly gay. While he went to work on me with his comb and scissors, he was touchy-feely, letting his fingers linger on my neck and shoulders longer than they would have during an ordinary haircut. I did nothing to dissuade him. When he finished, he said I was his last client of the day.

"Would you like a beer?" he asked.

I looked at my watch. "A quick one, sure."

He put the CLOSED sign on the front door, led me to a back room with a well-stocked refrigerator, a sofa and shower.

I laughed when he showed me the sofa was a pullout.

"You've got everything," I said.

"And now I've got you," he said, unbuckling my belt.

* * *

I had imagined if I married Maggie, I would go on having encounters with men behind her back, but I hadn't anticipated the same urges after I moved in with Ted. In some ways, maybe even stronger. In some ways, it was as if a door had opened to something long suppressed.

I didn't see any need to shut it. Though it did startle me sometimes, my sexual appetite, how it gnawed at me compared to its rather timid nibbles in college. I told myself my body had simply matured, was feeling its hormones as I entered my late 20s, though I knew deep down there were emotional as well as physical drivers for my seeking sex apart from Ted. I could look at it one of two ways: My excursions either had nothing to do with Ted—I was simply sowing my gay wild oats—or they had everything to do with him, a response to some grievance on my growing list.

In some ways, I was like a little kid not getting enough attention at school or throwing a tantrum after losing a game on the playground. My tantrums involved secret places, dropped trousers, quick goodbyes. It was the easiest possible way to get attention. I didn't realize it at the time, but there was an element of my own homophobia in what I was doing, too. I ran from my pleasant, out-of-the-closet life with Ted to man-on-man sex in the shadows, where part of me believed it belonged.

For me, it was a relief to acknowledge that sex between men was an everyday fact of life. It didn't have to be cloaked in some romantic dream of Achilles and Patroclus to blaze furiously, satisfyingly… until the next time. I wanted to be part of that reality—and yet I knew that returning to it time and again meant not only winning something briefly, but losing something, too. Losing the lovestruck guy who wrote those letters to Ted when he was in Ann Arbor. Cheapening the thing we had.

* * *

Ted was also changing in ways we wouldn't have predicted our first summer together.

The smart political scientist and statistician dropped out of grad school.

"Why did you do that?" I asked him on a spring morning in 2020 as he drove me to St. Joseph's Hospital in Atlanta for a follow-up appointment six months after my open-heart surgery. As I drafted this memoir, I couldn't remember his reasons for dropping out.

"I hated it," he said without hesitation. "My scholarship money had run out. I needed a job. And I found out I didn't like teaching. Why go on with something when you know it's not going to work?"

(All good answers, but I remember thinking when it happened that Ted left grad school because he was unsure about me after my abrupt departure from the *Banner*, that he realized it was time to start making more money in case I did something else impulsive.)

After he left Vanderbilt, he got a job working the front desk at the new Hyatt Regency Hotel in downtown Nashville. The job introduced us to a whole new stratum of Nashville's 20-somethings and 30-somethings. My colleagues at the *Banner* had been driven by devotion to their careers. The folks at the Hyatt, at least the ones Ted worked with, weren't like that.

They just wanted to party. So that's what we did.

A little too much. With Ted untethered from grad school and me untethered from journalism, the latter part of 1978 through 1979 was a wild time for us. I led the charge. Fortunately, no one had heard of AIDS at the time.

At a Halloween bash thrown by a manager of the hotel front desk staff, Ted reprised his Nashville tourist costume, the award winner at the Rosewood Avenue party a year earlier. My costume was the same tired one I'd worn. Though I had added a mustache drawn on with an eyebrow pencil I'd bravely bought at the drugstore, my costume hardly required the kind of creativity another guest displayed. He wore a yellow-and-white-checked tablecloth with paper plates, cups and plastic eating utensils stapled all over it. He was a picnic.

I discovered, though, that my costume had an advantage over anything more carefully thought out I might have put together: It made everything handily accessible for the late-night dalliance with Mr. Picnic, a cute hotel clerk who asked if I'd like "to go out back for a while."

Afterward, Mr. Picnic and I rejoined the party by separate entrances. Ted was nowhere around, so I figured I'd done a good job covering my little secret. Then Ted approached me in the living room with a red Solo cup in his hand and a quizzical look on his face.

"Where's your mustache?" he asked.

"My mustache?"

"It's gone."

I shrugged. "I guess it gradually wore off through the evening."

I went to the half bath off the living room and saw the proof in the mirror. The mustache had indeed not survived my lusty 15 minutes with Mr. Picnic. Not even a tiny smudge of the eyebrow pencil remained on my upper lip.

"Shit," I said to my reflection.

Today, the word would be *busted.*

* * *

Another time, after a weekend of sniping at each other over little things—"why would you put a gallon bag of chili in the refrigerator without being sure the bag was sealed?"—Ted and I went to a disco called the Carousel. Fueled by liquor (with my newfound freedom from the discipline of journalism, I was drinking more) and jealousy over the kiss one of his ex-boyfriends planted on his lips when we entered the place, I became acquainted with two young men with military haircuts. They had driven down from a small town on the Kentucky-Tennessee line to go dancing.

"We're doing a foursome," I said after I slurred through my introduction of the two eager-looking fellows to Ted. Donna Summer's latest blared from the dance floor. Pink lights whirled above.

"A what?" Ted asked.

"A foursome. We're going back to our apartment and we're going to have sex."

Ted was speechless.

"Lead the way," one of the Kentuckians said with a grin.

Angry, Ted pulled the car keys from his jeans pocket, dangled them in front of me and then clasped them noisily in his fist.

"Let's go," he said.

Our foursome never happened; the poor guys were stopped by the police as they followed us back to our apartment. My heart sank when I saw the flashing blue lights behind their car in the rearview mirror, watched them pull onto the shoulder of Hillsboro Road. I knew we couldn't stop or we'd risk arrest, too. So, we escaped scot-free.

"Satisfied?" Ted asked.

"No."

"You scare me sometimes."

"I'm sorry. I'll do better, okay?"

It didn't sound convincing. The truth was, I was scaring myself.

* * *

I couldn't blame Ted for doing some exploring on his own.

He told me about a handsome tour guide who brought substantial business to the Hyatt, how the two of them had had a make-out session in the fellow's car one evening after a group happy hour at the Gold Rush, a trendy Elliston Place watering hole, "but it didn't amount to anything," he said. I could hardly complain, given the fact that I was usually doing more than making out with the guys I met.

At another party one summer night in 1979, Ted disappeared much as I had done the previous Halloween with Mr. Picnic. I found him behind the host's house, where he sat on the brick half-wall that enclosed the outdoor air conditioning unit. Standing before him was a lanky fellow with shaggy blondish hair like John Ritter on *Three's Company*. I hated that show. I hated this guy.

Ted appeared to like him, however. He was laughing at something the fellow had said, then looked up and smiled as the fellow leaned closer. They kissed. I went inside and splashed more wine in my cup. *Let him have his fun,* I thought.

And he did. Soon Ted was heading my way. He told me he was leaving with his new friend, in the fellow's car, to go to our apartment.

"You're leaving me here?" I asked, stunned.

He shrugged. "You've got your car. You can go wherever and do whomever you want. You usually do." He snapped his fingers, as if a bright idea had dawned. "Maybe you could try a foursome."

He turned and walked away. Chastened, I nursed my drink.

I didn't try another foursome, but I did stay long enough to get invited to another party.

At midnight, after several more drinks and a group-shared joint, I found myself naked in a Belle Meade (zip code 37205) swimming pool with a dozen other gay men. Christian evangelicals would have reveled in it; in and around the pool was just the kind of decadent behavior decried from their pulpits then and now. Men entwined themselves in groups of two and three in the amber light from the French doors that lined the back of the house. Poppers were passed around freely. We were a poster shot for "the gay lifestyle."

One guy sat on my shoulders. We played Horse in the turquoise, chlorine-scented water with another impromptu couple. It was a weird, nighttime reversal of the game from my childhood summer days at the country club pool, when I'd sit on my favorite lifeguard's shoulders. Here we were naked. Here we could touch whomever and whatever we wanted.

It was like a scene from *Dancer from the Dance,* Andrew Holleran's unsettling novel about the gay party life on Fire Island. When it was published in 1978, it was one of the few mainstream books available about gay men. Reading it, I felt I had missed something—the parties, the clubs, the nightly sex with no strings attached. I asked myself if I might have settled down too soon.

I'd even dreamed about an orgy-in-the-pool scene one night while I was reading the book, and now here I was… taking part in one. Here, in real life, I was getting my wish—and all I could think of was Ted. What were he and the John Ritter-ish guy doing in our apartment? Why hadn't I resisted when he announced they were leaving the party? It had been a balmy, starlit night in Nashville, rich with the green smell of summer, a perfect night for falling in love. Were they? Could this mean the end of us?

Three would be a crowd indeed if the guy was still there with Ted when I got home, but I had to do it. I climbed out of the pool.

"Leaving so soon?" It was the slender, red-mustached guy who'd sat on my shoulders.

"Yeah. It's late." Whatever his sweet smile promised, I didn't want it tonight. "You guys have fun."

I grabbed a towel from the stack on a lounge chair and crossed the flagstone terrace to the house.

The living room was empty, eerily quiet. Our 50ish host was upstairs with one of the young guests. I found my shorts and Hang Ten T-shirt where I'd left them on the arm of the leather sofa. I dressed quickly, slung the damp towel over the wrought iron banister in the marble foyer and headed out the front door.

I don't know how I drove back to Rosewood Avenue that night. Somehow I made it without any blue lights appearing behind me. I unlocked the door to our apartment well after 2:00 Ted was asleep in our bedroom, his guest gone. *Good.*

I took off my shoes and crashed on the daybed. Home. Pressing my throbbing forehead into one of the pillows, I patted Copy as she curled next to me.

Cats are indispensable in troubled times.

* * *

"Want some coffee?" Ted asked the next morning. He had showered and dressed. Sunday morning sun streamed through the living room window, whether I was ready for it or not.

"Yes, please," I said.

"Breakfast?"

"Maybe some toast."

I sat up on the daybed. Big O was chowing down on her dry food in the kitchen like any other morning. Copy stayed by me.

"Did you like it last night?" I asked.

"No, I didn't like it," Ted said from the kitchen. He loudly snapped the lid in place on our yellow plastic percolator, as if to add an exclamation point to the end of his words. "What did you do?"

"I went to another party. Where else was I going to go?"

"Have fun?"

"No." I walked to the kitchen, where Ted put bread in the toaster. "I missed you."

"I missed you, too."

Relief flowed through me. "I'm glad we both got home okay."

He took butter and strawberry preserves from the refrigerator. "Can we have a normal day today?"

It's one of the best questions anyone has ever asked me. "Yes," I answered.

I was ready, so ready, for normal.

* * *

We did laundry. We went to the flea market. We went to RadioShack and bought a new set of speakers for the stereo. We went to Kroger and picked up the makings for spaghetti that night. Comfort food before anyone had coined the phrase.

One messy piece of business was Ted's date from the night before calling to ask if he could see him again. Ted said no thanks.

"I've got something here," he told the fellow. "I don't want to give it up."

Thank God, I thought, love filling my heart. The guy was hanging in with me. I was lucky. Luckier than I deserved.

Alcohol was not on the menu that evening. The television stayed off. We talked and talked. We cleaned up the kitchen together and turned the living room lights off by 9:00. When we got in bed, Ted put his arms around me.

"This is what I want," he said. "Right here."

I thought of the Paul Jenkins print hanging over our bed. An explosion of color. A mess, some might say, but a beautiful one, a painting with an underlying structure that was clear if you looked closely. Like my life with this man. Color and structure—even though at times all I wanted was to run away from it. I felt like crying as I pulled him close.

"I'm sorry I get angry with you sometimes," I said.

"It's okay. I get angry with you sometimes, too."

"Can we get back on an even keel? Stop the craziness?"

"I'd like that."

"Me, too." I inhaled his toothpaste scent. "Why can't we just love each other?"

"We can." He stroked my back, his breath soft on my shoulder. "If you'd let us."

Chapter Thirteen: Point of No Return

My 26th birthday celebration in 1978 at my parents' apartment, while I still maintained the fiction with Mom and Dad that Ted was "just a roommate."

"Letting us" wasn't as easy as Ted made it sound. I faced another hurdle—coming out to my parents.

The thought terrified me. So, during those years when Ted and I struggled to make a go of being a couple, I continued to avoid telling my parents the full story about us. They knew I had broken up with Maggie because, as I told my father and later my mother, when she returned from the Presbyterian women's retreat in North Carolina, "I'm just not ready to get married," but they didn't know the full story. They had their suspicions about Ted and me, I'm sure, but I hadn't told them in so many words that we were lovers.

We had some good times with my parents. There was one rollicking birthday party for me at their apartment when Ted came with me. He liked my parents, though he was sometimes bemused by their idiosyncrasies. One winter evening when he and I went to their place for dinner, they had the heat turned so high that Ted went to the guest bathroom and lay down on the floor, his cheek against the cool ceramic tiles.

"They're fun people," he said to me later. "But why do they keep it so damn hot?"

My reluctance to talk with them about my homosexuality got in the way especially around Thanksgiving and Christmas. Ted wanted us to spend the holidays together with his family or mine; I would have been content with splitting up on holidays, the old "we're just roommates" game. We'd done that a time or two our first years together, like the Christmas we thought the cats had turned on the tree lights. I had gone to my parents' apartment later that morning to spend the day with them; Ted had loaded up his car and driven to South Carolina for a few days with his family. I understood why Ted didn't want the practice to continue, but I still felt pressured. He was impatient, dissatisfied with my limbo state, especially since he'd told his folks about us not long after we'd moved in together.

It made me anxious, left me dreading the holidays I had loved as a kid. I found myself wishing we lived in Australia so we could avoid our families entirely at Thanksgiving and Christmas. But we didn't. Something had to give.

As it turned out, it was my sister Pat who explained the facts to Mom and Dad when she was visiting them. She was one of the first people I had told about my relationship with Ted, not long after he and I met in 1977; she'd grown tired of having to conceal the truth from our parents whenever my name came up. Yes, she outed me.

Memoir is a strange animal. Sometimes it's a disconcerting visit to the memory bank. Small incidents shine through crystal clear in my memory. The major ones sometimes not so much. The biggest challenge Ted and I have in remembering things from our early days together is where to place them on a timeline. What year did that happen? What was the weather like? Where were we working at the time? Were both kitties with us, or had Big O crossed the rainbow bridge, which she did several years before Copy?

Maybe it's a defense mechanism that neither Ted nor I remembers the exact date that I had "the discussion" with my parents, or some of the logistics of that day. But if that's what it is, a defense mechanism, it's not a very good one. Sometimes I think if I had a specific date, it would be easier to close the book on it. As it is, the memory hovers untethered, floating into my consciousness when I least expect it, even now, some four decades later. It's a painful, horrible memory. I don't think it's hyperbole to say it's a ghost that perennially haunts my life… if I let it.

My best guess is that it occurred in the summer of 1979 when I was 26, not long after my *Dancer from the Dance* night in the swimming pool in Belle Meade. Not long after Ted and I pledged to get back on an even keel. Despite the timeline fogginess, I remember precisely the things that were said that day. And I remember exactly how it felt.

* * *

Pat phoned me from Mom and Dad's that day. Ted and I had been planning to go see them for a spaghetti dinner that night, but Pat counseled it might be best if Ted didn't come. Mom wanted to talk to me alone.

"It's not good," Pat said.

Part of me was angry that Pat had told them without asking me; another was relieved that she had spared me that job. Whatever, the confrontation came at last.

It was late afternoon. Ted and I agreed that he'd be on his own for dinner. "I'll do something with Leslie," he said. Alone, I drove my yellow Volkswagen Beetle across town to my parents' apartment by Percy Priest Lake. Not knowing what to expect, I could feel my body tightening, as if someone had placed an icy hand on my back.

The apartment was oddly quiet when I arrived. Pat answered the door and headed out for a run. Dad was nowhere in sight. I walked through the living room, the smell of Mom's spaghetti sauce wafting from the kitchen. Mom was seated at the dining table that occupied one end of the L-shaped living room, where the big jade plant caught the setting sun's mellow light from the corner window.

"Hi Mom," I said. I could tell by the look on her face that there wouldn't be any hugs that afternoon. I'd never seen her look so grave.

"Aren't you going to say hello?" I asked.

"Sit down, Michael," she said.

Fear invading my heart, I sat. She had some paperwork in front of her, probably an application form for one of the many art shows she entered. I knew she and Pat had spent the previous day shopping. Today was one of her stay-home-and-paint days, her fair skin gleaming with the cream she applied on the days she didn't wear makeup. It smelled like roses.

"I have a few things to say to you." She put down the pen she'd been holding, looked at me fiercely. "You… are a liar."

It was a kick in the stomach. Such harsh words, and not at all what I'd expected. I'd thought her tone might be more sympathetic, more "help me understand this, Michael," instead of this direct assault.

"What do you mean?" I asked.

She proceeded to tell me how the minister at the Presbyterian church she and Dad attended had reported seeing Ted and me one weekend on the interstate east of Nashville, our car loaded with what looked like camping gear, sleeping bags and the like. She was right. I had lied. Mom and Dad had wanted me to do something with them that weekend—lunch and another art show, probably—and I had told them I needed to stay home and work. I had seen the minister and his wife when we passed them on the highway and thought, "Oh shit," when it was clear he recognized me, too.

"You've got me there, Mom," I said, my mouth dry. "I didn't want you to know Ted and I had plans to go camping together that weekend. I'm sorry." Despite my deferential tone, anger brewed inside me to think that the minister had reported my whereabouts, and to see the pride on Mom's face that she had known my secret all along.

"We knew then something was up," she said. "But it's not just the lying. You're a taker, too."

"A taker?" *What is this?* I wondered. *A recitation of my deadliest sins?*

She drummed four fingers of one hand on the tabletop, like a neat row of dominoes falling. "I've seen for years how selfish you can be. I've never said a word about it. But now. This. It's time someone told you to your face. You are a taker."

A weight settled in my stomach. Bittersweet bile rose in my throat. I thought I was going to be sick. *A taker?* I gripped the wooden slats on the sides of the chair seat, took a few deep breaths. Where was Dad? I had seen that his and Mom's bedroom door was open when I entered the apartment, and now I could hear the soft shuffling of books, pages being turned in their room. Was he just sitting there listening? Why wasn't he part of this conversation?

I swallowed. "I don't think doing something you don't approve of is being a taker. Just because—"

"I'm not talking about you and Ted. We'll get to that. I'm talking about the way you are, always thinking of yourself."

"When? What are you talking about?" I relaxed my grip on the chair, tried to calm myself, but anger was building in my gut. The cold hand pushed harder between my shoulder blades. "I've been working my tail off since college making a career for myself. If that's being selfish…"

She was shaking her head. "I'm talking about the little things. A million little things."

"Like what?"

She gave a laugh. "Like helping yourself to our record albums when we were in Florida."

"What?"

"You know."

"But…" Why in heaven's name was she bringing this up? I was here to talk about Ted. But I followed her path. "That's why I came and got them. You were in Florida. I brought them back after you got home."

"It surprised us, though, that you just waltzed in."

"I was watering your plants. I have a key, remember?"

My parents had been avid record collectors, though they no longer had a record player since their return to Nashville when Dad retired. They had a cassette tape player now. The albums sat on the floor in the guest bathroom closet, untouched. I hadn't told them that the main reason I took a few of the albums home one afternoon was that I wanted Ted to hear the song "I Loved You Once in Silence" from the original Broadway cast recording of *Camelot* with Julie Andrews and Robert Goulet. Though the song was written for Guinevere to sing to Lancelot, I thought it was a perfect song about hidden homosexual love. I wanted us to listen to it together. While looking for the album, I found *Fiddler on the Roof* and *Funny Girl,* which I had taken home, too… after watering the plants.

"You should have asked us," she said.

"I should have called you long distance to borrow a couple albums?"

"Courtesy has a cost. I guess that doesn't matter to you."

"Courtesy?" I felt the chasm grow between us. It wasn't that I borrowed the albums without asking. It was that I was no longer entitled to share family property without seeking permission, like a stranger or a mere acquaintance. That wouldn't have happened, I felt sure, if I had borrowed the albums to share with Maggie. Mom would have told us to take the entire stack. My anger kicked up a notch.

"Come on, Mom. If I hadn't moved in with Ted, we wouldn't be sitting here talking about record albums."

"He's a taker, too."

That one made me angrier than the record albums. "Ted has been nothing but nice to you since you met him. He cooked you dinner recently, remember? The veal?"

"I don't remember that."

"He worked all day on it. You and Dad enjoyed it. Or you said you did."

"That was some time ago."

"It was only a few months ago!" This was getting crazier and crazier. I put my elbows on the table, covered my face with my hands. Her feigned forgetfulness was infuriating.

"It's very hurtful to us," she said, "that you've let him lead you down this path."

I slammed my hand on the oak table. "Dammit, mother, he hasn't led me anywhere." I enjoyed the startled light in her eyes. "I'm sorry about Maggie, but Ted and I are in love with each other. You can accept it or not. But you will not call me a taker just because I'm not acting the way you want me to. And you will not insult Ted, either."

Dad was in the doorway, apparently summoned by the smack of my hand on the table, my raised voice.

"I can't listen to this." Mom stood, pushing up the cuffs of her painting shirt, an old dress shirt of Dad's with a slash of cadmium red on the sleeve. She looked at Dad. "He's lecturing us now, Bob."

"Honey," he said to her. "We can work this out, can't we?"

She said, "I don't want to work it out. I want…" She looked from Dad to me, her eyes brimming with tears. "I want Maggie to be your roommate." She went to the kitchen. From my spot in the dining room, I could see her standing at the sink, head down, dabbing at her eyes with a paper napkin.

That got me. After all I'd done and undone in the past few years, I owed her this. I knew she loved Maggie. I stepped through the kitchen doorway. "Mom, I'm sorry."

"Sorry?" She faced me with cold, hard light in her eyes. "You can take your sorries and go… to… hell."

* * *

I was stunned, heartsick. How had this gone so wrong?

"Will you come in the den and sit for a while?" Dad asked me as I left the kitchen. His voice was calm, patient.

The front door was opening. Pat was back from her run. I didn't want to see her, so I crossed the living room and turned down the short hallway to the den. It was cooler back there, at least, the curtains drawn. On the wall behind Dad's easy chair were the framed crayon drawings I had made in the second grade. One was of a hummingbird nest with three tiny eggs in it, mama and papa hummingbird suspended in air on either side of it, carefully guarding their bounty. Above it was my drawing of a blue jay perched on a tree branch, a musical staff with eighth notes flowing like a ribbon from its beak across the paper.

I lifted the drawing from its hook on the wall. On the back was the blue ribbon it had won at the Maury County fair in Columbia; Mom had taped it there when the fair was over. She had been so proud of me. The sweet memory tugged at my heart, but soon a grim, poisonous feeling overtook it.

I had known all along, hadn't I? Even in the second grade when I drew the pictures, when I was a happy little kid with a box of Crayola crayons and not a trouble in the world. I had known this day would come. The day everything would change.

I returned the drawing to its hook on the wall. Feeling as if I'd been slapped, harshly but rightfully punished for the disappointing son I was, I sat on the sofa, my pulse pounding in my ears. In the next room, my father and Pat spoke in low, dire tones. They were talking about me. Me. The liar. The taker.

A fresh jolt of anger, thrilling and scary, drew me to my feet. I was not going to sit and listen to them talk about me as if I were an outsider, as if I were a sick patient in the next hospital room. I pulled my car keys out of my pocket and strode down the hall to the living room, my heart doing double-time in my chest. It seemed just as scared and excited as I was, as if it were struggling to keep up with me, with the decision I had made.

"Mike!" Dad said, overly cheery. "I was just coming in to talk with you."

"I don't want to talk anymore, Dad. I'm going."

Mom was still in the kitchen, her back to our conversation in the foyer.

"You're not staying for dinner?" Pat asked, her voice oozing with condescending sympathy that brought my blood to a boil.

"No. I'm not. I don't want to be accused three months from now of taking food that doesn't belong to me."

"Come on now. Can't we talk about this?" Dad asked, gentle light in his clear blue eyes.

"Not as long as she feels the way she does." I looked in the kitchen again. "Good night, mother."

No reply.

"Good night, everyone." I slammed the door behind me. Standing on the front porch of the apartment, I savored the fresh evening air, a blessing after being bottled up in the apartment. I was free—just me, the pounding of my heart and the fading pink sky overhead.

I unlocked the door to my Volkswagen, slid onto the seat and started the engine.

The front door to the apartment opened. Dad pushed on the storm door and stepped onto the porch.

"Mike!" he called. He knew what had transpired at the dining room table was wrong. I could see it on his face.

Then why didn't you do something? I wanted to say to him. *Why did you sit in your goddamn bedroom and let it happen?*

"Hey, Mike!"

I put the car in reverse, backed out of the parking space, shifted to drive and stepped on the accelerator.

"Mike!"

I looked in the rearview mirror, saw him standing alone on the porch in his plaid cotton shirt, face drawn, arms hanging at his sides.

Once when I was in junior high school, Dad left us. It wasn't for long, only an hour or two. It was when everyone knew DuPont's Corfam project was dying after a disastrous product rollout, the disaster multiplied by the over-expenditures on the big house we had built in Nashville in the days Corfam was expected to be a glowing success. He and Mom had argued; Dad had walked out, pulled the car out of the garage and simply driven away, leaving us alone for a brief but terrifying time.

I remembered how it felt, being abandoned like that without a goodbye. Like the bottom had dropped out of the world.

"It's my turn to leave now, Dad," I said to the mirror. I pulled to the apartment complex's exit, waited for the automatic gates to creak slowly open. It seemed to take forever, but soon the way was clear. I stepped on the accelerator and turned the car toward home.

* * *

I was relieved to see that Leslie had come back to our apartment after dinner with Ted. I could be spared sharing all the gory details while she was with us. I didn't have the strength to go into those details with Ted now. She sat in the bentwood rocker in the living room. Ted sat across from her on the daybed. They drank herbal tea.

"How did it go?" Ted asked.

"Lousy," I said.

"Aw," said Leslie, the mug of tea cradled in her hands. "I'm sorry." With her kind smile and gentle voice, she was a comforting, intelligent presence, an ally when I needed one.

"No surprise, really." I went to the kitchen, got a glass of water, chugged it, as if I'd completed a 5K run.

"Have you eaten?" Ted asked.

"No."

"Want something?"

"No, thanks." I came back to the living room, sat next to Ted on the daybed. "I really am exhausted."

"Here. Lie down." He placed a pillow at the head of the daybed for me, took another one and sat cross-legged on the floor between Leslie and me.

At this point, all I could do was follow his instructions. Limbs heavy, I stretched out on the daybed. I felt like one of those wooden figures held together by a string pulled tight. Push the button on the bottom and the whole thing collapses.

I pictured my dad standing on the porch, watching me go. He looked so dejected. I hoped he was okay. It was a major thing, my leaving after decades of good son-ism. It was anybody's guess what the next step would be, or who would take it.

Folding my hands over my belt buckle, I took slow, steady breaths, trying to quiet the voices in my head. I took comfort listening to Ted and Leslie revisit their time in grad school, gossip about one of their professors in the program at Vanderbilt. Their banter was funny, carefree. After a while, I caught only snatches of what they were saying, and soon I drifted off to the sweet oblivion of sleep.

* * *

Mom phoned the next morning while I made the bed. I hoped for an apology, but all Mom said was that she wanted to speak with Ted. Just out of the shower, he stood by the door to his closet in our bedroom. I handed the receiver to him and went to the kitchen for coffee.

I could tell she was asking him questions. I heard him say, "Yes, I know." There was a slight laugh, then another, "Yes. I know." Then, "No, we'll be all right. Yes, I'll tell him."

I took my coffee into the bedroom after he'd hung up.

"What do you have to tell me?" I asked.

"That she loves you."

"Fuck that."

"Now, Mike—"

"Don't 'now, Mike' me. She owes me an apology for the things she said. Everything else is bullshit."

"She wanted to be sure you were okay. She asked me to keep an eye on you."

Another shot of rage leapt through me. "What, so I don't kill myself? Maybe I should."

"She's just concerned about us, Mike."

"I don't want her fucking concern." I looked at him. "Doesn't that make you furious, too?"

He stepped toward me, put his hands on my waist. "The important thing is the truth is out. We just need to give them time to get used to it. Baby steps. Meanwhile, can we stay calm and get on with our life?"

"No," I said. "We cannot."

* * *

A door slammed shut inside me after that phone call.

I wasn't about to stay calm for anybody. Instead, I developed a plan.

Newspaper work was what I knew best; it would have to be my lifeline now. My resume was decent. If I wasn't ready for the big leagues,

I could get a job at a smaller paper. Maybe I'd try Florida again, or Burlington, Iowa, a picturesque Mississippi River town in the area where Dad had been assigned with DuPont when I was in college. It was scenic and hip, with a street called Snake Alley that wound its way up a downtown hillside. Locals proudly called it "The Crookedest Street in the World."

Burlington had a decent paper, too—the *Hawk Eye.* While I visited my parents one Christmas, it had run a positive front-page feature about the one gay bar in town. That impressed me. I could make Burlington work. I knew it. And once I'd put in my time in Burlington, it would be just a hop, skip and a jump to a job with one of the Chicago papers. An Amtrak train ran daily from Burlington to Chicago in just a few hours. Interviewing there would be easy. Or maybe I'd try the highly respected *Des Moines Register.* Once I was free, anything would be possible.

On Monday, I dutifully went to work. At lunch, I drove to the bank, withdrew the money from my checking and savings accounts and had most of it converted to traveler's checks. It wasn't a huge amount, but enough to get me to Burlington and help get me started there, enough to tide me over while I found work. Hell, maybe I *would* wait tables. I'd do it if I had to.

"I'm moving," I told the bank officer.

"Best of luck," she said. "We'll miss you. Where are you going?"

"I'm not sure yet," I said, relishing the lie. She'd be questioned, I knew, once I was reported missing. I wasn't about to leave a breadcrumb for her to share with the police.

Ted was working nights that week at the Hyatt, so when I got home at the end of my workday, I had plenty of time to pack a suitcase and make my getaway. I wouldn't even bother leaving a note. Let them figure it out. What pleasure I took in imagining the truth slowly dawning on Ted and my parents and Pat. *He's gone*, they'd say. *He took Copy and left us*. How long would they wait before filing a missing person's report? It was delicious to think about.

My mother might even get a laugh over it.

"The taker took himself away," she might say with a knowing smile. "Good riddance."

If my parents didn't like me as I was, then I'd spare them the agony. Ted, too. He'd put up with a lot from me during the time we'd had together in this apartment. I'd simply remove the inconvenience of me from their lives. Mom and Dad could have their peaceful retirement without the embarrassment of a gay son. Ted could find someone doing a better job of *this whole gay thing*. And the association I worked for could easily find someone better suited for my position. Everyone would be happier once I made my exit.

I'd be leaving a lot of things in the apartment—books, my mother's Peace painting, clothing I wouldn't have room for. But I'd have the essentials with me, my portfolio of the choicest news and feature articles I'd written, and Copy. I'd bought a leash so she could get out of the car with me for potty breaks on the road. There'd be room for my typewriter, too. I didn't have a map but didn't really need one. I knew I would go north to Kentucky, then west to St. Louis, where I'd follow the river north to Iowa. If I drove steadily, I could reach Burlington by the next morning.

Or maybe I'd take my time. Explore St. Louis. Find a bench by the Mississippi and sit, enjoying my freedom, the peace of having to make no excuses, no apologies, to anyone. The welcome escape from all the accusations, too. On that bench, I'd settle on a new name for myself, figure out the steps to make it mine. *Coleman Michaels*, maybe. It had a much nicer flow to it. A classier ring. Or maybe something even more different. Something so different no one would ever find me.

I went through my closet and chose the clothes I'd take. Then I pulled my suitcase out of the storage closet in the second bedroom. On the shelf above the rack of winter jackets and coats was the shoebox of letters Ted and I had written to each other a few summers before. *Old news,* I thought. I'd leave those, too.

But the image of the box nagged me while I packed my suitcase, drew me back to the second bedroom where it sat on the closet shelf. I took the box down. I'd take one letter with me. Just one.

I sat on the gold whipcord spread that covered the single bed. Dust motes swirled in the air when I took the lid off the box. I retrieved the envelope at the top of the stack inside. There was the house plan Ted had drawn up for us. And the letter that went with it.

Ted had written: "At this point I think I would live with you in a tent just to be with you all the time. I don't ever want to leave you again. I know I'll hate it when you get sent out of town in the future, but, as long as you come back to me."

I unfolded the drawing. It had been a long time since I'd seen it. Or even thought about it. How could I have let it sit there untouched all this time?

I studied the details Ted had drawn so precisely, the furniture labeled and placed just so. Chaise. Piano. Sectional sofa. And the kitchen. Worktable. Open counter space. DW. Sink. Stove. A study with two desks. Bookshelves lining every wall.

The sweetness of it brought an ache to my throat. I hadn't even finished packing and already I felt homesick. Already I missed Ted.

I can't do this, I thought, looking around our little apartment. The place where we'd started building a life together. *Our life together.*

I carefully folded the letter and put it back in the envelope. Then I put the envelope in the box, put the box in the closet and closed the door. I left the sheet open with the drawing on it. I placed it on the small bookcase by the bed. I'd show it to Ted when he came home. We'd talk about it, about what our next steps should be to make the plan a reality. The plan for a happy life together. Whether my parents were part of it or not.

As I unpacked the suitcase and put my clothes back where they belonged, Copy looked up at me from her spot on the green carpet.

"We're not going anywhere, kitty." I picked her up, held her close to my chest, stroked the velvet bridge of her tiny nose with my thumb. "We're staying right here."

Chapter Fourteen: You Got to Have Friends*

With Alana White, early 1980s,

** Author's note: Unlike the other chapter titles in this memoir, this is not the title of a song from a Broadway musical. However, Bette Midler performed it, so I figure it can squeak in.*

Dad invited me to dinner a few nights after my aborted trip to Burlington, Iowa. He liked Tony Roma's, the rib house on Elliston Place in Nashville, so I met him there. We settled in a booth and ordered drinks.

"I'm looking forward to a nice rack of ribs," Dad said, rubbing his hands together. "You hungry?"

I had to credit Dad for starting us off as if nothing had happened. "Maybe we could split a rack?" I asked him.

"Let's each get a whole one. My treat. You can take what we don't eat—make a good lunch or dinner for you and Ted."

Although I'd expected Dad to extend an olive branch tonight, I hadn't anticipated it coming so quickly. The evening might be easier than I'd thought.

"Dad, I want to pay for my own meal." I was still smarting from Mom's "taker" remarks.

"Phooey," he said. "Keep your money."

"Really, I insist."

"You can buy the drinks. How's that?"

"Deal."

He smiled. "Be careful, now. I might have two."

"Go ahead."

"No thanks. One is my quota."

I don't know if it's typical of other families, but mine would usually put off talking about the rough stuff as long as possible. So, Dad and I talked about other things during the meal. He was recording a new book for the blind through a Lions Club program. He and Mom were planning another trip to Florida. They'd had dinner recently at a Korean place with a church friend who once lived in Korea. It felt good to be with my father just like before.

"Did you like the Korean food?" I asked him.

"It was good if you like kimchi," Dad said. "I'm not real fond of it."

I don't think I ever heard Dad say he hated or didn't like something. It was always, "I don't care for it," or "It's not my cup of tea." When the Beatles first appeared on the Ed Sullivan show in the 1960s, he simply held two sofa pillows over his ears. Sometimes he'd say, "For crying out loud," or "Good night, nurse," if the thing was really bad. (It was his usual response to anyone performing country music.) He was a gentle soul who didn't care to see the atmosphere around him colored with unpleasantness. That's why I knew he wanted to calm this turmoil in the family as quickly as possible. Given my decision to stay in Nashville with Ted, I wanted it, too.

After the meal, the waiter poured coffee.

"Have you been doing okay?" Dad's smile indicated he hoped for a positive answer. I felt a rush of affection for him, for what looked like sincere concern about me.

"I think so," I said. It was hard to stay mad at Dad.

"We were worried about you, running off the way you did."

"I didn't have much choice. Mom said some pretty horrible things."

"She didn't mean them."

"Maybe she could tell me that." I took a quick swig of coffee.

He was silent a moment. "Give your mother some time, okay?"

I puffed out my cheeks, blew air through my lips. "It's not like I'm a drug addict or something, Dad. Or living in a commune." That was one of the things that frustrated me most about my mother's reaction. Young people "dropped out" a lot in the 1970s. I hadn't. Ted and I had had our troubles, but we were trying to live a decent life. I had hoped that maybe my parents would want to be part of it.

"I know that. We're proud of you. It's just—" He shrugged. "In my day, it was okay to have boyfriends. I understand that, but…"

His words surprised me. Did he mean male friends, or boyfriends you had sex with? He hadn't lowered his voice or anything. Maybe Dad understood more than I thought he did. I filed the thought away for another time.

He continued, "But this thing with you and Ted. If you have feelings for each other… well, it's not what I would have picked for you, but if it's what you want, then…"

"We like being together, Dad. We have a lot in common. I like to think it might be a long-term thing. I hope you'll accept that."

"Like a marriage?"

"Maybe."

He rubbed his chin. "We want *all* of you to be happy, you and Pat and Marsha." He started to take another swallow of coffee, then set his cup down, as if he were considering something. With an apologetic smile, he said, "It does seem that ever since I retired, it's been one thing after another. Pat's divorce, and Marsha…"

I swallowed over what I wanted to say, that I was sorry my sisters and I had inconvenienced him and Mom. Pat had been through a divorce recently. Marsha had become a Jehovah's Witness, which had upset my Presbyterian parents greatly; more so, I think, than Pat's divorce. They had never been fond of her first husband, anyway. With Marsha, it took years for them to accept that her newfound religion was not just an experiment but a new way of life. The man she married in California was a member of the faith, too. My mother, especially, was horrified. "How do you feel about what's happened to our dear Marsha?" she asked in one of her weekly letters to me while I lived in Montgomery. In fact, Mom's reaction to Marsha's conversion was one of the reasons I delayed telling my parents about Ted and me.

I said to Dad, "I'm sorry we've upset you. Maybe things will settle down now." I sat back in the booth. "There's a book called *Loving*

Someone Gay. It's about families dealing with… when someone in the family is… gay." It felt good to be so blunt, so honest with my father. "It's popular right now with all the Baby Boomers coming out to their families."

A pained look crossed his face.

I shouldn't have said that, I thought, but I went on. "You can have our copy. It might help."

"I don't know, Mike." He looked down at his cup, then up at me. "I don't want to have a book like that in the house." He said it in his usual quiet, calm way, but showing me part of the wall was still up.

"Well, we have it… in case you ever want to see it."

"Okay."

Any other time I might have been angry that he'd refused the book. But I was tired of being angry. At least he hadn't said, "Over my dead body." That was something, at least. A sign he wasn't a total lost cause. I reminded myself he had warmed to the Beatles in their later years, despite his first pillows-over-the-ears reaction. I reminded myself, too, that my parents weren't spring chickens. They were retired, in their golden years. I could see how my coming out must have felt like engine trouble at the end of a long, relatively smooth flight. But we could still land safely, couldn't we?

"Well, gentlemen?" boomed the waiter as he approached our table. "What else can I get you?"

He had such a kind smile under his dark mustache, such a cheerful light in his eyes. It was as if he knew we'd been having a serious conversation. He came close to convincing me that maybe, just maybe, life was going to be all right after all.

* * *

Driving home from Tony Roma's, I looked back over the past few years with Ted. He could have/should have walked out on me numerous times. The good news was that he was still with me. Dad was with us, too, in his own way. It seemed to me that, despite his personal feelings about homosexuality—he didn't want that book in his house!—he was putting his responsibility as a father first. He hadn't rejected me as Mom had. Hadn't told me to go to hell. That meant more than a lot. It meant everything to me.

Turning my VW into the parking lot of our apartment, I said a prayer of thanks that I hadn't run to Burlington, Iowa. That I hadn't intentionally hurt the people I loved—people who still loved me. I hoped Mom was included on that list.

* * *

I drove out to see my parents a week after my dinner with Dad at Tony Roma's. I felt such a rush of love for my mother when I saw her that it nearly knocked me over, made my legs weak. I wanted to cry.

"You look so pretty," I said, swallowing over the tightness in my throat. She wore a shirtwaist dress that buttoned to the hem with a plaid pattern in pale blues and pinks. I noticed her hair was in a new style, clipped shorter on the sides and back. Guilt reminded me of the curses I'd flung at her from across town. But I told myself she had flung some curses, too. Still, I was determined to keep things positive tonight, a way of telling her and Dad that what we had as a family mattered to me, that I wasn't going anywhere. I had come, too, hoping for a hug and an apology from her.

"Thank you. It was my day to sit at the art gallery. You're looking awfully sharp." There was a brightness to her voice. *This is good*, I thought.

I was wearing khakis and a polo shirt the color of tomato soup. I started to say Ted told me I looked like heaven in the color, but decided against it.

"We just have macaroni and cheese and salad for dinner. I hope that's enough for you."

"Sure. I love your mac and cheese." She made it from scratch, finished it under the broiler with a sprinkling of wheat germ on top. It was crisp and gooey and wonderful.

"I made it this morning. With my cholesterol up, we're trying to have some meatless meals during the week. Although macaroni and cheese is pretty high on the charts, too. It's a constant battle." She sighed. "How's Ted?" I could tell it was an effort, as if she were asking about my pet snake. My mother hated snakes.

"He's gone camping with his parents. Edisto Island."

"Is that the one off the South Carolina coast?" Dad asked. "He's told me about that place."

"It is. His family has gone camping there for years. There's a state park there amid the hanging moss."

"Sounds buggy," Mom said.

"It sounds beautiful to me. He's promised to take me there sometime." I felt brave making it clear that Ted and I were very much an item, that the previous week's trauma hadn't shaken us. He had wanted me to come with him on the trip to Edisto, but I had thought it would be better not to leave the situation with my parents hanging, to stay and see if I could help move along their adjustment to the new reality.

"And how's little Copy?" Mom said as Dad started setting the table. She was smiling again.

"She's fine. These are nice." I gestured to the pieces of her artwork she had set around the living room. A pink female nude in pastels. Watercolor flowers. Two girls standing on a bridge in a lush garden.

"I'm entering the nude in the Art League show. Your father's going to take some pictures for slides tomorrow."

"I'll have to show you the new tripod I bought," Dad chimed in from the kitchen, silverware clattering.

I offered to clean up the kitchen after dinner. When the dishes were done and the leftover mac and cheese put away, I joined my mother in the living room while Dad went for an evening walk. It wasn't his usual habit. He was giving Mom and me a chance to talk. He poured us each a glass of champagne before he left. My mother loved her evening champagne. Then he was out the door.

"You know, I've been thinking about the estrogen therapy the doctor in Buffalo gave me when I was pregnant with you. I think that might have been the source of the trouble."

My jaw clenched. "What trouble?"

"With you."

I set my glass on the coffee table. This was going to take patience. "I don't think anybody knows, do they? What causes people to be gay?"

"It's one theory. And then sometimes I think…" I heard something catch in her throat. She sniffed and her eyes grew wet. "Sometimes I think I must not have been a very good mother."

I found myself wishing there were another mother seated across from me, anyone else's mother, someone who could accept the fact of me and move on. Who wouldn't stir up the black sludge of guilt inside me. But then another voice told me I had some accepting to do, too. This had all been a shock to her. As Ted and Dad had said, she needed time, encouragement. "You were a great mother. I hope you still will be."

"There were things I could have done differently," she said.

She wiped her eyes with a tissue, sipped some champagne. "When I saw you that morning in Columbia, kissing Richard Crenna on our television set, of all things… I knew. I knew."

That was a surprise. She knew. She remembered. We had never spoken of it.

"What did you think?"

She shrugged. "Children go through phases."

"Did you tell Dad?"

"No. I wasn't 100 percent sure of what I'd seen. It happened so fast. I didn't want to… start something if there wasn't anything there. But we should have dealt with it."

"What would you have done?"

With one hand, she straightened the collar of her dress. "We were very easy on you when you were growing up. Maybe military school—"

Anger prickled the back of my neck. "Maybe if I'd had a lower number in the draft. Would that have made you happy, if I'd come home in a box from Vietnam?"

"Michael," she scolded. "That's a horrible thing to say."

She was right. In my mind, I took my foot off the accelerator, chose a slower, easier course. "Military school wouldn't have changed the feelings I have. It might have even…" I let it go, but I had to smirk inwardly at the image of me in the barracks with the boys in military school. I probably would have had one hell of a time—and been kicked out, yet again a disgrace to the family.

"People can live without sex, you know. Just because you have impulses doesn't mean you should—"

"Mom, you had three children. Why would you expect…" I shook my head. These sessions with my mother were like wrestling matches, emotional tugs of war that left me physically drained. "I'm not going to argue with you about sex. How do you think it makes me feel when you say things like that? Ted is the best thing to ever happen to me. It should be something to celebrate." As I said it, I knew it was too much to ask. Now, at least.

She gave a harsh laugh. "I don't feel like celebrating, Michael."

Fighting the urge to run, I focused on the artwork Mom had set around the room. The scenes were all bright, beautiful. My mother never painted trouble. But she sure knew how to inflict it. I'm sure she felt the same about me.

Dad returned. "Everything all right here?"

Our silence said it all.

"Then let's put it away for tonight," Dad said. I was grateful for the break. He showed me the tripod and the new floodlight he'd bought for photographing Mom's work. The conversation turned to other things—Marsha's travel, another friend's retirement, the latest state government scandal. Even though I joined in it all, I felt as if there were a coil of barbed wire inside me beneath all the pleasant words. Mom had hurt me to the core last week, yet it appeared nothing more would be said about it tonight. No apologies. The world was back to the one she depicted in her paintings—trouble-free. On the surface, at least.

"Who's ready for dessert?" Dad asked. He dished up ice cream, handed a bowl to Mom, then me, sat in his easy chair next to her. "The important thing to remember is that we're a family and we love each other, and we'll get through this. You agree, Mike?"

"I've never not agreed," I said, though I had an addendum. "But I expect Ted to be part of our family, too."

He turned to my mother. "Honey?"

She closed her eyes for a moment. "I can't believe we're even discussing it."

With nothing left to offer, I dug into the Baskin-Robbins.

One of my mother's favorites. Pistachio almond fudge.

It should have been rocky road.

* * *

My mom's reluctance to accept my life with Ted kept me unsettled over the next few years.

Sometimes it seemed I was still in free-fall after jumping off that cliff when I left the straight life behind in 1977.

I'm not placing all the blame on her. Call it what you like—my shame for not being "all boy," my deep-seated suspicion, planted at an early age, that love between men wasn't right, my growing up as an American male in a culture some describe as aggressively heterosexual—the beast of my own homophobia still lurked inside me, even as I made convincing arguments to my parents and myself that everything was going to be okay. What I didn't know then, but know with certainty today, is that the beast does not go away overnight. It pops up when you least expect it. It wears various disguises. And it takes more work than I'd ever imagined to put it to rest. One-step-forward, two-steps-back kind of work.

The next few years were like that for us. Some progress. Some setbacks. Some bad decisions. Some good ones. A bumpy, searching time, but there was light at the end of the tunnel.

* * *

After nearly a year at the healthcare association, I quit. I was going to write a novel.

I pledged to Ted that no matter what it took, I would work odd jobs to uphold our agreement to share our living expenses equally.

Today, our great-nieces Olivia and Sarah use the word *sketch* to describe something iffy, something not up to standard. They would describe me as a sketch partner during this period of my life—dropping jobs on a whim, screwing around, bringing a load of family baggage into the relationship. I'd be the first to agree. With all the good things I had, and there were many, I wanted more.

And was willing to sacrifice a lot to get it. Why I would bring on such financial trauma at a time when I was undergoing the emotional trauma of coming out to my parents is a mystery to me from my perspective in 2020, but I remember feeling a great urgency to start the novel and get it finished. Maybe I thought, with a novel to my credit, my parents would look more fondly on the idea of having a gay son. "The extremely talented aren't like the rest of us," I could imagine Mom and Dad's friends saying, as if to forgive them for having a son who was different. Like my going to work at Camp Sunup when I was in college, like my involvement with Maggie, it was a clear case of wanting to prove myself to them again, this time with a literary twist. And like my seeking other men for sex, it was a case of wanting to prove something to myself, too.

What I needed was a good kick in the pants, but with no one around to do the job, I got my way and went merrily on. The best that can possibly be said is my intentions were good.

I had dabbled in fiction writing while I was in college, taken a creative writing course, published a short story in the campus literary magazine. In Montgomery, a group of us reporters started a short-lived, one-sheet literary journal called *possum*, in which I published a poem and a short story. With this meager experience, I felt qualified—and mature enough—to write a novel. Oy, oy, oy!

It was a young adult treatment of the Bernard Whitehurst shooting case I had covered in Montgomery. My protagonist, 12-year-old Andrew, would witness the shooting of Bernard by the police, witness the planting of a gun on his body and, through the course of the book, realize that his father, the mayor's press secretary, had helped engineer the plan to cover up the story. Andrew would face a choice of going public with what he knew or keeping silent to support his father.

So, I had my story. Now to have an income. I got a job at the Green Hills YMCA not far from our apartment. I opened the place at 6:00 in the morning, manned the front desk until 8:00 a.m. when the regular staff came in, then went home to write. In the afternoons, I'd go back to the Y to lifeguard and teach swimming to grade-school kids.

The job required that I refresh the Water Safety Instructor certification I'd earned in college. True, there were times when I felt as if I were moving backward on the board game of my writing career, but then I'd tell myself that I had thrown the old board away and was starting a new game entirely. That view gave me the energy to keep at it, to keep doing whatever I needed to complete my book.

Still, it was not a great arrangement. Without my income from the association, we struggled financially. I had to ask Dad for a loan to cover my share of the rent one month. I didn't like doing that. He had loaned me money to buy a car when I worked in Montgomery, but otherwise I hadn't relied on him for financial help since college. I'd been proud to be making it on my own. Still, I was determined to finish the first draft of my book, no matter what it took. After that, we'd see what happened.

As part of my new venture, I attended a writer's conference at Vanderbilt. Jack Mathews, author of the acclaimed short novel *Hanger Stout, Awake!* and one of the speakers at the conference, threw considerable shade on my grandiose plans after I proudly told him I'd quit my job to write my book. "Working a steady job AND writing a novel? That's the real discipline," he said. He had done just that. He'd have none of my false heroics about the sacrifice I'd made for my dream.

As if to spite him, I threw myself even harder into the writing of the book. I believed the more intense I was about it, to the exclusion of just about everything else, the greater chance of its success. When my parents flew to California for one of their visits with Marsha and her husband, Ted drove them to the airport. It was Tuesday night, after all, and I refused to miss a meeting of the Nashville Writers' Alliance, a group I had become involved with at the Vanderbilt conference. We met weekly, read passages from projects we were working on and critiqued each other's work. Their response to each new chapter of my first draft kept me going.

* * *

The group kept me going for another reason.

All of its members were men and women who lived heterosexual lives in Nashville. None of them knew my previous straight self; I told them I was gay and had a partner named Ted. Just saying the words felt like a big accomplishment, a forward step in the development of the gay me. The best part was that my homosexuality made no difference to them. They accepted me wholly and without reservation, and it felt terrific.

One of the members, Alana White, was the first in the group to meet Ted. She and I had bonded immediately at the Vanderbilt conference. We were both working on young adult novels, but it was more than that; Alana was and is a social animal, friendly, energetic, eager to share her love of writing and to hear about my love of it, too. I was drawn to her quick wit and the sparkle in her green eyes. And I admired her writing ambitions. With family roots in rural Kentucky, she was currently writing a novel set in 1949 in the Smoky Mountains, but her next project was going to focus on Lorenzo de' Medici. She spoke of learning Italian to help with her research in the stacks of the Vanderbilt library. That impressed me. The country girl had an academic bent.

Alana seemed drawn to me, too, among the dozens of other writers and would-be writers at the conference. I felt honored she had singled me out. And I was thrilled when she graciously invited me to join the writers' group meetings on Tuesday nights.

I had ridden with Alana to a meeting at the house of another group member who lived in Goodlettsville, a northern suburb near Old Hickory Lake, a long drive from our part of town. When she dropped me off at the Rosewood Avenue apartment after the meeting, I asked her to come inside and meet Ted, who had tried his hand at making spinach lasagna for a late supper when I got home.

"It smells wonderful," Alana said, pushing her curly brown hair behind both ears, gold hoop earrings dangling from her earlobes.

Ted pulled the bubbling dish from our avocado green oven, the aromas of cheese and garlic invading the air. Alana applauded.

"It looks wonderful, too," she said, smiling, putting a hand on my shoulder. "So, when are you inviting us to dinner?"

Over the next few months, Ted and I began a close friendship with Alana and her husband. Buddy was a Vanderbilt graduate, a devout Catholic and member of the Hillwood Country Club set.

One night we went for a movie and pizza together.

"It's our first double date," Alana said, smiling. It was a wonderful way to put us at ease.

Ted and I had Buddy pegged as a conservative Nashville businessman. Even in jeans and a sweater, he looked distinguished and Republican with his full head of white hair neatly combed and parted. But he didn't seem to have any problem with us. We met their teenage children, who didn't appear to have a problem with us either. When Alana and Buddy asked us to join the family for a long weekend at Buddy's brother's place in Destin, Florida, I felt we'd entered a sort of utopia, the way life should be lived when there are gay and straight people in the equation.

At a time when the wounds of coming out to my parents were so fresh, the support of our new friends was a balm in Gilead. Alana—and all the members of the group—taught me there was a life beyond the hurt, a place where Ted and I were welcome without judgment. They weren't just colleagues in the process of writing books; they were allies. And eventually they became like a second family to us. A stress-free family.

It felt good, too, knowing I had brought these friends into Ted's and my world. Sketch behavior and all, I had done something good for us.

* * *

To supplement my income from the Y while I wrote my book, I worked part-time at a call center selling subscriptions to the Broadway series at the Tennessee Performing Arts Center downtown. I was hired as a gaffer for a film crew shooting a documentary on an Olympic runner who lived in Nashville. Through my *Banner* connections, I wrote freelance for a respected local publication that offered an insider's view of Tennessee government and politics, got sent to Knoxville to write an investigative piece about the curious plans for a world's fair there, scheduled for 1982. I wore myself out going from job to job… when I could have been working on the book.

Then I took a job at a branch of Nashville's biggest independent bookstore. I made the mistake of being good at it. With my knowledge of books and my newfound ability to sell them, management quickly noticed and transferred me to the company's busy flagship store near the Vanderbilt campus.

I'd used the quiet times at the other branch to think about my novel, work out tricky plot points and dialogue, jot notes on a notepad to add to my manuscript when I got home. But at the bigger store, there was no time for that. The owner was onsite most of the time, offering tips on what to say to customers and how to speed up the incredibly cumbersome inventory process at the manual cash register. A pink slip had to be filled out with the title and other details for every book that was sold. If it was only a single sale, no problem. But at Christmas and other busy times when customers lined up at the register with foot-high stacks of books in their arms, it was insane.

There were perks, however. When a well-known gay author came to town promoting his new book, a well-connected friend from the store invited Ted and me to a big party at his house. Ted and I arrived late. I don't remember why. We walked into the living room to find one of the guests on his knees, performing fellatio on another guest on the sofa. A crowd had gathered around.

"Come on," I whispered, as if speaking to the couple, as if to say, "You've got to be kidding." I could hear my arrogant tone. I'd put the days of cheap sex behind me now that I was working on my book, so I judged and dismissed them, wanted nothing to do with them. I was going to be a published author. I wanted to meet the guy whose book we were celebrating.

"Come on," I repeated, but with a different meaning this time. I was talking to Ted. I was saying, "Let's go somewhere more interesting." We ventured through the rest of the rambling house to find the published author. I led the way.

When we found him and introduced ourselves, he didn't give two hoots that I was working on a young adult novel. He wasn't mean about it. He simply gave a vanilla reply like, "That's good. Keep it up."

What he seemed more interested in was the fact that Ted and I were a couple. He wanted to know how long we'd been together. How we'd met. He wanted to know about us, not me.

I was crestfallen. Those weren't the things I wanted to talk about. Sure, the author signed our copy of his new bestseller, but I was hoping I might get his card, an offer to "let me know when you finish your book. I'd love to see it."

No. Nothing like that. We should have stayed in the living room and watched the blowjob.

* * *

I titled my novel *The Dream House*. After spending 1980 and much of 1981 completing it on my electric typewriter, I found an agent—Jean Naggar, the founder of the reputable Jean V. Naggar Literary Agency in New York City. Signing and returning my contract with the agency in September 1981 was an exciting moment. Ted and I celebrated at a local restaurant called Spats. We ordered drinks and ribs and an ice cream-topped brownie for dessert. My writing future looked bright.

So bright, in fact, that the Naggar contract convinced me that I was living life the right way, working odd jobs to pursue my creative writing career. The last thing I wanted was to go back to "a regular job." I had other projects in mind that I wanted to explore. So, I took two more years doing it. Ted's patience was heroic.

In the months that followed, rejections arrived… from Macmillan, Scribner, Farrar Straus & Giroux, and others. Some offered praise for the writing but pointed out problems in characterization, motivation and weak development of the conflict between father and son.

Meanwhile, I sent Jean another manuscript, a children's book I wrote with Nashville photographer John Netherton, another ally and friend to Ted and me. John and I had written several magazine pieces about photography. I was proud that one of our articles was translated and published in a German photo magazine. I had titled our book *Things that Go Hum in the Night.* John's photographs featured treefrogs, praying mantises having a nighttime snack on moths, all the typical creatures kids might see if they explored their backyards at night equipped with a flashlight and some curiosity about the natural world.

More "thanks but no thanks." From Scribner, Holiday House, Lothrop, Lee & Shepard…

I knew rejection was part of being a writer, but there didn't seem to be anything else in my life to balance it out—other than Ted. Was our relationship enough to sustain me? Ted had a strong personality. How would I keep from losing myself if I weren't a published author with a book to my credit? Somewhere in the back of my mind, I heard Liza Minnelli as Sally Bowles urging me to be "a most strange and extraordinary person." Extraordinary or bust.

At the very least, being a published author would justify my decision to leave the *Banner*. "No wonder he left," people would say. "That novel was just waiting to burst out of him."

So far, though, it was more of a fizzle.

* * *

While my professional life was hardly on an even keel in the early '80s, our social life was doing better. Ted and I curbed our partying with the Hyatt crowd, though we still made appearances occasionally at a downtown mostly-gay restaurant and bar called World's End. We ate stuffed mushrooms, played a new game called Pac-Man, talked with friends, went home and went to bed.

We got involved with a group that was opposed to I-440, a road that would connect two of the interstate highways in Nashville and cut through some of the city's oldest, most beautiful neighborhoods. In the bulldozer's path were the tangled woods that our apartment's living room window faced. We loved those woods. We were passionate about saving them.

I read part of my novel on a city bus one day as part of an arts celebration program. People liked it.

I discovered the thrill of making darn good money for quick ghost-writing jobs. My bookstore colleague Lisa had a wealthy boyfriend who had lost his mother to cancer. He wanted an experienced writer to help with her obituary and the eulogy he would deliver at her funeral.

The pay was extravagant—a nice surprise. With fresh cash in hand, I treated Ted to another dinner of ribs and a brownie at Spats.

I took advantage of the Y's employee discount and enrolled in a scuba diving class the center offered. I lusted after another student, a guy in his mid-30s, a high-profile local executive with clear hazel eyes and thick, chestnut-colored hair on his chest.

I thought he was straight. Yet I had seen him in the showers and had wondered about his head-to-toe tan. This was before tanning beds; you had to be creative to bronze your butt in those days. Was he successful enough to have his own secluded pool at home, or did his story include clandestine getaways to nude beaches? Might some of those beaches include Key West, Fire Island or Provincetown?

After the classes were over, he phoned me one morning while I was revising a draft of a short story I was submitting to a local publication. He asked if I'd like to meet him for a drink and dinner that night. (In those days, if you wanted to call someone, you just looked up their name in the phone book and dialed.) It would have been easy; Ted was working nights at the Hyatt. But I politely declined.

In doing so, I followed an unspoken rule in my relationship with Ted. Our occasional dalliances during our years on Rosewood Avenue had never been consequential. Neither of us looked for romance with another guy. This fellow from the scuba class was different. He was substantial. More than a quickie. As great as he looked, he was also smart, funny, a good conversationalist. Going out with him would have crossed an unspoken boundary; I wasn't willing to risk it. Still, I saw him a week later washing that chest of his in the showers at the Y, creamy suds sliding down his stomach and legs. *Damn*, I thought. I hoped Ted might one day appreciate the magnitude of my sacrifice.

It was just as well. In 1981, AIDS made the news. Though at first it seemed confined to the bathhouse crowd in New York and San Francisco, the stories about the "rare cancer" scared us. It was not the time to be fooling around with anyone—executive, hairdresser or hotel clerk.

Ted and I kept up our interest in camping—and didn't care any longer if nosy Presbyterian friends of my parents spotted us on the road. We spent many weekends at some of the beautiful, well-tended state parks outside Nashville, where we hiked, swam, read and perfected the art of cooking on a camp stove. We took pleasure in wholesome living… for a change. I stopped dreaming about swimming pool orgies.

Life was good. I was past the days of keeping secrets from my parents. But Mom continued to be a challenge.

* * *

It wasn't that she was opposed to progressive ideas. Even when I was little, I'd known she was different from other moms. On snow days, she didn't make snow cream like Terry's mother; she taped on the living room wall the sketches she had made of the nude models in her life drawing class so she could study them, see which ones might be contenders for figures in a new painting or pastel.

Then there was the story of Ambrose. When I was an infant in Columbia, a wealthy family at the foot of our hill had "a man," or a butler, as my mom called him. Elderly Ambrose had worked for the family for years. One of his jobs was walking the grandchild of the matriarch and patriarch daily around the circle of our subdivision. It just so happened his walks coincided with my mother's walks with me in my stroller. She and Ambrose started walking together. Mom enjoyed talking with him and found him to be a lovely man.

Well, the neighborhood was not pleased that a black man was walking with a white woman—a Yankee woman who wore pants in the 1950s, no less—but it didn't bother Mom. She and Ambrose continued their practice of walking around the circle together.

A woman like that could accept a gay son now, couldn't she?

Her response to being robbed at gunpoint on a shopping trip to Green Hills after Dad retired was another example of her progressive views. She was surprisingly unperturbed by the incident. What upset her was the number of people who asked if the robber was black when she told them what had happened. "Why do they want to know that?" she asked me. "It's appalling. I tell them, 'No, he wasn't black. He was a skinny white kid with a pimply face!'"

Since moving back to Nashville from Montgomery, I'd seen her generous views of other gay people, too. She was friends with several gay men—some of whom were quite flaming—from the art classes she attended and the art organizations she joined. She didn't seem to have any problem with them.

Let's face it: Mom was cool. But the coolness stopped when it came to having a gay son, much to my dismay. As one of the older members of the writers' group had said one evening, it was like a death finding out one of your children is gay. Coming from a staunch Democrat known for her liberal views, the statement shocked me. I thought she'd address the topic more gently, but the woman had grown sons of her own, so I figured she knew what she was talking about.

Maybe my mother felt the same way, that my being gay was like a death, but I was very much alive, thank you. I wasn't perfect, but why couldn't she celebrate the life I was trying to stake out for myself? Why did she seem so… bruised sometimes?

She continued to meet Maggie for lunch occasionally. "Can't two ladies who enjoy each other's company get together for lunch?" she asked me. I couldn't help but feel she was meddling, still hoping for a future for Maggie and me, still refusing to accept the truth.

Fortunately, Dad held steady. He listened. He was never short with me. He was always patient and kind. So, I kept on, hoping Mom would eventually soften.

When Jean and Gene, Ted's mom and dad, came to visit from Anderson, South Carolina, I got tickets for all of us, including my parents, Bob and Beulah, to see Carol Channing in *Hello, Dolly!* at the performing arts center when the revival of the show toured in 1982. It was the first time the two sets of parents had met. Mom cried during "Before the Parade Passes By." I knew she was thinking of my sister Marsha, who had recently lost her husband to colon cancer. And I think we all got a little choked up when the title number began, when Carol and those waiters started singing. It was a fabulous show.

Afterward, my parents joined us at our apartment for sauerbraten with egg noodles. (It was one of my trademark dishes in those days, a recipe Mom had shared with me after college, when I had my first apartment in Montgomery and Mom was helping me, long-distance from Iowa, set up housekeeping.) Everyone got along well. But I ask you, how can anyone have a bad time when Carol Channing is part of it?

After Bob and Beulah had gone home, when bedtime came, Ted and I went to our room and left the door cracked open so the cats could get in and out. Jean took the single bed in my office, Gene the daybed in the living room. I couldn't imagine my parents doing the same thing… but I felt Ted and I had made a little progress by getting our folks together—thanks to Carol and those singing waiters.

* * *

Ted left the Hyatt and took a job as a junior underwriter at a major insurance company that had an office in Nashville. I was finishing up a second novel. It was called *Losing Time*. It was about a friendship between a gay man and a married woman, Jeff and Kathy.

Though the book was inspired by my friendship with Alana, my heart wasn't in it. I was worn out. I kept thinking I should get a real job like Ted's. I kept thinking I should focus on improving *The Dream House* instead of starting something new. But how to improve it? I'd received some valuable feedback from the publishers who read it, but I wasn't sure how to work their general comments into specific improvements to the characters and the storyline.

I finished *Losing Time*, though, and sent the draft to Jean Naggar.

She responded with a letter in the fall of 1983. She wrote:

"I continue to feel you are a very talented writer, and capable of a fine, publishable, adult novel, but I do not feel I can present *Losing Time* to publishers, given my own strong sense of the novel's problems."

After recounting all the places she'd sent the other two manuscripts without success, she added:

"We don't seem to be getting anywhere, and perhaps in view of my lukewarm response to *Losing Time*, you might want us to make a break (possibly a temporary break) in our association so that you can explore other options?"

It was the nudge I needed. *We don't seem to be getting anywhere.*

I responded cordially to her letter and thanked her for her interest.

Then I called my former boss at the healthcare association and asked if I could have my old job back. To my surprise, he said yes. It just so happened that the current communications director, the woman who had replaced me, had submitted her notice and agreed to work through the end of the year. My new job would begin Monday, January 2nd, 1984, at a starting salary of $20,000, considerably higher than my salary on my last stint with the association and twice what I'd earned at the *Banner*. Being a PR hack didn't sound nearly as awful as it had five years earlier.

"All I ask is that this time you don't quit after a year to write a novel," he said.

"You have my word," I answered.

That evening, while Ted was out of town with his insurance job, I had my own quiet celebration. In the refrigerator was a bottle of Perrier water some friends had brought over. I poured what was left of it into a glass with a lime wedge, took it outside and sat on the steps of the breezeway. Watching the setting sun's soft glow behind the woods that flanked our building, I considered the fact that life was about to change. Becoming a successful novelist overnight—well, in a few years—wasn't going to happen. It was a relief to put those hopes away for a while. What if I wasn't the "strange and extraordinary person" I'd tried to be with my feverish novel writing? I was tired of trying to prove myself.

Maybe I finally had accepted me for me. Not the legendary *Coleman Michaels*, the name I was going to adopt if I had run to Burlington, Iowa. No, I was plain old Mike Coleman, an ordinary guy with an ordinary job and an ordinary life. Okay, a maybe not-so-ordinary life with Ted.

"Thank God," Ted said when we talked on the phone later that evening. I knew he'd be relieved.

I was ready for a steady schedule. A regular paycheck. A life without rejection letters. For the first time in my life, the 8:00-to-5:00 world looked like a fine place to be.

I was 31. It was time for real life to begin.

Chapter Fifteen: It Takes Two

Ted's parents, Gene and Jean, 1971

With the help of friends from the Nashville writers' group, who contributed manpower, womanpower and a truck, we moved to a bigger apartment the following month. It was on Cedar Lane between Belmont Boulevard and 12th Avenue South. The Belmont area had been one of Nashville's first suburbs, but in the 1980s it was considered an in-town neighborhood.

Our new apartment occupied the entire first floor of an old stone house built in the 1920s. Our landlord told us the home's original owner was a Nashville businessman with a wife and three daughters— "and one bathroom, if you can imagine," said the landlord, rolling his eyes. The upstairs had been converted to a separate apartment with a recently added bathroom and outdoor entrance. The indoor stairs in the back hallway of our apartment had been closed off at the ceiling. We had access to the basement, which had connections for the washer and dryer, a nice change from the apartment on Rosewood, where the washer had to be rolled to the sink and the hose fastened to the faucet whenever we did a load of clothes.

I loved our new place. Because I wasn't starting work at the association until January and I'd dropped the part-time gigs, I had nearly two months to play house-husband full-time.

I got down on my hands and knees and scrubbed the tiny white and blue hexagonal ceramic tiles on the bathroom floor with Spic and Span.

I painted the living room and dining room brandied peach, the "it" color in 1983. "It looks like Pepto-Bismol," one of our friends said. "It does not," his wife quickly countered. "It's yummy."

I thought it looked great with the stone fireplace, heavy white woodwork, which included crown molding, and blond hardwood floors. I enjoyed watching the paint color deepen as the afternoon light faded from the tall windows facing the street. Gone were the textured dark green carpets of the apartment on Rosewood Avenue, the avocado green appliances. Make no mistake, the place had a romantic flair that we both liked.

I painted the back hallway aubergine. I liked the sound as well as the look of it. "Could you please say purple?" Ted asked. "You sound so gay."

For the first time in my life, I didn't care.

I removed the hardware from the built-in cabinet in the breakfast room and scraped off several coats of paint to discover gleaming brass underneath. With a fresh coat of white paint on the cabinet and the brass fixtures polished and oiled, we had a beauty on our hands.

"Mike, it's only a rental," Ted said.

"I know. I want to make it nice for us."

We found out that my efforts might not be in vain. The landlord told us the owner was considering putting the house on the market. We liked it and the neighborhood so much that we discussed the possibility of making an offer if the time came.

Still, I think I would have continued the work anyway.

"It's like we're newlyweds," I said.

Unlike the apartment on Rosewood, there was no more pretense that we had separate bedrooms. In the spacious second bedroom on Cedar

Lane, I set up my desk and bookcase and put the single box springs and mattress directly on the floor with a blanket and pillow. You had to look inside the room to see the mattress. If guests walked by the office on the way to the bathroom, they'd only see the desk. It might not seem like a big deal today, but that frank arrangement in 1983 was an enormous step forward for me. We no longer needed a "beard" bedroom. No more hiding. I was telling the world: It is what it is. We are who we are.

I cooked dinner most every night. When Ted got home, I'd greet him at the door with a scotch. There'd be enticing aromas wafting from the kitchen and classical music on the stereo. If our time in the apartment on Rosewood Avenue was our Scott and Zelda period—or Scott and Scott—things were different now. We were Laura and Rob Petrie on *The* Dick van Dyke Show. Our Laura and Rob period. Or Rob and Rob. I was the Rob who stayed home and vacuumed. I didn't mind.

It was a taste of stability. Copy liked it, too. Sadly, Big O had left us while we were on Rosewood Avenue. She died of kidney disease at a young age for a kitty. Ted had had her for six years; he estimated that she was maybe seven or eight. We missed her.

The kitchen of the place on Cedar Lane had a mudroom with a porch and steps going down to the backyard. It was perfect for the litter box. The morning sun through our bedroom window made a nice warm spot on the bed—perfect for a napping kitty.

All of us were happier after we moved to Cedar Lane.

* * *

Except my parents.

Ted and I invited them to our housewarming party along with friends from the writers' group, new friends of Ted's from work, old friends from Vanderbilt and the *Banner.* My friend Frank had taken a job in Yakima, Washington, shortly before the Mount Saint Helens eruption. (He jokes that a Yakima resident told him before the move, "Nothing ever happens here.") He was fine, but I regretted his being unable to celebrate with us.

Around 3:00 p.m. that Saturday, I was putting a coat of paint on our bedroom ceiling. I had painted the walls a cool, pale blue and wanted the ceiling to match. It was the last surface in the apartment to be painted. It was not cooperating. The more I painted, the more chips of plaster flaked off the ceiling and onto the roller. I was getting frustrated. I'd planned to finish the painting an hour earlier because we had food to prepare, ice to pick up for the coolers—all the last-minute party details.

The phone rang. I shifted the plaster-specked roller to my right hand and picked up the receiver with my left.

It was my mother. "I don't think we're going to be able to come tonight."

"Why not?" I sat on the foot of the bed. "Is everything okay?"

"We're fine. It's just that… we don't feel it's a reason to have a party, Michael."

"What?"

"You and Ted playing house together. It's not… well…"

Anger bolted through me. I sat up tall, back arched. "Well then don't come. If you can't be happy for me, I don't want you here. We don't want you here."

"Michael—" There was that scolding tone again, as if I were the one being mean.

I slammed the receiver in its cradle.

"What was that all about?" Ted stood in the doorway.

My shoulders slumped. Had I just hung up on my mother? I pressed my thumb and fingertips against my forehead.

Ted sat next to me. "Did someone die?"

"Me," I said.

He rubbed my back. "What do you mean?"

"They're not coming. Bob and Beulah."

"Why not?"

"They don't feel like celebrating. They don't feel like celebrating us."

He sighed. "Good Lord. I thought we were past this. It's been years since—"

"No… the hits just keep coming."

"Is it their church?"

"I don't know what the fuck it is."

I stood, took a deep breath. I'd been excited about showing my parents what we'd done with the place. I'd hoped my mother might even make cowboy cookies for the occasion. So much for that. I hadn't seen any of those in years.

And where was Dad? Why had he allowed this crap? It was her idea,

I felt sure. Maybe I'd been wrong about his support of us, of me. What happened to his pledge the night of the should-have-been rocky road ice cream? *The important thing to remember is that we're a family and we love each other, and we'll get through this*. All talk, I guess.

"Why don't you put the paint away for now," Ted said. "It's fine."

"No." I wiped my eyes with the rag draped over my shoulder. "I am going to finish this goddamn ceiling. For the party. For the people who care about us."

* * *

It was a successful party. Our dining room table (a hand-me-down from Ted's parents) fairly groaned under the weight of food our friends had brought, including my favorite, Alana's hot artichoke dip. The sideboard, a flea market purchase, was covered with gifts, mostly bottles of wine with ribbons and cards attached. For several hours, I enjoyed the pleasant hum of a house where people are talking, laughing, having a good time. Our house.

At one point, Alana squeezed my shoulder and asked if I was okay. Ted had told her about the call from my mother. I raised my glass. "I'm celebrating being an orphan," I said. "It's kind of fun." I wanted it to sound like a joke, but as I said the words it seemed as if a dark pit opened at my feet. I didn't want to be an orphan. It felt scary and strange. Alana furrowed her brow, a skeptical look in her eyes. "Let's talk tomorrow, okay?" she said.

After midnight, after our guests had gone home, Ted and I put dishes in the sink, got coffee ready for morning and fell into bed.

"That was fun," I said. "Thank you."

"Thank you." He stroked my hair. "You okay?"

"I guess so." I rested my cheek on his chest. "Why do they care so much? Why do they care what I do with my dick?"

"What?"

"That's what it boils down to, isn't it? Why does it matter to them?"

He laughed. "Whole cultures and religions have been built on what men do with their dicks."

"It's crazy, isn't it?"

He yawned. "I'm not sure anyone can answer it, Mike."

I lay back on my pillow. "I wish your parents were my parents."

"That's because they're not your parents. They've had their moments, too, you know. With me. When I broke up with Lynn."

"But they're great now."

"For the most part." He kissed me. "Goodnight now. My dick and I need some sleep."

* * *

Unhappy thoughts simmered in my head, keeping sleep at bay.

Ted got up to pee around 3:00 a.m. As he padded to the kitchen for a glass of water, I went to the bathroom and peed, too. We returned to the bedroom at the same time. He handed me the tumbler of water, half-full. I drank.

"Thank you," I said, setting the tumbler on the glass-topped table on my side of the bed. Then we slid under the covers together. Pale moonlight shone through the sheer curtains at the windows, giving the bedroom a dim, black-and-white glow.

"You're not sleeping, are you," he said.

"No."

"Want to tell me?"

I let out a long breath. "I've been thinking about how clueless they are. If you have a gay son, shouldn't now be the time you'd want him playing house with someone?"

"What do you mean?"

"AIDS. The virus. Mom and Dad should be thrilled the two of us have each other. They see the same news we do."

It was true. By 1983, the disease was frequently making national headlines. *Time* magazine did its first cover story on AIDS in July that year, and my parents were long-time subscribers. While the epidemic still seemed a long way away from our social circles in Nashville, we were wary of it just the same. I often wondered what my parents thought of it in relation to Ted and me.

Ted said, "I think your mom's so emotional about us, she hasn't thought that part through."

"Maybe not."

"It would be nice if you could talk with her about it."

"If I ever see her again." I pictured the dark pit opening at my feet again. I took his hand and squeezed it tight. "I'm glad we have each other."

"Are you saying the virus is the only reason you're playing house with me?"

"No!"

He laughed. "I'm teasing you." When he spoke again, his voice was serious. "We are lucky, though, aren't we? Especially now."

"Yes."

He pulled himself toward me, draped his leg over mine and gave me a full-body hug, so hard that the bones in my back crackled with that welcome feeling of tension released. It was as if he were trying to wring out all the bad thoughts and feelings that had welled in me since Mom's afternoon call.

He kissed me long and hard, as passionate as our first days together when we simply couldn't get enough of one another. Then he pulled away, his nose touching mine.

"We can't let them ruin us," he said softly.

"No. They will not," I said, and kissed him again.

* * *

1984 passed without much interaction with my parents. Still energetic retirees, they traveled frequently that year, which made the break seem not quite so harsh. They spent their usual chunk of winter in St. Petersburg, Florida, took long road trips in spring and summer to visit relatives north and west of Tennessee. While they were gone, I checked on their apartment from time to time, watered the plants, took care not to borrow any record albums from the stock in their bathroom, and talked with Dad occasionally when he called to see how things were.

"And how are you?" he'd ask. "How's Ted?" The struggle to sound cheerful, as if things were all okay, made my heart ache. So did the sheer surface-ness of it all. What hurt most was how my parents seemed to want to know less and less about me—how, at a time in my life when I felt I'd made significant strides in the growing-up department, they were more distant than ever.

I wondered how big a role my failure to produce grandchildren played in our troubles. My sister Marsha had miscarried a few years earlier, not long before the death of her husband from cancer. Remarriage didn't seem likely anytime soon. My sister Pat couldn't have children because of her diabetes. So, it was all on me. Is that what Mom was upset about? It was a sad business, sure, but did she expect me to change myself just to fit her expectations? Maybe another son would have. It was not the kind of son I wanted to be. And I couldn't help but believe that, deep down, it wasn't the kind of son she wanted, either.

Whenever our impasse threatened to freeze me in my tracks, I'd go for a swim or a run. I knew I had to keep moving forward. I'd go into the office on off-hours to get ahead of my heavy workload. I'd treat Ted to dinner or a play or movie. Afterward, I'd light candles in our bedroom for a little romance before sleep. I found that a glass or two of Folonari Soave—a slight step up from our Carlo Rossi days—also helped dull the pain over my parents, though I kept my drinking in check most of the time. My philandering, too.

Ted and I were even at the point where we could shake our heads and laugh about things like the failed foursome with the guys from Kentucky, though the longing to find them, apologize and be sure they were okay still tugged at me. I thought that should we find them, maybe they'd laugh along with us. Or kill us dead.

We spent Thanksgiving with friends that year, Christmas with Ted's family in South Carolina. In January 1985, when my Uncle Burton, Mom's brother, died in Minneapolis, Mom broke the silence between us and called to tell me the news. Time has a way of tearing down walls.

"I'm sorry," I said.

"Well…"

I made a mental note to stop saying "I'm sorry" to my mother. It never evoked the right response. Always left me feeling worse.

I went on. "I'm glad I got to meet Uncle Burton that summer." When I was 15, my grandfather took me to Minnesota to go fishing with Burton and meet my Aunt Audrey and my three cousins on that side of the family. "Are you going up for the funeral?"

"I don't think so. We were just there for a visit. I'll let you know if we change our minds."

I hung up, sad about Uncle Burton but glad that my mother had called.

* * *

After another week or so, I invited my parents to dinner. It was the least I could do, given Uncle Burton's death and all, but I was extending a dare to them, too. *If you don't come this time, we're toast,* I imagined saying to them.

I thought they would accept. They did. And this time they didn't back out.

I wasn't sure what had brought about the change. Maybe they knew another refusal to visit the place where Ted and I were "playing house" would be fatal to any future between us.

Whatever… I didn't question it. I was happy we seemed to be on the right track. Maybe the long tug of war between us was over.

Maybe Ted and I had won.

* * *

A few weeks later, Bob and Beulah joined us again when Ted's parents visited.

"What do you think of the bathroom, Jean?" my mother asked Ted's mother as we gathered on the sofas in our brandied peach living room.

"Good God," Jean replied. She was a handsome, silver-haired woman with a husky laugh.

"What's so funny?" I asked. I liked our bathroom with the clawfoot tub, the old-fashioned faucet handles on the sink, the hexagonal tiles on the floor. "It could use a vanity, but—"

"I've spent my life getting away from bathrooms like that," Jean said. "Now you two think it's the bee's knees."

"We shared a bath like that with another couple in our first apartment, before the war," Mom said. "I'd sing the whole time I was in the tub to be sure Mel didn't walk in on me." She pretended to be washing under her arms and sang, "Oh Danny Boy…"

Another round of laughs. It was a story Mom often told when the conversation turned to pre-war days or the struggles of early marriage. I couldn't tell whether she was on autopilot or genuinely having a good time, but I was grateful she was keeping the conversation rolling.

Another night, Fred LaBour got us tickets to the Grand Ole Opry. I had taught swimming to his two children at the Y a few years earlier. We met Fred and the rest of the guys from Riders in the Sky, the acclaimed western music and comedy group, in a dressing room backstage, then sat in a place of honor—the bleachers on the Opry stage. My parents did not like the Opry—the only time we went to the Ryman Auditorium was to see Victor Borge perform when I was in high school—and Jean and Gene weren't big fans, either, but everyone had a good time that night.

At one point, Porter Wagoner graciously stopped the show so the husband of a fan who wanted her picture taken with Porter could go bounding to the lobby to buy flash cubes. Our moms enjoyed the music more than our dads did, but Gene and Bob had to admit that Porter did a skillful job keeping everyone entertained while we waited for the fellow to return.

"He's a true showman," Dad said.

"That he is," said Gene.

It was great to see our dads talking so casually with each other.

Of all the joy the Grand Ole Opry brings to the world, I wonder what Porter would have thought if he knew he had helped deliver a little piece of it to two young gay men and their parents on the stage of the Opry that night. I have a feeling he'd just smile in his colorful sequined jacket and say, "Y'all come back and see us now, y'hear?"

* * *

They say money can't buy happiness, but when you've been without it and then watch it start flowing again, it's a lovely thing.

Thanks to my new job, I repaid the loan my father made a few years earlier when I couldn't pay the rent. We hired a woman to clean the apartment twice a month. (Now there's something that brings happiness, too.) I traded in my yellow Volkswagen bug for a brand-new Nissan pickup truck with a cassette tape deck, a big deal at the time. I put a camper top on the back for our camping trips.

Dad asked to give the truck "a spin" when he saw it. I rode with him as he drove around our neighborhood. "Drives good," he said. "Makes me want one, too."

I could have hugged him. I realized I couldn't hold a grudge against him for not standing up to Mom the night of our housewarming party. Despite the support he had given me, when push came to shove, I had learned he would always stand with Mom on the choices she made. It was foolish of me to expect otherwise. Maybe he had insisted they come to our place for dinner after Uncle Burton's death. I'll never know. The important thing was that things felt better between us, better than they had in a long time. Maybe we were a family again.

* * *

I didn't find the job at the association nearly as monotonous as I had previously. The organization had grown so much that I had a staff to manage—an assistant writer and a secretary. And while my boss had some difficult attributes, I admired the fact that he acknowledged my relationship with Ted and didn't seem to care who I was sleeping with as long as I produced good copy and kept the communications engine running. Along with having money, it was also nice to be rid of the terror I'd had at the *Banner* that "someone will find out."

You could make a convincing argument that this was more because I had changed rather than the world around me. I'd left a job and landed on my feet. If I got spooked at the association because people didn't like my "lifestyle," I could leave and likely find another decent job somewhere else. I had confidence. And maybe… just maybe… I'd grown a little more comfortable with the fact of Ted and me. The fact of us.

It was also a relief to have the novels tucked away in a drawer in my home office filing cabinet. I enjoyed not having to think about them every day. I was still sending out the photos and manuscript of the book I had written with John Netherton. That way, I felt I was at least keeping my hand in the game of getting a book published.

And while I stopped going regularly to the Tuesday night meetings of the writers' group, our friendships only strengthened with those kind, creative souls.

When Ted and I attended a terrific Bruce Springsteen concert with Alana and her teenage stepdaughter Rebecca (Buddy stayed home), it was one for the history books.

The concert was on a Sunday night at Middle Tennessee State University in Murfreesboro about 30 minutes from Nashville. It lasted until nearly midnight, when we left the arena to find that our car had been towed. We walked to a nearby fraternity house, where a lively party was in progress. We asked to use the phone to call the towing company and find out where our car had been taken.

It was a process that took much longer than it should have, but the complimentary beer the guys served us helped immensely. (Rebecca had soda, of course.) We were all struck by how kind the guys and their dates were, how they pitched in to make us out-of-towners feel welcome and—more important—feel safe. We also appreciated the fact that they didn't seem the least bit puzzled by our unconventional group: a married woman, her stepdaughter and two single guys in their early 30s. When we did get a location for the car, one of the brothers gave us a ride to the impound lot. Gentleman that he was, he didn't leave until we signed the paperwork with the attendant and drove out of the gate.

It was nearly 4:00 in the morning by the time we got to Nashville.

I was at my desk at the association at 7:45 a.m. We had a department head meeting at 8 a.m. sharp every Monday morning, and woe to those who didn't make it.

"Are you alive?" Alana asked when she phoned me at the office later that morning.

"Actually, I feel pretty good," I said.

"I wish I could say the same. We need to send a thank-you note to that fraternity."

"We do." I closed with a joke. "And don't we have a good story to tell the grandchildren?"

When I hung up, I had one of those moments where time seems to stop. The sun outside the window seems brighter and the sky bluer than usual, and you can't think of anywhere or anyone else you'd rather be. You're just happy to be alive—even with three hours' sleep.

* * *

Ted and I talked about taking a serious summer vacation, maybe a drive to New York and then up the coast to Maine.

"Or we could go camping somewhere around here and put the money toward buying a house," Ted said.

It was a conversation stopper for me.

Though we had considered buying the house on Cedar Lane where we were renting, it had always seemed like a bit of a pipe dream. And the more we considered a possible purchase, the less attractive it looked. We didn't want the hassle of renting the upstairs apartment or reconnecting it inside with the rest of the house. Then the owner told us he had decided not to sell it after all.

Nonetheless, Ted's dream of being homeowners persisted. It scared me a little. I feared buying a house with Ted might bring a cold end to the slowly reviving heartbeat of my relationship with my parents. But I went along with it. I told myself that two guys owning a house together was the right thing to do.

* * *

So, we bought a house.

We went looking and found a small ranch house on Pleasant Valley Road with a fully finished basement and more than an acre of yard. The lot backed onto Franklin Road, the Nashville thoroughfare that gained fame when George Jones drove his riding lawnmower down it to buy liquor the day Tammy Wynette hid the car keys.

In 1985, $86,000 bought a lot of house. We did it all on our own financially, although to meet FHA requirements, Ted's mother wrote a letter saying she would back us on the $3,000 we needed at closing. My parents were showing signs of progress, but I couldn't imagine making the same request of them.

I learned that when significant money is involved, people don't care about your sexual orientation. The realtor was more than happy to work with us. We got approved for the mortgage, no problem. The sellers refused to sit at the same table with us on closing day, but it wasn't because we were gay. The couple had received an offer that was higher than ours after we had signed the contract and put down our earnest money. The husband had called and asked if we would back out as a favor to him and his young family. We refused. He was pissed.

We had two sunny bedrooms, two baths with 1950s ceramic tile, a living room and a big kitchen. Hardwood floors throughout, except for kitchen linoleum, which could easily be replaced. I liked it a lot.

On our first night in the place, on the big back deck overlooking the deep backyard, we shared a bottle of wine while two thick ribeyes sizzled on the grill.

"Now this," I said. "This was a good decision."

We'd come a long way since the apartment on Rosewood Avenue.

And not only financially. Emotionally, too. Being first-time homeowners had a certain gulp factor, sure, but also made me proud. If this was what being half of an ordinary couple felt like—the writer half with no successful novels to his credit—it wasn't bad at all.

* * *

Thirty-five years later, in March 2020, just as everyone was realizing the coronavirus wasn't going away anytime soon, we met our Nashville friends Alana and Buddy in the Smoky Mountains for a weekend of togetherness and social distancing. We have spent Thanksgiving with them every year for over 30 years, but in 2019, we had to postpone the trip because of my heart surgery. This visit with them was Thanksgiving in March—or Friendsgiving, as another friend put it.

For dinner together on Friday, I made paella and served it in the big porcelain-glazed cast iron pan we'd bought at the old Miller Dinnerware shop in downtown Gatlinburg some 30 years before. During our meal, the topic of Ted's mom came up—I'm not sure how. Ted told one of his favorite stories.

The year was 1985. Ted and I had only been in our Pleasant Valley Road residence a few months when Ted's parents, Jean and Gene, came to visit. They came to work, more accurately. Jean hung grasscloth in the den. Gene helped get the yard in shape and worked with Ted to start a vegetable garden in the backyard. On Saturday, I tackled the stall shower in the bathroom off the den, the one I had claimed as mine. The walls were metal above the salmon-colored ceramic tile and were rusted and mildewed from years of neglect. I scraped off the old white paint, sanded and applied a coat of waterproof primer before painting. By the end of the day, the shower was beautiful. I was a mess.

We were going out to dinner that evening. Jean had already showered and dressed when I emerged from the bathroom. She looked cool and elegant in a white pantsuit and lime green blouse. I raised my arms and pretended that I was Sasquatch or a zombie coming after her with sweat, paint and grime all over me.

"He chased her all over the house, through the back hall to the living room and then to the kitchen, through the den with the new wallpaper and then to the hall and the living room again," Ted told Buddy and Alana over our paella dinner. "Mom was laughing and screaming—" His voice caught. "She loved it. It's one of the best…"

He wiped his eyes. I took his hand. Jean and Gene's visit that year had been the last time Ted saw his mother well and happy.

During that visit in 1985, none of us had known what was going to happen to Jean in a few months. But on a crazy impulse, I chased her around the house.

I was lucky. I did something that—all these years later—makes her laughter ring in her son's ears.

* * *

When Jean was a little girl, she picked up a blasting cap in an empty lot near her house. It exploded, leaving only a stub where her thumb had been. She'd push the stub into Ted's neck when he misbehaved growing up. The injury had also left her with a staph infection that lay dormant in her system for decades. It sprang to life when Jean had the flu in 1986, a few months after her wallpapering visit with us. The flu was bad that year, the largest influenza B epidemic in the United States since the 1960s.

The staph bacteria attacked her heart and eventually led to a stroke. This was the explanation her doctor gave us for what happened to Jean at 57.

The day Ted and I drove from Nashville to see her, she sat slumped at a table in the dining room of a rehab center in Greenville, South Carolina. We weren't sure she recognized us.

Ted took her hand. "Hi, Mom."

Her eyes were blank, her mouth slack.

"Are you going to eat?"

Meatloaf, mashed potatoes and lima beans congealed on the plate before her.

Without making eye contact, she shook her head.

I don't know what thoughts her brain was capable of at that moment, but it seemed to me that, wherever she thought she was, she was ashamed of it.

Eyes welling with tears, Ted looked at me.

"It's nice to see you, Mom," he said, stroking her hand.

* * *

I compare my boss at the association to Meryl Streep's character, Miranda Priestly, in *The Devil Wears Prada.* Working with him was ultimately good for me, but at times he was a royal pain.

He had a strict policy that staff members could only be approved for an absence to attend a funeral if the deceased was an immediate family member. A young attorney challenged the policy not long after he joined the association's legal staff. A well-known Nashville judge, the young attorney's mentor, had died; the funeral was scheduled mid-day on a weekday. The fellow was determined to attend that funeral, but our boss persisted. It was an absurd policy then and seems even more absurd today, especially when you consider its long-term effects. The young attorney took another job a matter of weeks after that experience.

And so, I wondered, when it came time to request time off for Jean's funeral if my boss would make an exception. One's mother-in-law was considered immediate family. But "my roommate's mom" was not a mother-in-law. I wasn't sure my boss would make the stretch.

"My roommate's mom died," I told him. We were on the phone. Some days, he didn't come into the office.

"Ted's mom? Please give him my condolences."

"I will." I swallowed. "I need to go to the funeral. It's this Friday in Anderson, South Carolina. Ted would like me to be there. I'd like to be there."

I held my breath during the silence.

"That'll be perfectly fine," he said.

"Thanks."

I loved him for bending his own rule that day. For his quiet acceptance of the way things were. I never had to have the "I'm gay" conversation with him. He knew, and it was okay. If only others in my life were as easy.

* * *

Ted's family was wonderful to me the whole time we were in Anderson for the funeral—even the Baptists next door who were in-laws to Ted's family, the parents of Ted's sister's husband. They all seemed to appreciate the fact that I was there, standing with Ted.

I figured they were following Jean's lead; she had always been wonderful to me, too.

I didn't speak at her funeral, but if I had, I would have talked about her generosity and the extra effort she put forward to make me feel part of the family. I would have talked about the first Christmas I spent with Ted's family.

That was the visit they got real about our sleeping arrangements. On our first visit one summer, they had relegated Ted and me to the camper van out back. But this time, we were graciously assigned to the double bed in the guest room. That was a major step.

Jean's gifts to me that year were thoughtful and special. (The gifts were technically from Gene and Jean, but I knew Jean had picked them out.) Ted had told her I liked classical music and opera. Imagine my delight when I opened two boxed LP sets that Christmas morning—the Leontyne Price, Richard Tucker version of *Madame Butterfly*, and Linda Ronstadt's turn in *La Boheme*.

Our lives were busy at home in Nashville—long workdays during the week and numerous household projects over the weekends. There was no time to focus on the music. When I came down with a bad cold early in the year following that Christmas with Ted's family, I got my chance. I stayed home from work, brewed some lemon tea. Liner notes in hand, I savored my day alone with Jean's gifts.

* * *

The nights following Jean's death weren't easy.

Early one morning, I woke up to find Ted's side of the bed empty. I got up and found him sitting on the sofa in the den, a little pile of wadded tissues on the cushion beside him. That pile of tissues broke my heart. He looked at me, started to say something, then pressed his thumb and index finger to his eyelids.

"I'm sorry," he said through his tears.

I put my arms around him. "Cry all you want," I said. "I'm here."

Rough as it was, working through Jean's death with Ted was an honor. It brought us closer together, yes, but there was something more. We were passing the same milestone many straight couples pass as their love grows and deepens. And because of that, I felt a sense of normalcy to our relationship, a legitimacy I hadn't felt before. We were no longer just fuck-buddies, two wayward guys who had found each other in a bar one Sunday night. We were a unit that stood strong in the face of personal tragedy, stronger together than apart.

As I held Ted that morning, protecting him in my arms, I knew I would have bitch-slapped anyone who dared criticize the love we had for one another.

And that—lovely record albums aside—was the best gift Jean gave me.

Chapter Sixteen: A Quiet Thing

Dad and I at my parents' 50th wedding anniversary party, 1988

My parents were married in Buffalo, New York, on July 30th, 1938. As their 50th wedding anniversary approached in 1988, two years after Jean's death, I got busy. With a house and a yard in a city that was somewhat centrally located (my sister Marsha had a small apartment in Marin County, north of San Francisco, and Pat had a house far away from everything in a place called Hephzibah, Georgia, outside Augusta), it made sense for me to host the celebration.

When I offered to do it, my parents said yes right away, which surprised me. I hadn't been sure how they'd feel about exposing family and old friends to their gay son and his partner, even though I knew they had made progress in the past few years. They genuinely were fond of Ted; I think Mom had outgrown her feelings that he had led her son down the primrose path. They couldn't argue with the fact that Ted had convinced me of the wisdom of buying a house. And I think Jean's death had further humanized Ted in Mom's view. "It's so hard to lose a parent," she had told Ted at the time, giving him a long, heartfelt hug. I'd been right about Jean's death legitimizing us, making us easier to love, at least as far as my mother was concerned.

Of German descent, my mother's father was Amil Tschache. (We called him Dapo.) He had been one of nine Tschache brothers, so my mom had cousins all over the place. She gave me their addresses; I sent handwritten invitations to all of them. Counting her brother Burton's daughters and granddaughters in Minnesota, my Dad's nephew and his family, who were now living in Texas, my parents' close friends from our Columbia days and new friends they had made in Nashville since retiring there in 1976, the guest list totaled over 50.

I was calm, at first. I figured Mom's cousins from Montana and other distant locales would decline. But that wasn't the case.

As the redbuds and hyacinths began blooming in Nashville, I had a total of more than 30 *yes* responses to the invitation. That's when reality hit me. This is going to happen, I thought. All these people are coming here. In July. What the hell are we going to do with them?

There was another aspect of the event that terrified me. Mom and Dad might have been okay with having the party at the house of their gay son and his partner, but as the event grew closer, I wasn't sure I was.

I'd be exposing myself to people who had known me since I was a little kid, relatives I knew and some I'd never met. Our life would be on display as never before. I wasn't sure I could handle it. After all the agony I had gone through with my parents, all the energy I had spent to help them accept my relationship with Ted, now I was the one who questioned it, who wished things were different. The party would shine a spotlight on our relationship for ALL THOSE PEOPLE to see. My own homophobia wasn't just revived again; it was chasing me around the house the way I'd chased Ted's mom. The only difference was, I wasn't laughing.

I told myself the party would be different from our housewarming on Cedar Lane, where mostly new friends were invited. These guests would be old-timers, including the parents of a girl named Kathy, my sweetheart when I was four. They also included a couple whose kids I'd babysat for when I was a teenager. Could I handle the disappointment in their eyes when they saw how young Michael had turned out? The idea made me queasy, made me want to turn back the clock to the days when Ted and I were simply roomies, not two guys "playing house."

Maybe Ted could go visit his Dad for the weekend?

I asked what he planned to do.

"I'm going to stay and help," he said.

"You are?" I hoped my voice didn't reveal my dismay.

"Of course. What did you think, I'd go visit Dad for the weekend?"

Bingo.

If Ted were away, it would be easier to pretend we were just regular guys. "Do you live here by yourself?" I could imagine relatives saying. "No, I have a roommate, but he thought he'd just be underfoot, so he went home to visit his family."

Instead, with Ted on the premises, it would be a different story. Everyone would wonder about the exact nature of our relationship, wouldn't they? There'd be whispering as the ladies in the group slowly worked it out among themselves. And I knew Ted. He'd be answering questions with we, we, we. "We bought the house three years ago." "We're really happy here." "We've got a list of improvement projects we want to tackle." And worse, "This is our room. That's the guest bedroom over there." Oh, I could hear it now. Ted's presence would make it clear to my family and long-time friends that we were a couple.

I was sorry I had ever thought an anniversary party for my parents was a good idea.

* * *

I suppose I've always been one to reach for a quick fix in times of stress.

With my parents' anniversary drawing closer, I didn't grab the Cold Duck as I had the night Blake spent the weekend with Kelly when we were in college. I knew of another antidote for stress.

I found a new Mr. Picnic.

Only this one brought ants and a thunderstorm.

* * *

It was just a one-time thing. That's all it was—with a steely-armed, itinerant construction worker from Arkansas in town on a job. I met him in a new downtown bar after work and we went upstairs, even though the bar and dance floor there wouldn't open until later that night. We had to step over a rope hanging between two stanchions to get to it. It was dark and private. That was all that mattered.

At first, it was a relief just having another pair of arms around me, an experience completely separate from Ted, from the simmering tension that awaited me every day when I came home from work. "What can we do tonight to get ready for the party?" Ted would ask, and he'd tick off a list of house-related or yard-related projects. Now, Ted and the house on Pleasant Valley Road might as well have been a world away. This guy felt good. He smelled comfortably of sweat and sawdust. We were just using our hands on each other, so we were being safe, but then he asked me to do more.

* * *

A month later, in early June, I started feeling weird.

Since the AIDS epidemic began, Ted and I had familiarized ourselves with the early warning signs of the virus—night sweats, fever, swollen glands. I didn't have any of those.

I chalked up my lack of energy and fierce heartburn to pressure at work and the stress of getting ready for the anniversary party. With so many people coming from out of town—I can't remember now whether I arranged a block of rooms at a hotel in the area or had simply provided a list of choices to book on their own—I felt obliged to entertain them not only Saturday night for the big party with dinner, cake and champagne, but also Friday night with a more casual get-together.

Looking back on it, I understand now that the guests probably would have appreciated a free night on Friday, but I didn't see it that way at the time. We planned a come-as-you-are gathering for Friday with barbecue, beans and coleslaw. And what to do with them Sunday morning? I planned breakfast at the Loveless Café, a local landmark that served the best country ham, biscuits and homemade peach and blackberry preserves in town.

In the middle of the planning, Ted thought a getaway was in order. He had been in Knoxville on business, opted to stay over Saturday night and invited me to join him. We'd spend Saturday at the hotel pool, go somewhere nice for dinner that night and take our time driving home to Nashville on Sunday.

In those days, Applebee's was still a novelty, at least in Nashville. They'd built one on the way to my office. I knew it wasn't great food, but the hamburgers were fine and I appreciated the convenience of being able to stop for dinner and have less than a mile to drive home, or pick up a dinner that was a step up from fast food.

Since Ted was in Knoxville, I stopped at Applebee's for takeout on my way home that Friday evening. Once home, I changed clothes. Fed Copy. Sat down, opened the lid of the carryout box that held my burger… and promptly closed it. Dinner wound up in the garbage.

I got to Knoxville the following day around 1:00 p.m. Ted and I went out by the pool at the hotel where he was staying. He swam. I dozed. I had slept for an hour when Ted woke me up mid-afternoon.

"You're going to burn if you don't turn over," he said.

Getting burned was the least of my worries. We had 35 people coming for a party the following month and all I wanted to do was sleep.

Nothing was really wrong, but by the same token, I knew something wasn't right. I'd heard the word *malaise* before, knew it could be a sign of serious illness. Now I knew firsthand what it meant: discomfort, fatigue, a general feeling of being unwell. That's what I had, in spades.

For dinner, we drove out Kingston Pike to Naples, a family-run Italian place that had been a favorite when I was in college, and had become a favorite of Ted's, too, on his frequent business trips to Knoxville.

I ordered spaghetti. The child's plate.

"Are you okay?" He sipped red wine.

"Just feeling a little weird lately."

"You slept so much by the pool."

"It's been a long week. I haven't been to the Y, either. I think that's why I'm kind of achy."

"Do you think you should go to the doctor?"

"Let's give it a few more days. I don't have a fever or anything." I sipped some water. "Winnie, Mom's high school friend from Moose Jaw, is coming to the party. With her boyfriend. She wants to sing."

"The whole night?"

"Only one song. She called Mom and wanted to know what kind of sound system we have, if we can play a cassette tape for her accompaniment. I think I'm going to slash my wrists."

"Don't be so dramatic. It'll be fine."

I looked at my plate. I wasn't at all sure.

* * *

Things went further downhill on Monday. My body's waste products were whacko. What was supposed to be brown was gray. What was supposed to be clear was brown.

By midafternoon at work, when I'd peed my darkest yet, I made a doctor's appointment for 5:00 p.m.

"You can go earlier if you want," my boss said.

"Thanks, but I've got a newsletter article to finish up. It'll be fine."

The doctor was a gay-friendly fellow I had found a few years before. He was straight and married; I wanted to know when I signed up with him whether he had a problem having a gay male as a patient. He said he did not, and he meant it.

I liked him from that very first visit for my annual physical a few years earlier. Before he gave me a rectal exam, he asked which way I preferred.

"I didn't know there was a choice," I said.

He explained that there was a painless way and a painful one. "Doctors learn both in med school," he said. "But they're encouraged to use the method that hurts. Straight guys get nervous if it doesn't."

I laughed. "I'll try the other one."

Instead of bending over the exam table, I followed his instructions to lie on my side, bend the knee of my upper leg and raise it slightly toward my chest while keeping it relaxed on the table. He was right. Easy as pie. But then I hadn't exactly needed a doctor to explain it.

"I can see how some guys would have a problem with that," I said afterward, wiping myself with the tissues he handed me and zipping up my pants. "Life is strange, isn't it?"

"Sometimes," he said with a laugh.

On the day of the brown pee, however, he wasn't laughing.

"It's your liver talking. Early-stage viral hepatitis, most likely," he said. "Your eyes are showing a little yellow. They'll get worse."

Something heavy settled in my gut. Hepatitis was serious stuff. With the whites of my eyes looking yellowish, I'd suspected I had it, but to hear the word spoken made it real. With all the information available about safe sex in the era of AIDS, I knew hepatitis could be transmitted through blood and semen during unprotected sex. The image of the construction worker from Arkansas flashed through my mind. What he'd asked me to do. My willingness to comply.

"Have you been sexually active?" The doctor's eyes met mine.

I guess you didn't get away with it after all, did you? I thought. *Shame, shame, shame.* I looked at my hands. "Just once, recently. This guy from out of town."

"How long ago?"

"About a month."

"That's the usual pattern for this stuff." He picked up the clipboard he had brought into the exam room, scribbled some notes on the paper it held. "There are different types of hepatitis. My guess is you have the B variety. It's the one I see most often. We'll draw some blood to confirm it."

"What do you do for hepatitis B?"

"There's no cure. You need to rest. Eat well. Stay away from alcohol. Usually, there's total recovery in four to eight weeks."

"I've got a big event coming up at the end of July. My parents' 50th anniversary."

"Six weeks from now. That's a good amount of time to get to feeling better." He put the pen in the pocket of his white lab coat. "We'll need to test for HIV, too."

My stomach tightened at the mention of the acronym, even though I had feared it might be part of the visit.

"What did you fellows do?" he asked, as casually as if he were asking what I had for lunch.

"Strictly oral."

He gave me a questioning look.

I shrugged. "I gave him a blowjob."

"Nothing else?"

"No." I silently thanked him for his poker face. I'd always known he was a good doctor, but his performance today was surpassing all others. No judgments here.

"And nothing since?"

"No." Though I viewed my indulgence with the construction worker as a welcome release, part of me had been appalled by the risk I'd taken. I'd walked the straight and narrow in the weeks since. No more trips to that bar.

"Didn't you tell me you have a roommate or partner?"

I felt my face flush. "Ted. We've been together 11 years. We get busy, you know, with a house and work and everything. Sometimes sex goes on the back burner… especially lately."

"That's lucky for him. For the moment, anyway."

I gave a laugh. *Lucky,* I thought. But sad, too. How long had it been since Ted and I had made love? I mean, really put some effort into it? Our sex life had been pretty dry and perfunctory of late. We needed to remedy that, once we cleared this hurdle, if we cleared it…

"About the oral sex…" The doctor scratched one salt-and-pepper eyebrow. "Unless you have an open sore in your mouth, the chances are good that HIV doesn't transmit—"

"I've read that," I said. I didn't want him to think I'd been totally careless. "That's why we just…"

"I understand." A small, kind smile crossed his lips. "But I still want to test to be sure. I'll send Connie in to draw some blood."

Before he left the exam room, he had one more question.

"Do you know how to get in touch with the fellow you were with?"

"No, I… didn't get his name."

"I don't mean to preach, but the sexual revolution is over."

"I know. I missed it the first time."

"Be safe."

"Thanks."

* * *

Good things don't always come in pretty packages.

While I'd never wish for hepatitis B again, it brought a few good things.

After my doctor's appointment that day, I drove back to the office. It was half past 6:00 on one of the nights my boss usually worked late. I felt it would be easier to tell him my diagnosis in person, but I was still scared. What would he say? Would he ask how I got it? Wouldn't everyone ask how I got it? And then there was Ted. How would I tell him? I'd been keeping that question at the end of the line in my head, afraid to face it.

You know what?

No one asked how I got it. Not a single soul asked me how I acquired hepatitis B.

My boss' first question was, "What do you need to do?" When I told him the doctor recommended two weeks of rest at home, I quickly added, "But I can keep working."

Assessing me, my boss chewed on his unlit cigar. He never smoked, but after a meeting there'd be little wads of wet cigar in the ashtray on his desk. I thought it was weird, but we all have our foibles. "We can deal with that. It's a good thing you live close. I can have Judy (his secretary) take your mail over every day."

I went upstairs to my office to get drafts of the articles my assistant writer and I were working on. Once downstairs again, I stuck my head in my boss' office to say goodnight.

"I talked with Dee," he said. She was the president of the association that year. It made sense that he would tell her about any serious new developments with a staff member. Dee was also a nurse. It wouldn't have surprised me if she'd filled him in on the details of how the disease was transmitted and assured him that my illness wasn't a threat to him or my other co-workers. But his wrap-up to me covered none of that.

"She said what you've got isn't to be taken lightly. I know your doctor is good and all, but I'd feel better if you get checked out at Vanderbilt Hospital, too. To get another opinion. Will you do that?"

"I will."

There was no question of "who'll pay for it?" The employee insurance plan at the association was a good one.

"Take care of yourself. And check in with me to let me know how you're doing, okay?"

"Yes, sir."

Little wads of cigar notwithstanding, the man had class.

When I got home, Ted was in the bedroom changing out of his suit from work. Because the company he worked for still allowed smoking in the mid-1980s, Ted kept his work clothes in the closet of the second bedroom across the hallway from ours. (He didn't smoke, but some of his colleagues did.) I waited for him to finish the back-and-forth while I put my words together. I had decided on the direct approach.

"I went to the doctor this afternoon. He thinks it's hepatitis. Hepatitis B."

What made breaking the news a little easier was the fact that hepatitis wasn't a strange word to us. A few years before, we had bought a copy of the original cast recording of *March of the Falsettos* by William Finn. We listened to it all the time. The character Trina has a song early on about the consequences of her husband Marvin's philandering with other men, including a case of hepatitis he brings home.

Shocking as it was to hear the song for the first time in a musical comedy, we got the blunt humor of it. And now I took some courage in the musical's message that other people got hepatitis. Funny people. Married people. Normal people. I knew life wasn't musical comedy, but anything to buoy my spirits.

I waited for Ted's response while he slipped the white T-shirt with the purple Furman logo over his head. He didn't say anything, so I soldiered on. "We won't know definitely until the blood test results come back. But he's fairly certain. My pee looked like coffee today."

Ted shuddered but still said nothing. That worried me, but it was too late to turn back.

"He wants me to stay home and rest for two weeks. I told my boss. He wants me to go to Vanderbilt to get checked out, too."

Ted stepped forward and put his arms around me. "I don't want you to be sick. We've got busy times ahead of us."

I groaned, but underneath I was vastly relieved by Ted's response to my news. Maybe this was going to be okay. Maybe, like Trina and Marvin, we could play this for laughs and go on with our lives. But there was one other thing.

"They're testing for HIV, too. Just a precaution."

He looked down at the floor for a moment, then his eyes met mine. Here it comes, I thought.

"You going to rest?" he asked.

"After I change clothes. Dinner's easy." Before work that morning, I had put two turkey drumsticks in the crockpot with onion, apple and rosemary, the seasonings Dapo used for roast turkey on his visits when I was a kid in Columbia.

He grabbed a baseball cap. "I'm going out to water the garden."

While I got out of my shirt and tie, I wondered when the other shoe would drop. Ted would mull over the news while he was outside. There'd be a confrontation over dinner. I felt sure of it. That's how it would play in a book or movie, wouldn't it, with tears and smashed dinnerware, the kitty hiding under the bed?

But that didn't happen. Trina might have confronted Marvin, but Ted never confronted me.

In the story about my friends putting me to bed the night I drank the bottle of Cold Duck, I mentioned the things that are unsaid among friends, how not talking about what's understood can sometimes be the best way to show love in our "let's put it all on the table" society. Here was another instance… this time between Ted and me. In the moment he looked down at the floor while he was changing clothes, I figured he processed a critical fact: When I fooled around, it was usually not the sexual activity that carried the highest risk. Anal sex had never really been my thing. If we weren't totally immune to HIV, at least I hadn't opened the most likely door to exposure.

There was probably another unspoken reason for his acceptance of my news. Ted's job required occasional travel, visiting insurance agencies across the Southeast. While I had no proof, I couldn't guarantee that he wasn't finding a Mr. Picnic or two on his overnight trips. How could he be angry at me for the same behavior? As long as we played it safe. As long as our extracurricular activities didn't go any further than sex, didn't involve romance or the possibility of falling in love with someone else.

Our love hadn't been shaken by our occasional shenanigans with other guys in our early days. Somehow I was proud of that—proud that our commitment had survived without a chastity belt, without demands of monogamy from one another. And now it appeared my illness—and how I had acquired it—wouldn't shake us, either. I'd learned it years before: There was room in our relationship to make mistakes. Even major ones.

The headline today was hepatitis, not "I'm leaving you for someone else." Not "I never want to see you again." In its own strange way, I thought as I set the table for dinner, it was good news, a reason to keep moving on and be thankful. And yet another reason to love Ted.

* * *

A few days later, the lab results came back positive for hepatitis B, negative for HIV. On the phone, my doctor's nurse sounded as relieved as I was. Once again, the ice on my metaphorical pond had held underfoot. If I'd had skates on, I would have done a triple Lutz.

My dad couldn't have been better about my illness. He didn't ask how I got it, either. I had thought he might have, but then I realized his silence was completely in character. It reaffirmed the strength I had found in him since my coming out. Once again, he was my rock. If he and Mom wondered about the possibility of HIV infection, they didn't mention it. Neither did I, but I hoped my breezily stated "all the other tests came back negative" would be enough to put their minds at ease.

The second week of my time of enforced rest, Dad took me to the doctor's appointment at Vanderbilt Hospital, where I was told the same things I heard from my doctor: Eat well. Rest. Don't drink. There'd be a follow-up test in a few months to see if I was rid of the virus. There was every chance of total recovery. After the appointment, Dad took me to lunch and then drove me to other places I needed to go, the drugstore for vitamins, the bank, the health food store for some good juices to drink during my period of prohibition from alcohol.

"You drove me all over town today," I said to him when we got home. "Thanks so much, Dad."

We didn't hug. We had never been a hugging family. That came later.

"You're welcome," he said. "Call us if you need anything. Take care of yourself."

We shook hands. I watched him back the Ford out of our driveway and pull away on Pleasant Valley Road toward home. I laughed at the irony. Here I was with a serious disease and yet I'd just had one of the best days I'd ever had with my father. Funny how life works.

In the days that followed, I started feeling better. The whites of my eyes were still yellow, but other things were returning to their usual color. Ted said some nights I'd be so still he'd listen for my breathing to be sure I was alive, but that awful malaise had passed. I slept. I had an appetite again. I was hopeful that I might even be back to normal by the time the anniversary rolled around.

* * *

The party was a great success. Both nights. Alana helped with food, and another married couple we had befriended—Matt and Sharon—made a watermelon fruit basket for the more formal, Saturday night event. I broke out the hundred or so spinach and feta spanakopitas Ted and I had made in May and frozen in preparation. Winnie sang an old tune from the 1920s. Mom cried. Toasts were made.

Most important, everyone loved Ted. He kissed all the ladies goodnight after the party on Saturday night.

For me, the ultimate compliment came from one of my parents' friends, a fellow DuPonter who had traveled from Philadelphia with his wife to attend the party.

"Hey, Mike, you forgot one thing," he said in his big trombone voice. "T-shirts. Where are the T-shirts?" Then he pumped my hand. "Seriously, great job. You did your mom and dad proud." He pumped Ted's hand, too. "Super evening," he said. "Thank you."

After everyone had gone home, I pulled Ted to me and held him tight.

"Thank you, thank you, thank you," I said. "I'm so glad you were here."

He kissed me. "I'm glad I was here, too." Then he pulled back and grinned. "You couldn't have done it without me, you know."

I thought of how I hadn't wanted him at the party at first. How the hell had I ever been so shallow to have wanted that? I thought of how the event and my illness had consumed most of his summer. I thought of how he held me the night before I got the results from the HIV test.

With the tension of the last two months slowly draining from me, all I could do was nestle my forehead against his shirt collar. "Of course, I couldn't have done it without you."

I stepped back and looked into his beautiful blue eyes, at the little beauty mark on the bridge of his nose. Who else was lucky enough to have this: a good man who insisted on staying no matter what I threw at him?

"You're the best," I said. "I love you."

What I didn't say, but what I hoped he knew, was that I would do better. No more picnics. Ever. That was a promise.

But then I remembered what I'd told the doctor, how sex often took the back burner when you've been with someone for 11 years.

I hugged Ted again and made a silent promise for more picnics. Lots of them. Picnics with just the two of us.

* * *

As I slipped into bed beside Ted that night, I began to see the most important benefit of his staying for the anniversary party. Now my family and my parents' friends knew about me, knew I was in a relationship with another guy.

They knew—and the house hadn't exploded.

They knew—and no one had left in disgust.

They knew—and I never had to hide from them again. I never had to hide from anyone.

My arm across Ted's stomach, I fell into a long, peaceful sleep.

Chapter Seventeen: Move On

Ted and my mom with Max at the house on Pleasant Valley Road

We took a vacation. We drove the Natchez Trace all the way to Natchez and then down to New Orleans and a week of camping in Florida on the Gulf Islands National Seashore. It was a beautiful trip.

Arriving home to normal life was a gift. No parties to plan. No spanakopitas to make. Just healing and getting back to our usual schedule.

When my sister Marsha, the Jehovah's Witness who had come to the anniversary party from Marin County, California, sent me a Watchtower pamphlet describing homosexuality as an abomination, I held it up for Ted to see. It was the only negative response we'd received from anyone who had attended my parents' 50th anniversary party—and from one of my sisters, no less.

"Unbelievable," he said. "Does your family not have anything better to do than pick on us?"

I looked at the pamphlet again. "There was a time in my life when this would have bothered me." I tried to sound tough, but deep down it hurt and angered me.

He grinned. "Come on."

He took my hand and led me downstairs to the basement, where we kept lighter fluid and matches for grilling out back. Then we went outside. Ted lifted the lid off our charcoal grill. We set the pamphlet on the grate and doused it with lighter fluid.

"You do the honors." He offered me the box of matches.

I struck one, tossed it on the grill. The pamphlet went up in a satisfying whoosh of orange and purple flame.

* * *

We told the story of the pamphlet the following weekend when Buddy, Alana, Matt and Sharon joined us at our house to celebrate my 36th birthday. Ted served spaghetti and pesto he made from basil in our backyard garden. It was late August 1988. Everyone applauded our incendiary response to what Marsha had sent.

"I just don't get it… why she'd do that to you guys," Sharon said.

"Now you know why we keep a healthy distance from the doors of every church," I replied. I was still upset by what Marsha had done, but I was experiencing yet again how much it helped to have friends to commiserate with, to have a family beyond my family.

Our friendship with Buddy and Alana had grown by two with Matt and Sharon, who had contributed the watermelon basket to my parents' 50th anniversary party in July. Matt was a contractor colleague of Buddy's and a serious hiker. He was determined to make serious hikers of the rest of us. We six had taken some long weekend trips east to the Smoky Mountains—trips that sealed our friendship.

"How are you doing?" Sharon asked as we cleared the remains of the pesto meal from the table. She knew about my case of hepatitis earlier in the summer.

"I still get tired sometimes, but otherwise fine," I said, wondering what she thought about my having the disease, about its clear message that I'd visited places I shouldn't have. Yet, like everyone else, she was polite enough not to probe.

"We're very glad you've survived," she said. "But we're even more impressed you're surviving without alcohol." Small and slender, Sharon often had a glint of mischief in her hazel eyes.

"Question." Matt rubbed his hands together in the kitchen doorway, a smile on his tanned, outdoorsman-handsome face. "How long must we wait for the BAs?"

It was a tradition among the six of us to whip up a batch of Brandy Alexanders for dessert after our dinners together.

"We have cake," Ted said. "I made it for the birthday boy and you're going to enjoy it. We do have brandy, though, if you'd like an AD."

I had to laugh at our acronyms—BAs for Brandy Alexanders, ADs for after-dinner drinks. I did miss drinking sometimes, wine especially, but I was following doctors' orders to make it through the end of the year without alcohol. And I did appreciate waking up Sunday mornings clear-headed, getting up early to read—Elizabeth George's *A Great Deliverance* was a current favorite—or have a jog around the neighborhood while Ted slept in.

So, after I blew out the candles, I had milk in a wine glass with my chocolate birthday cake while everyone else had ADs.

* * *

Ted and I considered it an achievement of sorts that our best friends since we'd moved to Pleasant Valley Road were two straight couples. We got together with Buddy and Alana, Sharon and Matt frequently for dinner and enjoyed each other's company immensely. Like Ted and I making it through Jean's death together, it seemed like validation, proof that we were an ordinary couple, that one's sexual orientation didn't matter.

Sometimes, though, we longed to have another gay couple as buddies. We kept in touch with Mark and Andy, the house-flippers on their way up to life in the plush 37205 area of town, but we just didn't click with them the way we did with our straight friends. Besides, we felt that our friendship with Buddy, Alana, Matt and Sharon had grown organically, naturally. We hadn't had to make the effort that "finding another gay couple to be friends with" would take. And truth be told, there just weren't that many opportunities in Nashville in 1988 to meet other gay couples. Not that we could see. So, we put the questions aside and enjoyed the friendships that had found us.

Matt and Sharon had two teenage children from previous marriages. Sharon's daughter, Amy, was a gem—smart and funny and, like Buddy and Alana's family, totally accepting of the two of us. Sometimes Ted and I called her "the daughter we never had." At the time, adoption just wasn't as realistic an option for gay couples as it is today. But sometimes I'd look at Amy with her bright eyes and shiny, honey-colored hair and think, "Wouldn't it be nice?"

Amy had come along on one of our Smoky Mountain hiking trips with Matt and Sharon, Buddy and Alana. On that trip, she astounded me by how whip-smart and big-hearted she was.

"I'm glad Mom and Matt are friends with you," she said to me at the end of the long hiking day, while we cooled off in the bend of the river that edged the campground. She was probably 14 or so at the time.

"I'm glad they are, too," I said. "Or we wouldn't be here with you."

She laughed, then grew quiet, watching her hands sweep through the water, her chipped, little-girl-pink nail polish gleaming just below the surface. "How did you and Ted meet?"

I decided not to sugarcoat the story. "We met in a gay bar. In Nashville."

"A long time ago?"

"Way back in the '70s. The decade you were born."

She kept watching her hands stir the water in front of her. I could tell she was considering something. Then she looked at me. "And... you've just always loved him?"

"Most of the time," I said, trying to keep our conversation light. We watched Ted stride across the campground toward us in his blue bathing suit, the faded one he brought for the weekend. A towel slung over one shoulder, he looked happy, his cheeks rosy from the day's sun, his flip-flops squeaking rhythmically under his feet. "I mean, how could you not?"

She pursed her lips, gave me a questioning look. Then she looked at Ted, her hands suddenly still. She smiled, as if something momentous had occurred.

"I get it," she said softly. She turned her eyes to me, her hands moving through the water again. "People want to make it into something weird. But it isn't, is it?"

That was the moment I fell in love with Amy Vandiver.

* * *

"Did you have a good birthday?" Ted asked as we cleaned up the kitchen, after Buddy and Alana, Matt and Sharon had gone home, bringing an end to my 36th birthday party.

"I did. Thank you." I squeezed water from the dishwashing sponge into the kitchen sink. "Have you ever thought about having children?" Amy had been on my mind through the evening. Our friends weren't inclined to brag about their offspring, but Matt and Sharon did talk at dinner about Amy's good grades, her cheerleading, her growing interest in the sciences. All the evidence showed they were rearing a well-rounded and well-grounded young woman.

"We're too old!" Ted said.

"We are not. We're still a long way from 40."

He put his arms around me, slid his hands in the back pockets of my khaki shorts. "I like it just being us."

"You know what?" Images of diapers, 2:00 a.m. feedings, endless carpool loops crowded out my sweet thoughts of Amy. "I like it, too."

* * *

With the abomination pamphlet, a chill descended over my long-distance relationship with Marsha in the months following my birthday party. Otherwise, my 36th year was a good one. It brought change, yes, but the changes were mostly good.

My relationship with Bob and Beulah continued on the upbeat. I didn't tell them about the pamphlet. Their anniversary party was such a success, I didn't want to sully the memory of it. Worse, I thought they might defend Marsha. "You're being who you are. She's being who she is," I could hear my mom saying. And I imagined my response: "I've never called what she's doing an abomination." And then we'd argue. I didn't want to get into it, didn't want to hear my sexual orientation equated to her religious choice.

I'm not sure Mom would agree, but I think seeing a touring production of the musical *La Cage aux Folles* also contributed to her ongoing acceptance of Ted and me. We all went together, Ted and I, Mom and Dad, and enjoyed the big, splashy, heartwarming musical. I think of any of us, Mom was moved by it, her tears flowing at the end as Georges and Albin, the two long-time male lovers at the center of the piece, walk into the sunset together. I might be stretching here, but by showing Georges and Albin as human beings, the play shed light on a new vision for my mom of what her son's future could look like, one that wasn't nearly as awful as she had imagined. It's the kind of thing theater can do, and it worked in our case. I like to think so, anyway.

Something else that helped was our pets. My dad was lukewarm about animals, but my mother loved them. After Copy died (in her mid-teens after developing the sniffles one weekend; I mourned that sweet companion for months), we got a gray tabby from the animal shelter and named her Lucy. In keeping with our love of musical theater, especially Sondheim's musical *Follies,* we had to have a Jessie, Lucy's alter ego in the show. We found one; a stray cat that hung out at my parents' apartment complex had had a litter of kittens.

My mother had been feeding the cat and treated the new kittens as tenderly as Mother Teresa would have. We took all of them to the animal shelter except Jessie. Mom was delighted not only that we took Jessie home, but also that we had a name for her even before we put her in Lucy's cat carrier and got her in the car.

Then there was Max, our puppy. (Musical theater fans will appreciate the consistency of our naming conventions—Max is also a character in *Follies*. We even had a Benjamin, a neighborhood cat who sat on an outdoor window ledge and watched indifferently as Lucy and Jessie hissed at him from inside.)

Over Easter weekend in 1989, the first Easter after the anniversary party, Buddy and Alana came for dinner on Saturday. They left around 11:00. As I was brushing my teeth and getting ready for bed, I heard a far-off sound like a baby crying.

"What is that?" I asked Ted. "Do you hear it?"

We went down the basement stairs and out the back door. After I grabbed a flashlight from the storage room by the garage, we walked toward the sound, across the wet grass, over the creek and onto the pavement of the parking lot behind the big red brick church that faced Franklin Road.

At the back door of the church was a little white puppy. Yelping. She sat on a lavender cardigan sweater. She was either so scared or so excited to see us that she peed as we approached her.

"Hello, baby," I said, picking her up. She fit neatly in my cupped hands.

She yelped back at me.

Ted stroked her head. "It's okay." He looked at me. "Somebody left her here with the sweater. Pretty smart. This place will be jammed with people in the morning."

"How could they—" The puppy's bark drowned me out, but she grew quieter, only whimpering when I held her tighter.

"What do you want to do?" Ted asked.

"We can't leave her here."

She came home with us. The plan was to keep her over Easter (we figured the animal shelter would be closed for the holiday) and take her there Monday morning.

We filled a cereal bowl with water. We found a box in the basement, outfitted it with a beach towel and put it at the foot of our bed. I don't remember if we tried to feed her anything. There was no dog food in the house, and she took no interest in the cats' food.

We tried to sleep, but the puppy kept yelping in the box. Lucy hissed at her once and then skulked into the other bedroom. Jessie followed.

I picked up the puppy and put her in bed with us. She scooted up my chest, snuggled against my neck and stopped barking.

I laughed and folded my hand over Ted's. "'night, Daddy," I said.

"That dog is outta here first thing Monday morning."

"First thing."

That was how I went to sleep that night—Ted by my side and a little white fluff ball curled against my collarbone.

* * *

Of course, Max stayed.

We invited Mom and Dad to go to dinner the next Friday. They came to our house to have a drink beforehand on our deck—and to meet the new puppy. Max snuggled against Mom's neck just as she'd snuggled against mine her first night with us.

"Aren't you a little cutie?" Mom cooed.

"We're going to build a doghouse for her and call it the Maxi-Pad," Ted said.

Mom thought that was hilarious.

Things were going great that evening. We talked about our plans to build a run for Max in the backyard. For now, we had bought a child's gate so Max could stay in the tiled workroom downstairs and not pee on the carpet that covered the rest of the basement floor.

"She's not house-trained yet, I guess," Mom said.

"I wish," I said.

Mom scratched the top of Max's head. "Your dads expect a lot from a little puppy, don't they?" she asked Max.

I was taken aback by her calling us dads. Progress indeed.

It had rained earlier in the day and the deck was damp. As we were getting ready to leave for the restaurant, Ted picked Max up to take her inside. I gathered the glasses from the round metal table that was part of our new outdoor furniture set.

"I'll get my purse," Mom said.

I heard a thud and looked behind me. Mom had slipped and landed flat on her back on the decking, arms outstretched like Jesus on the cross.

I thought she was dead. Mom was 73, after all. I thought it was the end of our pleasant evening on Pleasant Valley Road.

Instead, Dad, Ted and I helped her to her feet. No blood. No broken bones. The damp deck boards hadn't even stained her crisp taupe cotton dress.

"Goodness, I knew it was happening and couldn't do a darn thing about it," she said.

"I think you should sit down, Mom," I said.

"Oh, I don't need to sit down." She was never one for coddling. "I'm fine."

Ted stationed himself at one side of her, I on the other. Each taking an arm, we gingerly escorted her into the house. I think we all were relieved to set foot on carpet, away from the risk of any more slippage on the damp boards. Home free.

Mom took her purse and went upstairs to the bathroom I had painted the day I chased Ted's mother around the house. I rinsed our glasses in the kitchen sink, my heart still pounding from the shock of seeing her dead… then rising to her feet, a happy-hour Lazarus, saints be praised.

Like meeting Ted, like missing the Waverly explosion, like scoring negative on the HIV test, the ice had held under my feet one more time. If there were such things as guardian angels, mine was doing one hell of a good job.

"Thank you," I said to the kitchen ceiling.

Mom emerged from the bathroom and stood in the kitchen doorway, hair brushed, nose powdered, eyes bright. She smiled and clapped her hands.

"Who's ready to eat? I'm starved!"

On the way to the car, I put my arm around her. I felt proud that she was my mother, sorry for all the tough times between us. "I'm so glad you're okay."

"Thank you, honey," she said, her arm around my waist. Her voice lifted my heart. "It takes a lot to whip your old mother."

I had a feeling she meant more than just the fall on the deck.

* * *

In 1991, the insurance company Ted worked for offered him a promotion to the company's Atlanta office. After eight years at the association, I'd been considering a career move, too. I'd bought a Tandy computer and was playing around with desktop publishing. I was also playing around with thoughts of freelance writing, taking my newspaper experience and my experience directing communications for a nonprofit organization and putting it to work for me.

"Atlanta is bigger than Nashville," I said to Ted on a late afternoon walk down Pleasant Valley Road. "There would be more opportunities for freelancing."

"You're sure?" he asked. I could tell he was excited by the offer.

"Let's do it," I said.

Even though I missed our Nashville friends, Atlanta was good for us. It was not only bigger than Nashville, but also more gay-friendly. In Nashville, Ted and I avoided going out to dinner to a nice restaurant on the weekends. It wasn't seemly for two men to look as if they were out on a date together. We'd go during the week, where our date could appear to be a meeting between business partners or some such. I know it sounds weird today, but that's the way it was in Nashville in the 1970s and 1980s. In Atlanta, the South's "Gay Mecca," it was routine to see male couples and female couples dining out together any night of the week, even on Saturday with candlelight and wine.

I also liked another aspect of Atlanta.

"In Nashville, I always felt that I was running into my old self, the person I was in high school, the person my parents expected me to be," I told Ted one night on the screened porch that ran half the length of our four-bedroom split-level house in Atlanta.

"It feels better here?" Ted asked.

"Much."

We'd made money on the sale of the house on Pleasant Valley Road in Nashville. The split-level in Embry Hills just inside the I-285 loop on the northeast side of Atlanta was more room than we needed, but the location was great. The neighborhood had a pool and tennis courts. We even spotted a rainbow flag on one of the houses nearby.

To put it another way, I felt less confined in Atlanta, less self-conscious, more secure. That made me more comfortable with my gay self, closer to that person I'd kept hidden for so long. And oddly, even with nearly 250 miles between us, I felt closer to my parents, too. A little distance was good for us.

In Nashville, when we met somewhere for dinner or ate at each other's respective abodes, we'd always have to go our separate ways at the end of the evening. When Bob and Beulah came to visit us in Atlanta, the evenings were longer and more relaxed. I'd open another bottle of champagne after dinner instead of retrieving car keys from my pocket. We had good talks during those times. And I can say without hesitation that my mother and my father both fell in love with Ted. For me, it was as if we'd finally put behind us the old hope of being a family together in Nashville with Maggie and our children. I had my own life now. I had my own home. And Mom and Dad were always welcome there.

The Christmas open house Ted and I hosted in the early 1990s was the realization of what I had wanted our housewarming party on Cedar Lane to be a decade earlier in Nashville. Many of our neighbors came. No one had any doubt about the exact nature of our relationship. And there were my parents, chatting away with everyone and looking as if they were genuinely having a good time. Mom and Dad would drive on to Augusta the next day to spend Christmas Day and New Year's Eve with my sister Pat and her husband, but for now they were celebrating the season with us.

That felt good.

A friend of ours from Ted's Hyatt days had told us that his parents wrote him out of their will when he came out. Over the years, no matter how stable and upstanding he and his partner proved themselves to be, the will was not changed. His parents didn't budge. In contrast, I was proud of the progress my parents had made, and the progress I had made along with them.

Their will, my dad had mentioned casually one morning at

breakfast, left their estate to be "shared and shared alike" among me and my sisters.

And since Dapo had taken me fishing that summer with my Uncle Burton in Minnesota, since I had been the only grandchild who had attended his funeral in Winter Park, Florida, after his death in 1977, my mother gave me his ornately decorated confirmation certificate and certificate of his birth in Janesville, Minnesota, in 1892. She had had them beautifully framed. I hung them in our dining room in the house in Embry Hills.

A little part of the family history.

My family.

And ours.

Chapter Eighteen: Freak Flag

A warm welcome in New Orleans, mid-1990s

Atlanta was good for my writing career, too.

I went to the print shop by our Embry Hills neighborhood one afternoon to pick up copies of my new resume and a tri-fold brochure I had written and designed to market my writing services. Another customer at the counter was a striking, dark-haired woman who had also recently started her own business. She was picking up her own printing project.

"I'm looking for a writer," she said.

I held my hands palm up. "Here I am."

It was the beginning of my 12-year association with Char Baxter and what she called her "boutique" marketing agency for high-tech companies. Her first client was SAP America, which meant nothing to me at the time, but I quickly learned. Today, SAP is the biggest business software vendor with clients like Walmart, Exxon, Apple, CVS and General Motors. I had landed in a nice pot of jam.

Working with Char was a stretch for me. I had a whole new subject to learn. She taught me about client/server computer systems, about a new concept called business process reengineering, where companies were automating the processes their sales, financial, inventory and distribution teams used to get their work done.

She explained that, because the field was so new, it was filled with language gobbledygook. Technology geeks with brilliant minds, mind you, were trying to promote their companies and their products in their own computer engineering vocabulary. People with MBAs from places like The Wharton School, the Massachusetts Institute of Technology and Georgia Tech were brought in to build the businesses. Skilled as they were, they weren't communicators, either. The industry needed writers who could dispense with the mishmash and write about the companies and the products in a way that was clear and concise.

That was my challenge and my opportunity.

"I like your journalism background," Char said. "We need that. We need someone who knows how to ask the right questions."

I liked knowing that the work with Char somehow made sense. It wasn't a random thing. I was applying skills I'd learned across 20 years as a professional writer. Though I was taking my career in a new direction, the stars were aligned in a logical progression. It made me feel that our decision to move to Atlanta was right, that there was order to our lives. It felt good. Best of all, I got to work from home at a time when that was a rare privilege. There was travel, too.

Char and I would fly to Boston, for example, for a six-hour session where the founders of a new technology firm or a consulting firm that installed the technology would try to explain what their company did. At the end of the day, their flip charts and whiteboards looked like the walls of a cave filled with ancient hieroglyphics scratched out by someone on speed, acid or both.

I'd fly home with a briefcase full of notes and microcassette tapes on which the entire dizzying day had been recorded. My first assignment? To condense their presentation down to 35 words that made sense. That would be the "elevator statement," a company's essential story that could be communicated in the time it took to get to your floor on an elevator.

From the elevator statement would come a more detailed "positioning paper" that laid out how the company would talk about itself to the world. From that document would come the usual marketing pieces—brochures, product sheets, case studies, websites (the new kid on the block in the early 1990s) and advertising.

Char handled the contract side of our relationship with the companies, brought in graphic designers to create a logo and whatever piece I was working on, and set the overall strategy of our work. While we were at it, sometimes we'd name, or rename, a company.

We were a good team.

The money was good, too.

Ted and I were able to indulge our interest in travel and theater. We went to New York, stayed in nicer hotels and saw many shows with the original casts—*Angels in America, Falsettos*, the 1992 production of *Guys and Dolls* with Faith Prince, Nathan Lane and Peter Gallagher. (We both had the hots for Peter Gallagher.) We took cruises with RSVP, the gay men's charter cruise company that offered a chance not only to visit New Orleans for Mardi Gras one year and later sail into the Panama Canal, but also to test our fidelity. (We succeeded. We were old enough—I turned 40 in 1992; Ted in 1993—to say the late-night partying and 'round-the-clock hook-ups weren't for us. We weren't married, of course, but we were acting more and more like an older married couple. I think that's how the young guys on the cruise saw us, anyway.)

In the late 1990s, the agency had done so well that Char bought a building in an office park located about halfway between her house and mine. I would no longer be a stay-at-home freelancer, but I made the sacrifice. Char promoted me to vice president and brought me and the other freelancers inside the new office as full-time employees.

At one point, there were nearly 20 of us—graphic designers, website developers (kids in their 20s making outlandish salaries because they knew how to do what no one else could: build a website for a company), account executives, extra writers to help me, an assistant for the woman who did our billing. We were riding the crest of the growth of the technology industry in Atlanta. It was an exciting, often stressful, time.

The best part was that I could be open at work about who I was. Two decades had passed since my days at the *Alabama Journal* and the *Banner*, my skulking around to the Other Side when I wanted to meet others of my persuasion and my secretive calls to Ted from the payphone in the *Banner* downstairs lobby—if the security guard wasn't at his desk. A lot had changed in those years.

The other employees on Char's team were straight, gay, married, single, Christian, agnostic, vegetarian, carnivores. Nobody cared about anyone's life choices. Ted came to our Christmas parties, where clients were invited, too. He was invited to happy hours on Fridays, Scrabble games on Sunday afternoons. He was also appreciated by Char for helping create the kind of home environment that kept me stable, kept me in Atlanta, kept me thriving.

My comfort in my new workplace, and my confidence in my relationship with Ted, made me more confident in myself, too. I look back on that time with Char and I think I can say that I was a warmer person, more relaxed, funnier, more willing to reach out than I had been once upon a time.

And more comfortable around openly gay people. Of all my memories of the time working with Char, one of my favorites is taking out the garbage. And making a friend.

* * *

Char asked all of us on staff to take turns each Friday gathering up the garbage from deskside bins in the offices upstairs and down. We took the stuff outside to the dumpster in the office park before we closed up shop for the weekend.

One Friday, it was my turn. I carried the jumbo black plastic garbage bag to the workstation of one of our best graphic designers, a guy named Rob. He was very smart, very funny, very out. Just being around him made me happy to be out, too.

I held the open bag to him and said, "Trash?"

He hooted. "Who you callin' trash?"

I laughed. "If the shoe fits."

"Mm-hmm," he said.

From that day on, it became a game between us. When it was Rob's turn to gather the garbage, he'd stand in the doorway to my office with a hip slung out and a black plastic bag in one hand.

"Trash," he'd say, looking straight at me. I came to look forward to the days it was my turn or Rob's to take the trash out so he and I could play our little game. God bless him, he even made garbage pickup fun.

Rob is gone today. When the tech bubble burst, Char closed the agency in 2005. I started my own writing business. Rob went on to another ad and marketing firm in Atlanta, where he brought me in many times to be the lead writer on new projects.

Nearly a decade passed. Then I lost touch with Rob. It wasn't until 2020, after Ted and I had moved back to Atlanta from our place in the northeast Georgia mountains, that I did a search for him online and found his obituary. I cursed Google for its dutiful robotics, for not bothering to prepare me, for delivering up the news as if it were a pie recipe. I don't remember making a sound, but I must have done something because Ted stuck his head in my office to see if I was okay. Through tears, I read that in 2016, Rob died of complications from pneumonia in an ICU bed while his mother sang him his favorite lullaby. He was 50 years old.

Time goes fast. Life is funny. During my time with Char, we won awards, had great weekend parties at her lake house, had company dinners at some of the best restaurants in town, met interesting people from all over the world who were making a name for themselves in the technology industry in Atlanta, but trash days with Rob are among the memories I treasure most. I suppose there was some sublimated flirting going on in our little game. I'm not sure. Rob was single, nearly 15 years my junior. I don't know if he felt any attraction for me. I know I did for him.

He and a young woman on the staff took smoke breaks in the afternoons on the sidewalk outside my office. There were steps down from the sidewalk to our office entrance, so from my window on the first floor, I could see only the lower extremities of whomever was outside. One day, Rob wore shorts to work, and when I looked out my window to where he and the young woman were smoking, all I could see was a pair of skinny but nicely shaped, ginger-haired legs. Loafers. No socks. And those legs.

I sat down at my desk, hoping he hadn't seen me looking, hoping he hadn't seen the sudden activity in my khaki pants while I stood at the window. Or maybe, I was hoping he had.

Look out, I cautioned myself. *You could get in trouble here.*

I never did get in trouble with Rob. I think maybe we could have, but we were just friends through the years we worked together. As vice president, I was technically his boss, but that didn't mean we couldn't cut up together.

One Friday a group of us went to happy hour at a Mexican restaurant near the office. I was on my second margarita when the conversation turned to the husky blond Georgia native who worked as a rep for the company that printed most of the materials we produced for clients. He came to the office frequently to pick up new jobs on computer disk or to deliver proofs for our scrutiny before the presses rolled. Sometimes he wore a suit. Most days he was more casual, his shirt collar and tie loosened, sprouts of golden hair peeking out from under the crew neck of his white T-shirt.

One of the designers at the table was relaying the rep's story of his and his wife's recent visit to Italy. They'd toured a town called Poggibonsi, a Chianti village that Ted and I had visited a few years before.

"Poggibonsi." She imitated the rep's slow southern drawl. "I mean, he literally made it sound pornographic."

"I think everything he says sounds pornographic," I said.

That got everyone's attention.

I continued. "He's not movie-star handsome or anything, but some days I just want to rip the clothes off that man."

The response was howling laughter, groans, handclaps, gaping mouths.

"I can't believe you said that," one of the designers said.

Frankly, I couldn't either. Imagine me a decade earlier saying anything so gay to a table of co-workers. I guess I had come a long way.

Rob pointed one index finger at me and stroked the top of it with the other. "I'm gonna tell Ted on you."

I took another sip of margarita. "If Ted saw him, he'd feel the same way."

"I know I do," said Rob.

The laughter died down. So did the group conversation. Staff members talked in twos and threes as baskets of chips emptied and glasses ran dry.

Rob turned to me. "I really like working with you," he said.

"I really like working with you, too."

He lifted his glass. "To Poggibonsi."

I laughed. "To Poggibonsi."

We clinked our glasses together.

It was the last time we would.

* * *

Unfortunately, from our very first days in Atlanta, Ted's workplace wasn't as congenial as mine.

I could sense it. He dreaded going to work every day. Every morning, his face clouded with the same misery I had felt when I was trying to make a go of covering the Davidson County courthouse in Nashville.

Ted had a few friends among the team in the Atlanta office, but in that straight-male-dominated corporate environment, he remained closeted to the higher-ups. Some of them made life difficult for everyone. I don't think the phrase "toxic masculinity" had been coined in the 1990s, but if it had, you could have said Ted was knee-deep in it in his new job in Atlanta.

He told me about a meeting where human resources staff members had encouraged white male executives to build a more diverse team. I won't repeat one of the exec's responses here, but imagine saying the following line in the most racist, sexist, offensive way possible, and you'll get the idea: "I might bring in a black man but I'm not hiring any black women."

I didn't know what to do about it except listen to the grim stories he brought home. I tried my best to be a good partner to Ted during those days. It was unsettling to think that his job dissatisfaction could threaten the happy equilibrium we—or more accurately, I—had found in Atlanta.

Late one afternoon, while we walked Max around the circle in our neighborhood, Ted suggested looking for another job.

"It could mean moving somewhere new," he said.

"But I'm just getting started," I said.

I didn't like the idea of pulling up roots again, though I felt selfish staking a claim for me instead of supporting Ted, instead of saying I was open to the possibility of moving. I reminded myself how steadfast Ted had been through the years—while often I was the one struggling. It was my turn to be steadfast now.

"Still," I said. "If you think there are better opportunities somewhere else, then sure, I'd be up for whatever." Score one for me, I thought, even though I felt as if I'd let go of something dear and was watching it sink to the bottom of the ocean.

"We'll see," Ted said, uncertainty looming before us.

Instead, he stuck it out, God bless him. Maybe my willingness to go somewhere new was all he needed to hear. Happily, our Atlanta roots grew deeper in the months that followed.

We made friends volunteering every Wednesday night with Project Open Hand, a nonprofit organization that provided meals for Atlantans with AIDS. We packed the meals in an assembly-line setup that was ideal for getting to know the other volunteers. We had good conversations. We had fun, too. Instead of hairnets and caps, some of the guys wore Easter bonnets one evening. I wasn't ready for drag yet; I wore a baseball cap, but I admired the other guys' willingness to be silly for silly's sake. Amid the laughter, we figured those who got our meals would want us to have a good time while we put their dinners together. It was Ted's idea to seek friends in a more wholesome setting than the clubs and the bars in Atlanta, and he was right. Several of these fellows—and one wonderful woman named Cherry—are still friends to this day.

We were with these friends at Atlanta Pride in 1993 or 1994 when a bluetick hound puppy came by our tarpaulin-shaded spot on a hillside in midtown's Piedmont Park. She was under the watchful eyes of a lesbian couple who ran a Shar-Pei rescue center in one of the suburban counties north of the city. I don't remember how they happened to find Blue, but they were looking for a home for her.

What happens between a couple when you make a significant life decision? Seems to me there is a complex network of verbal and physical cues to be navigated and interpreted. I've come to know that Ted might say he wants something if he sees I want it when in fact he doesn't want it. He's better than I at understanding the true meaning behind the said and the unsaid, though I've worked through the years to improve, to be more sensitive to what he wants.

On that day at Pride, I don't remember who said first, "We should adopt this baby," but I do remember knowing the feeling was mutual, remember being 100 percent convinced that Ted wanted Blue as much as I did.

The two women visited us the next day. They came to inspect the environment Blue would be adopted into before they signed her over to us. We passed.

We'd known it all along, but it's always nice to get confirmation. Ours was a certifiably good home. A little stressed, at times, but good.

* * *

Ted found a job with another insurance company. A company in Atlanta.

The end of his previous job wasn't pretty, but he landed on his feet. He was hired by a smaller but highly regarded company in midtown Atlanta. When he told his boss at the old company that he was leaving the same afternoon he gave his notice, the fellow objected, saying if Ted left so quickly, "it will make us look bad."

Ted packed his briefcase and was out of there.

He started the new job two weeks later.

And life was better in our house on Embry Circle.

* * *

So much better, in fact, that Atlanta remained our home through the 1990s. A home both of us thrived in. We had good friends. Work was going well for both of us. We considered new investments, new ways to grow together. New escapes, too.

We'd seen on maps how the Blue Ridge Mountains begin their northward crest in northeast Georgia, home of the Appalachian Trail's southern terminus. But it took our lesbian neighbors in Embry Hills to introduce us to the lovely landscapes in that part of the state.

One neighbor was a high school principal who had smartly invested in a small cabin near Lake Burton, which is tucked about as tightly in the northeast corner of Georgia as you can get. She and her partner, an elementary school teacher, invited Ted and me up for a weekend at the cabin.

One of the graphic designers who worked with Char said he knew about Lake Burton when I told him Ted and I were going there for the weekend. In his early 30s, he was most impressed by the Bose sound system his in-laws had installed in their boathouse on the lake. "It's sweet," he said. He also described the setting as "very European."

"What do you mean?" I asked.

"It's hard to describe, the way it's kind of nestled in the mountains. It could be in Germany or Switzerland somewhere."

The mountains that surround Lake Burton aren't nearly as tall as the mountains in Switzerland, but once I saw the lake, I understood what he was getting at. It didn't look like Georgia. It was a blue gem, the ice-cream-scoop mountains around it a dazzling green. It was special, a world apart.

And it came along at exactly the right time.

We'd both been working hard in Atlanta. The traffic drove us crazy sometimes. Our neighborhood in Embry Hills was declining, too. Recent break-ins had been reported. And whenever there was an accident or other problem on the interstate highway near us, our street became clogged with drivers using it as a cut-through. Lake Burton was an escape from all that.

We swam. We water-skied. At the grill by the Cherokee marina where our neighbors kept their boat, we had some of the best burgers and fries we'd ever eaten.

We also got a kick out of the quirkiness of the place. The sparkling river that ran through the area was the Soque, the Cherokee word for pig, our neighbors told us. When we drove to the marina for the July 4th fireworks on the water, a pickup truck blocked access to some additional parking space. About a dozen local guys, "bubbas," as our neighbors described them, simply picked up the truck barehanded and moved it out of the way. Cabbage Patch Dolls had been born in a community a few miles down the road. The "Babyland General Hospital" offered tours. We liked the way people in the area seemed stubbornly determined to be unsophisticated, a refreshing change from the highfalutin, "my building has a doorman" airs of some folks we knew in Atlanta. And the scenery—the open pastures, the wooded hillsides, the gravel roads meandering through thick mountain laurel—was drop-dead gorgeous.

"What do you think about buying a place here?" I asked Ted when we got in bed in the guest room of our neighbors' cabin, tree frogs trilling outside the screened windows.

"Sure."

I searched his face.

"You're serious?" I asked.

"I was going to bring it up a while ago. I didn't think you'd go for it."

"I'm going for it!"

On the drive back to Atlanta the next day, we spotted several homes for sale. I wrote down the realtors' phone numbers. We called them when we got home.

"We'll find you boys a little cabin in the woods," said the realtor who took us out one Saturday a few weeks later to look at houses. Ted and I rode with him in the front seat of his big old pickup truck. His family went back generations in the Lake Burton area. I think he qualified as a bubba, too, but he didn't seem to have a problem with us at all.

We had similar experiences all through our time in the mountains. No one seemed to give a flip that Ted and I were obviously more than fishing buddies. It was pleasant surprise after pleasant surprise.

Maybe the world really had changed since 1977.

One of our new mountain friends summed it up in her typically local way. She was a gravel-voiced lady in her 60s who owned a bakeshop near the cabin we eventually bought. In that shop, she turned out fabulous Italian cream, chocolate/peanut butter and fresh strawberry cakes. I'd watched her ice those cakes with a cigarette dangling from her lips, the ash growing longer and longer—yet miraculously never befouling the buttercream. "A lot of folks come here to get away from something," she said. "They're not gonna judge because they don't want to be judged either."

It sounded good to us.

The cabin we bought in the north Georgia woods was outside a little town called Clarkesville, in a subdivision called Skyview. It was just what we were looking for. Seventy-five miles northeast of our place in Atlanta, we could reach it easily on a Friday afternoon after work, even spend Sunday night there and drive to Atlanta early Monday morning if we felt like it. With a wood stove as its main source of heat, it had a small bedroom and bath downstairs and an open loft on the second floor. The floors were a lovely natural pine. In the fall, our no-upkeep, one-acre lot looked like an Eliot Porter photograph from the living room window. The evening light turned the mountains to the north a deep turquoise.

"They're not called the Blue Ridge for nothing," Ted said. "I love it here."

I did, too.

For a while, our little cabin in the woods was just a weekend getaway.

Later, it was the thing that saved my life.

Chapter Nineteen: Ah! But Underneath

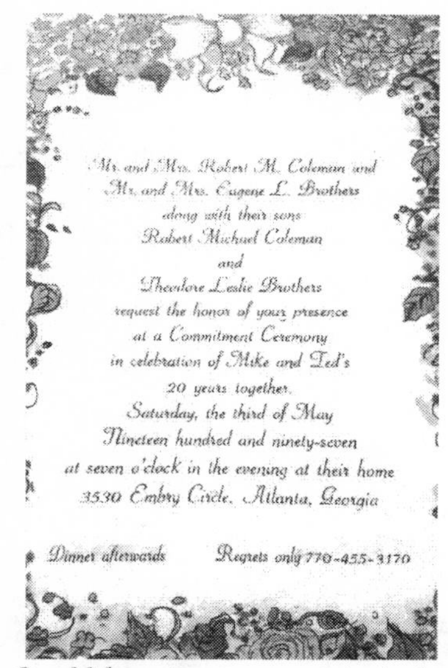
Mr. and Mrs. Robert M. Coleman and
Mr. and Mrs. Eugene L. Brothers
along with their sons
Robert Michael Coleman
and
Theodore Leslie Brothers
request the honor of your presence
at a Commitment Ceremony
in celebration of Mike and Ted's
20 years together.
Saturday, the third of May
Nineteen hundred and ninety-seven
at seven o'clock in the evening at their home
3530 Embry Circle, Atlanta, Georgia

Dinner afterwards Regrets only 770-455-3170

Our 20th anniversary party invitation
Flowered border painted by Beulah Tschache Coleman after the event

The next part of the story isn't easy to tell. I considered leaving it out of the memoir, but it shaped the person I am, the couple Ted and I are today. It can't go untold.

Some years ago, I attempted a fictionalized treatment of it in a third novel I started. But I realized that just because something happens in real life doesn't necessarily mean it will work in fiction. That is the case with this part of my story. The unfinished manuscript sits on a thumb drive today, ignored, probably as it should be.

In the novel, the events and my protagonist's response to them didn't quite match up. My protagonist seemed, at best, unsympathetic, self-centered, grandiose; at worst, a downright crazy drunk. I have accepted the fact that I was all those things during this period of my life.

It was more than a rough patch; it was a runaway merry-go-round for a few years, like the climactic scene in Hitchcock's *Strangers on a Train.*

But that's not quite an accurate description. This crisis happened quietly, under cover of what appeared to be the happy, successful life Ted and I had built together. Not many people knew about it. My parents knew some parts of it but not the whole story.

Even Ted didn't know all the gory details. But that was just as well. I had started down a road I had to travel alone, started on a journey I had to complete myself.

* * *

On May 3, 1997, Ted and I hosted 50 of our friends and family members for a commitment ceremony and party at our house on Embry Circle in Atlanta to celebrate our 20th anniversary. The ceremony was Ted's idea; it was as close as two men could get to a wedding in 1997, with the two of us publicly repeating vows to one another and a minister asking God's blessing on us.

Ted was emboldened by what had happened the previous year, when the U.S. president himself, Bill Clinton, liberal though he was, signed into law the Defense of Marriage Act, which defined marriage as a union between one man and one woman. Its sweeping provisions prevented the federal government from recognizing same-sex marriages and gave states the right to deny recognition of same-sex couples. We were disappointed by Clinton's action; we had voted for the guy. As a positive protest, Ted wanted us to make a statement that our union was worth celebrating, too.

I wasn't thrilled that he wanted such a public display. I thought we might be rocking the boat, thought we might be asking too much of my parents to join us, but to my surprise, they agreed to drive to Atlanta from Nashville and stand with me during the ceremony.

Still, there was trouble. What stunned me was where it came from.

Across Ted's and my years together, my mother had told me to go to hell in the late 1970s. My sister Marsha had called our relationship an abomination in 1988. In 1997, it was my sister Pat's turn to lay a curse. (I've never written it in these terms before, but it does seem as if each of them picked a decade, doesn't it, to keep the fun rolling? I can imagine the conversation: "Mike has been looking entirely too happy and successful over the last ten years. Who wants to harass him this time?")

Now on her second marriage, Pat had a circuitous spiritual life. She seemed to be always searching. She attended the Episcopal Church when she was in school in Atlanta, but once she moved outside Augusta, she and her husband explored other congregations, some traditional, some not. There was time spent with an Anglican congregation, then with one calling itself the Vineyard. I had given up keeping track of it all. Whatever theology she and her husband were espousing in 1997, it was not a gay-friendly one. She refused to make the two-hour drive from Augusta to Atlanta to attend the ceremony and celebration.

"I can't ask God to bless your union," she said to me on the phone one night.

Another man might have said, "That's my sister," and gone blithely on with the celebration. But I took it as a real blow. It shocked and hurt me. I thought we were close. Pat had been one of the first people to whom I had introduced Ted after he and I met.

One weekend before she moved to Atlanta for graduate school, we visited her in Johnson City, Tennessee, where she had a job working with handicapped children. Pat had an infected toe on that visit, not a huge concern for most people but a red flag for a diabetic with possible circulatory issues. On Sunday morning after the throbbing pain had kept her up most of the night, she decided she should go to the emergency room. The challenge was that several inches of snow had fallen during the night.

It didn't stop us. We piled in my yellow Volkswagen Beetle and to the hospital we went.

Of course, nearly two decades had passed since that winter morning in Johnson City. Pat had shown her capacity not to be my ally when she outed me to our parents a few years later. Still, I couldn't understand how anyone could refuse to ask God to bless the union of a couple who had risked life and limb to make a hospital run with you.

* * *

And yet, I wondered if part of me didn't share Pat's objection to what we were about to do. Since Ted and I had met, God had not been part of our lives. At least, I hadn't thought so. I think it's accurate to say that I stopped believing in God when I left home for college. And then when I came out, I thought there was no way one could be a practicing homosexual and a practicing Christian at the same time. I made a choice.

I'd thought Ted agreed with me, but now I was learning that a tiny flicker of the God from his Episcopal upbringing had glowed inside him all along. I thought it was sweet but disturbing. Where had I been all these years? And now that we were planning a ceremony with a minister asking God to bless our union, how did I make the transition? Why did I need to? But Ted was so enthusiastic about the celebration, I put the questions aside. I contacted a young pastor at Atlanta's Metropolitan Community Church, part of the denomination founded primarily to serve gay and lesbian congregants, to perform our ceremony. And I wrote an outline of what we wanted him to say during the service.

I enjoyed doing it. It gave me a chance to express my pride in the years Ted and I had logged together. It also made me feel that a flicker of the Presbyterian God from my youth was alive in me, too. Maybe, just maybe, that God would be with us while we said our vows. The same God in whose name I'd been baptized as a kid.

Still, I was cautious. Just because we were having a ceremony with a minister didn't mean we were going to become born-again Christians or anything. And deep down, I looked forward to the ceremony being over, to the day we could go back to our comfortable, churchless life, whether God had truly blessed our union or not.

* * *

A little after 7:00 o'clock on the evening of the ceremony, Ted's father, the lady friend he had taken up with since Jean's passing, and my parents flanked us on our green lawn while we said our vows. We stood under the tall pines that edged our backyard, the day's bright sunlight nicely softening.

"Dear God, we ask that you bless these two men, honor and protect the love they have for one another," said the pastor. In tuxes, Ted and I faced our guests. "If all of you here pledge to support Ted and Mike in their life journey together, please answer by saying, 'We do.'"

"We do!" answered the crowd, which included Buddy, Alana, Matt and Sharon, our Brandy Alexander friends who had made the trip down from Nashville to be with us.

I was grateful they had. They were my allies in the absence of both my sisters from the ceremony. And then there was Ted's family, who came in droves and showered us with love that day. His brother and sister were there from South Carolina with their spouses and children, who volunteered to greet guests and make sure they signed the guestbook while Ted and I got ready upstairs. Ted's aunt Denise had flown up from Jacksonville, Florida, and brought her mother from Clearwater. She was Ted's grandmother. Nearly 90 and wearing a stunning peacock-blue pantsuit that set off her carefully coiffed white hair, Olive was the belle of the ball that evening.

"Isn't she wonderful?" I said to Sharon during the catered Asian dinner we served after the ceremony.

"She's a hoot," Sharon said. "I hope I look that good at her age."

"You will." I picked up a napkin one of the kids had dropped on the dining room rug. "I wish Amy could have joined us," I said, referring to Matt and Sharon's daughter, the one Ted and I called "the daughter we never had."

"She wanted to be here, but the wedding is running her ragged." Amy was engaged to be married later in the summer in Memphis, where she had attended college and met her husband-to-be. "Running us ragged, too."

"We're looking forward to it." Ted and I had already made plans to attend. We would travel to Memphis from Atlanta and make a weekend of it.

Ted's hand was on my shoulder. "When do you want to cut the cake?" he asked, nodding toward the elaborate, three-tiered confection on a table at one end of the living room.

"Let's give it a few more minutes. People are still eating."

I looked across our dining room and living room, where our family and friends were finishing their meals. Other guests were eating in the den or on the screened porch. We were fortunate to have beautiful weather that evening.

My mother and Char were on the sofa, having an animated conversation about Picasso. Dad and Gene were helping themselves to seconds from the food we'd set out on the dining room table. In the foyer, Ted's grandmother was holding court with a group of young gay men, our friends from our volunteer work packing meals at Project Open Hand. They were all laughing. She obviously had said something funny. She had a knack for that. Ted's aunt Denise had told us that when she'd asked Gramma a few months earlier if she'd have a problem being around "lots of gay people" at our celebration, Gramma had replied, "Nonsense. I've always had friends in the theater."

As I watched the scene, people talking and laughing, enjoying an evening in our home, I regretted the misgivings I'd had about the celebration, was glad that Ted had pushed us to go ahead with it. No matter what Pat said about it, on this evening, the truth had never been so clear to me: *This is good,* I thought. *This is right.*

* * *

Nearly two months later, on July 1st, 1997, the phone rang shortly before 8:00 a.m. I was still working from home then. With a busy day ahead, I was already showered, dressed and at my desk, putting the finishing touches on the ad copy I'd written the day before.

I wondered who'd be calling so early. With my parents getting older, any call before 9:00 a.m. signaled possible trouble. Or maybe it was Ted, who was traveling on business, but he was in Los Angeles—where it was only 5:00 a.m. He wouldn't be calling so early, would he? Besides, we had talked last night. The next logical choice was Char. She was an early starter, like me. I picked up the receiver, hoping for the best.

"Mike. It's Matt."

That surprised me. Sharon's husband, our friend from Nashville, was the last person I'd expected to hear on the other end of the line. It was only 7:00 in Nashville. Maybe he was calling with some details about Amy's wedding next month, though he didn't sound like the usual, energetic Matt. His voice was faded, slack.

"Hi, Matt," I said. "What's up?"

There was a long pause. A scary one.

"Matt?" I asked.

"Amy died," he said.

* * *

Amy had been diagnosed with tachycardia, a rapid heartbeat caused by heart rhythm disorders. We weren't aware of her condition, but apparently it had reached the point where her Memphis doctor recommended a relatively routine procedure to correct it. We were told it involved putting a catheter in the heart and ablating it, or removing cardiac tissue causing the rhythm problem. With her wedding coming up in August, Amy decided to go ahead with the June 30 procedure, one more item to scratch off her to-do list before the Big Day.

We never knew the exact details, but the procedure went haywire somehow. Amy died on the hospital table. She was 24.

Matt told me he had already phoned Buddy and Alana with the news. After our call, I wanted to talk to Ted, but it was still so early in L.A., so I went downstairs to the kitchen, poured more coffee. The news hadn't quite hit me. *Amy died.*

Was this numbness natural? Aside from my grandfather's death, I had never experienced the death of anyone so close to me. My body wasn't responding at all the way I'd thought it would. Tears weren't flowing. My heart wasn't aching with emptiness. Instead, as I stirred the coffee in my cup, what I felt was dread, a dark anxiety awakening inside me. *Amy died.* A bomb had dropped. The fallout, I knew, would be like hard, freezing rain, transforming everything on this sunny summer day.

But that wasn't the thing that scared me most. What did was the fact that Amy's death came as no surprise.

* * *

She was golden.

In looks and personality, Ted and I sometimes remarked that Amy resembled Kellie Martin, the young actress who played the daughter on the early 1990s TV series, *Life Goes On*, a favorite of ours. Or maybe I should say that Kellie resembled Amy. She was beautiful. Even when she came into our lives as a young teenager, there was a brightness about her, a glow she shared with us from the very beginning.

After Ted and I moved to Atlanta in 1991, we kept our tradition of meeting Buddy, Alana, Matt and Sharon in Gatlinburg for Thanksgiving each year. (The kids spent the holiday with their other respective families—Buddy's, Sharon's and Matt's former spouses.) It was a way to stay connected after our departure from Nashville. The six of us pledged that the long weekend would be ours only—no other family members were allowed. But one year, we'd made an exception for Amy when she attended a special college program at the University of Tennessee in Knoxville, which wasn't too far from the house we were renting in Gatlinburg. I believe she was in her early 20s then. We were impressed by how easily she fit in with us "oldsters." She helped prepare the dinners, joined us for a dip in the rental house's hot tub at cocktail time, discussed books with our decidedly bookish crowd and was, all in all, a genuine pleasure to have with us. She was worth breaking the rules for.

And now… all I could see was Amy the way she had looked while we cooled off in the river on our Smoky Mountain hiking trip when she was a young teenager. "I get it," she had said. "People want to make it into something weird. But it isn't, is it?" I remembered how she'd made me feel that afternoon: blessed.

* * *

After Matt's phone call, I considered not interrupting Ted's business trip, waiting to tell him the news when he came home later in the week, but it just didn't seem right. He needed to know. Besides, early hour be damned, I wanted to hear his voice, hoped it would chase away the growing chill inside me. At 8:30 a.m.—5:30 his time—I called his hotel and asked to be connected to his room.

"Are you okay?" he asked sleepily.

"No," I said. But even then, the tears didn't come. The news about Amy had scared them right out of me.

* * *

Ted cried, however.

He'd shaved and showered after my call, dressed, gone to breakfast in the lobby of the hotel. He told me later he'd felt numb, moving through his morning routine like any other day. With a full agenda, he'd been planning to get up early, anyway. It wasn't until his colleague from Atlanta came downstairs, said "Good morning," and took a seat across from him that Ted burst into tears.

Ken was a good guy. He and Ted had appointments booked through the day with insurance agents in the area. Ken canceled all of them. They found a cheesy map in the hotel lobby and spent most of the day playing tourist, driving around in their rental car to the homes of the Hollywood stars. Ken caught instantly the magnitude of what had happened, what Amy had meant to Ted and me, what Matt and Sharon meant to both of us. It was a death in our family. For one day, work could wait.

* * *

A few days later, we gathered around Amy's freshly dug grave on a blazing hot afternoon in a Nashville cemetery. Hysteria lurked beneath the surface of Matt and Sharon's gray faces. They were our dear friends, yet they seemed oddly removed from us by the tragedy, exiled to a strange new land while we watched helplessly from the other side of the figurative fence. Misery looked as if it had taken up permanent residence in their frightened eyes.

As Ted's hand gripped mine and sweat trickled under my shirt collar, a bird sang in the tree up the hill. The Episcopal priest cleared his throat and began the service.

I tuned out his words, one thought repeating in my head as I stared at the gaping hole in the dark earth: *We are standing at the mouth of Hell.*

* * *

It's a sign of maturity when one accepts that life is a series of random events that bear no relationship to one another. To put it simply, in 1997 at age 44, I wasn't there yet.

Somewhere in the deepest, most insecure part of me, I viewed Amy's death as a consequence of what we'd done on May 3. That's why Matt's call that morning hadn't surprised me. Pat had warned us: "I can't ask God to bless your union." We had. And look what had happened. A statement had been made.

Sure, part of me knew it was ridiculous to connect the two events—our ceremony, Amy's death. In the weeks after the funeral, we were in close contact by phone with Matt and Sharon—and Buddy and Alana, too. They hadn't made the connection, so why should I? Ted hadn't made the connection, either. So I kept silent, even though it was all I could think about.

If I'd had a firmer foundation in theology, the answers might have come easily. But lacking that, especially after a drink or two, the questions would rise like ghosts in the night, ruining my sleep. Were we somehow responsible for what had happened to Amy? Could someone prove absolutely that we weren't? Maybe our exuberance over being so public about our relationship after we moved to Atlanta hadn't been such a good thing after all. If we'd kept a lower profile. If we hadn't dared to bring God into our union. If... if... if...

I considered going to the pastor who had performed our commitment ceremony, talking with him about the questions that troubled me. But he had told us he was leaving Atlanta the week after the ceremony. I didn't know how to reconnect with him.

What I wanted to say to someone was this: It wasn't as if the God I'd grown up with in the Presbyterian church was one to hurl fire and brimstone. He wasn't that kind of God. He did have a code of conduct, however. Follow it, live righteously, and certain protections would stay in place. That was part of the bargain, wasn't it? Step outside the boundaries, and all bets were off. Oh, it was okay to stray once in a while. The prodigal son. The lost sheep. The difference was that they had returned to the fold. On the other hand, stand before friends and family and proudly celebrate your transgression as Ted and I had done at our commitment ceremony? We had asked for trouble. I should have listened to my misgivings and put a stop to the celebration before the plans got off the drawing board.

When I raised the questions with Ted, his response was just as I'd expected.

"Are you kidding me?" he said. "We had a beautiful ceremony. We have friends and family who love us."

"What about God?"

"God loves us, too."

"I'm not sure I believe that."

"Then I think you need to talk with somebody. Find a psychotherapist. Because you will not use this bullshit to ruin what we did." Clippers in hand, he headed outside to trim the roses, but he stopped at the back door and turned to me. "It dishonors Amy, you know, to make her part of your problem."

That was the deepest cut of all.

* * *

I found a psychotherapist.

One of our early sessions went something like this:

"Ted and I have ignored God for decades. Starbucks is our church on Sunday morning."

"Ours, too," she said. Her name was Brenda, a soft-spoken woman who dressed beautifully.

"And then all of a sudden we come knocking on his door asking him to bless our union. I didn't even ask the minister to read from the Bible. I had him quoting Kierkegaard, for God's sake."

"So, you think God has singled you out?" she asked, her hand at the neckline of her yellow blouse. "Isn't that a little arrogant?"

"Not singled us out. Turned his back on us. There's a difference."

"Have you heard of a thing called faith?"

"You're not going to go all Billy Graham on me, are you?"

She laughed her gentle laugh. "I think I hear you saying that you don't have the theological… ammunition to counter your sister's stand. Is that right?"

"I should… but I don't."

"Even the book of Leviticus, where sex between men is right up there with eating shrimp as a major sin?"

I laughed, then looked at my hands. "If it's that obvious, why don't I feel it?" My eyes met hers. "Why don't I feel that God is okay with us?"

"That's a very good question."

I glanced at her immaculate desk, the handsome batik print of irises on the wall behind it. If only my life looked so cheerful, so calming. "Ted and I have had some good times and made some good friends since our move to Atlanta six years ago. But everything that's happened since our ceremony has made me realize I've been afraid to look too deeply… into why Ted and I are the way we are. Into what our place in the world really is. Into what God, if there is one, thinks of us. What if I don't like the answer?"

She laced her fingers together on one knee. "Have you always felt guilty about being gay?"

I looked to the ceiling, bumping my head against the wall behind me. There was a moment of intense, surprising pain. I tried to rub it away. "You're not going to make this about that, are you?"

She held her hands palm up at her sides, as if to say, what else is there? "Just remember that not coming to your commitment ceremony says a lot more about your sister than it does about you."

"What does that buy us?"

"Maybe something. We'll see. Now… you look like you could use a hug."

Brenda always ended our sessions with a hug—her not-so-subtle way of saying "your time is up."

She stood. I stood. We hugged.

"I'm mad at Ted," I said when she released me. "I guess I need help with that, too."

"Why are you mad at Ted?"

"For wanting to have the ceremony in the first place! For setting up this whole question that is driving me fucking crazy!"

"You need two hugs," she said, hugging me again. "Take good care. We'll see you next week."

On the way home, I stopped at the liquor store and bought a bottle of pinot grigio, the liter-and-a-half size. Why not two? I asked myself. I had a free hand. Besides, pinot was better than hugs.

* * *

At least I told myself it was. But I knew the downside. I turned 45 in August 1997. My body wasn't processing alcohol as handily as it had in my younger days. Even though I had given up hard liquor since the hepatitis in 1988, I was putting away plenty of wine.

I'd wake up at 3:00 in the morning—many times, precisely at 3:00, the hour the devil walks the earth, someone told me—and stay awake for hours with questions dancing through my head. If I was lucky, I'd drift off to sleep around 5:00 or so, only to wake to the 5:30 alarm. I thought I was covering pretty well at work, although one day I did something I had never done—I called in sick because I'd had too much to drink the night before. I'd worked my way to the bottom of one of those 1.5-liter bottles of wine.

"I have a terrible sinus headache," I told Char. We were meeting with new clients that morning. She met them without me.

My denial of the problem was so ironclad that I even called my doctor for an appointment that afternoon.

"I have a terrible sinus headache," I said.

I went to his office, trying my best to make true the lie I had told that morning. I don't remember if he gave me a prescription for anything, but by the time I got home I had almost convinced myself that it was the truth. I had had a terrible sinus headache.

I poured a glass of wine before I even changed clothes.

Ted was traveling frequently in the months following Amy's death. I did my heaviest drinking when he was gone, so I don't think even he knew the depth of the problem. What he knew, however, was that things between us weren't what they'd been before the 20th anniversary party. I wasn't the same. I withdrew. From Ted. Our families. Our friends. Our life.

I stopped seeing Brenda, too, after the third time she suggested that I consider going to a meeting of Alcoholics Anonymous. I didn't want to hear it. Another form of withdrawal. Of denial, too.

Ted would say:

"We should have Jeff over for dinner this week."

or

"Dad wants to come to the cabin next weekend."

or

"Want to have a cookout for your birthday?"

My response? "Sometimes I feel my life is leading me instead of the other way around."

"Well, excuse me if I'd like to have a good time."

"I'm just tired, Ted."

"You know what? I'm tired, too."

Meanwhile, Matt and Sharon's lawsuit against the Memphis hospital where Amy died moved forward. It required exhuming Amy's body from her grave in Nashville. Were they there when Amy's casket was unearthed, or did they stay home? Which would have been worse? And then, when it was opened, who was there to see what was inside?

Waking up at 3:00 in the morning with those questions spinning in my head, I would stay wide awake until the alarm went off at 5:30, head and heart pounding, half hoping the devil would find me.

* * *

In the spring of the year following Amy's funeral, I found a receipt from a local budget motel on the dresser top in our bedroom in the house in Atlanta. The address was north Atlanta. The date was the previous Friday afternoon. Ted had not traveled at all that week. On Friday, I had thought he was at his office in midtown.

I considered hiding the receipt and saying nothing about it, having it framed and presenting it to Ted on Christmas morning. Wouldn't that have been rich?

Instead, I chose instant gratification.

I marched downstairs, anger building. I'd thought we'd left our time of picnics far behind in Nashville when we'd moved to Atlanta. So much for our elaborate "commitment ceremony"—a joke in more ways than one.

In the dining room, Ted was setting the table for our dinner with friends that evening. The event had been Ted's idea. He was preparing most of the food, too. As had become our recent habit, I'd been relegated to making the salad.

"What's this?"

I showed him the receipt. He tried to take it from me, but I jerked it away. I was still considering the satisfying thought of having it framed.

"Mike, I—"

"Did you leave it out on purpose? Were you hoping I'd find it?"

Ted got crystal wine glasses from the china cabinet.

"I have needs, Mike," he said, setting two glasses in their proper place on the table. This infuriated me, too, that he could continue with the evening's preparations as if nothing were wrong.

With the back of my right hand, I sent one of the glasses flying against the wall. It shattered, leaving a gash in the chair rail molding I'd painted so carefully a few years before.

"Feel better now?" Ted asked, his voice icy.

"No." I pulled out a chair and sat down. "Is it someone I know?"

"It's a guy I met at Colony Square. At lunch one day. He started talking to me."

I had wondered about the opportunities Colony Square might present to Ted. At the suburban office of the previous insurance company he worked for, things were pretty insular. Ted only interacted with his colleagues. But Colony Square in midtown was a huge multi-office and hotel complex. Its buildings shared a common food court an elevator ride or short walk away for thousands of people who lived and worked in the area.

"Is it serious?" I asked.

He brushed a piece of dark lint off the cream-colored tablecloth.

"Is it serious?" I asked, louder this time.

"No." The anger left his face. What remained was something softer, a little boy with hurt feelings. "But it's nice to be noticed."

That got me.

"I'm sorry," I said.

"I do love you, Michael. But lately, it hasn't been easy."

"I know."

I set the receipt in the center of the table. He could have it, throw it away if he wanted to. My anger ebbing, I stood, feeling tired, washed out.

"The dogs need their walk. I'll clean up the glass when I get back." And then, wishing it didn't sound quite so much like an afterthought, I said, "I love you, too."

Chapter Twenty: Epiphany

Blue Ridge Mountain view from the cabin

Over the next year, we worked hard at getting our relationship back to a good place. And I worked hard at being strong, at making sure Ted felt noticed and appreciated… by me, not by some young guy at Colony Square.

With the help of Ted's dad and his nephew David, we built a deck on the back of the cabin. The following weekend, Ted and I installed the railing around it all by ourselves, a task we enjoyed, with results we were proud of. We hosted a Halloween party at the house on Embry Circle in Atlanta with our neighbors and friends from Project Open Hand. We visited Ted's aunt Denise in Jacksonville, where a friend's February oyster roast went on until midnight, at which time someone's gay uncle stood and sang *God Bless America* in the style of Kate Smith. "That's the way to end a party," Ted said.

I worked hard at work, too. I won regional awards and got national recognition when a spiral-bound, booklet-style brochure I wrote and helped "concept" for a client was cited for excellence by *Print* magazine, a big deal for a small ad agency.

I knew life had to go on, but Amy's death remained a puzzle to me. And the questions about God did bubble up occasionally… but I pushed them away. If God had turned his back on us the day of our 20th anniversary celebration, I turned my back on him, too. I took pride in telling people I was the one child in my family who wasn't a religious freak.

* * *

In the year 2000, three years after we lost Amy, Ted and I went to Italy with Buddy and Alana. Working on a historical mystery novel set in Tuscany during the Renaissance (with Lorenzo de' Medici as a major character, *The Sign of the Weeping Virgin* was eventually published in 2012), Alana was a great guide for us, especially in Florence, where she took us to the Bargello to see Donatello's David and the animals of Giambologna, the Basilica di Santa Croce to see Giotto's frescoes and other sites off the typical tourist track.

She also found a villa for us to rent on the cheap in a town called Castellina in Chianti, where the open, unscreened windows let in the sweet—and bug-free—nighttime breezes.

My mother had loved Florence when she and my sister Marsha visited there in the 1960s, so when Ted and I came home, I wrote Mom and Dad a long letter detailing the things we saw on our trip.

My parents had invested in a primitive email device, but they didn't use it, and we didn't have a computer at our first cabin in the north Georgia mountains. I didn't have a laptop yet either, so I wrote the letter by hand on notepaper on the deck Ted's dad had helped us build behind the cabin. It was autumn; leaves drifting down from the oak branches were gold against the brilliant blue sky.

It was such a nice day, in fact, that I opened a bottle of white wine and had a glass while I wrote.

Ted had gone to his hometown of Anderson for an event of some sort. If I remember correctly, it was the wedding of a high school friend's daughter. I don't know why I had chosen not to go. Maybe I had simply said I needed the weekend to rest after the trip to Italy. Whatever the reason, the dogs and I had the cabin all to ourselves that weekend. (Lucy and Jessie stayed in Atlanta.)

What should have been—could have been—a beautiful, relaxing weekend turned into something quite different.

I finished the letter, returned the half-empty bottle of wine to the fridge and took the dogs for a walk. We did our usual route—up the steep hill that climbed to the top of the crest in our subdivision, then down the other side of the circle to the small lake at the bottom. Blue waded. Max didn't. I sat on the picnic table on the small sandy beach, took a bottle of water from my pack and the paperback book I was currently reading.

After an hour, we walked up the hill toward home. I swept the leaves off the front porch and back deck, got the grill ready for the steak I was having for dinner, made a note to check about getting a post office box in town rather than having our mail sit in the box at the end of the driveway all week.

I put fresh water in the dogs' water bowl, washed and scored the potato I was baking for dinner, put a simple salad together.

Then I got my book and climbed into the hammock Ted's dad had helped me hang the previous year.

He had even attached a long cord to an adjacent tree.

"What's that for?" I had asked.

"It's your remote," he said.

"Gene, you're a genius."

Now, with the remote in one hand and my book in the other, I swung the hammock from side to side while I read. I passed another hour this way, enjoying the breeze and the mellowing afternoon sun. These were the days without smartphones, when downtime was downtime. We had a TV at the cabin but rarely watched it unless we had rented movies in Atlanta and took them up with us. I even let the remote go and dozed.

When I woke up, it was only 6:00 p.m. I had a nice long evening ahead of me. For the first time in a long time, a cocktail sounded good.

* * *

The tree frogs start chirping in the woods in north Georgia when night falls. On this night, the voices in my head started chirping, too. And I, downing my second Jack Daniel's over ice, had no one to listen to but them.

I lit the grill, opened a bottle of red wine to go with dinner. As often happened when I was alone, a long evening of self-analysis began.

"Everybody wants to be you," a friend had said to me recently while I grilled burgers at our Atlanta house for our group from Project Open Hand. His candor surprised me.

"Come on," I had said.

"It's true."

I understood what he meant. The Open Hand group was made up of mostly single guys; it made sense that some of them might envy us, our longtime partnership, the travel, the nice house, the yard, the good jobs, the dogs, the cats. For many, we were living the dream. I knew some envied me, too. Ted was a catch.

And now, I was spending a picturesque weekend in our picturesque mountain cabin sheltered by golden oaks.

Sure, I knew how things looked. Perfect. I also knew how things felt. The two hadn't matched in a long time.

I was good at covering the gap. The letter I'd spent an hour writing to my parents that afternoon, for example. It was the kind of thing any good son would do to reach out to parents who loved him. There were several flaws, however.

One was how Bob and Beulah had accepted Pat's reason for not attending our 20th anniversary celebration. I'd been hoping they might have challenged her. But then I realized it wasn't their nature. Their relationship with Pat went along just as before. I viewed it as tacit approval of the pain she'd caused me.

Something else bothered me. Since the day Mom told me to go to hell, she had never once sat me down and said, "I'm sorry. I didn't mean to say that." Or, "I was upset. You know I would never intentionally wish you harm."

Did I know that? I remained a son cursed by his mother.

I wondered why the apology had never come. I still longed for it, even after all these years. In its absence, the relationship I'd had with my parents for the past 20 years or so since my coming out had been a bit of a sham, hadn't it? That was the thing I really wanted to tell them, not pleasant stories about our trip to Italy.

I compared the unconditional love and respect Ted got from his family—and the sniping and preaching I got from mine. It wouldn't have been allowed in Ted's family, I thought, would have been immediately silenced by the bulwark of support around him. That hadn't happened with me. My dad might have been a bulwark, but it hadn't stopped my mother and my sisters from taking their shots over the decades. Why? Because they knew they could get away with it. I was entirely too nice. I should have faced them down, should have fired some shots of my own.

Then there was Amy's death. The same old question it raised about how God, if there is one, really felt about Ted and me. I continued to avoid facing that one down, too.

Wine glass in hand, I even went back to what I had done to Maggie, stringing her along all those years. In my darkest hours, I viewed it as a kind of rape. I stole four years of her life for my ego, my safety, my fears about who I was. No wonder she had never forgiven me. She hadn't gone back to Bud Rose, by the way. She had married a successful music business executive in Nashville; I had reached out to her a time or two in the years after our breakup but met with a lukewarm response. And why should it have been otherwise? Why would she want to be friends *with me*? And yet Lynn, Ted's former fiancée, had forgiven him. They spoke occasionally, like best buddies with lots of catching up to do. Why? What unassailable goodness did Ted possess that I didn't? What was it about me that made even my own family come after me time after time after time?

"Have you always felt guilty about being gay?" my therapist, Brenda, had asked.

Maybe that was at the heart of it all. The source of all my demons.

Maybe I kept coming back to one answer.

"It's wrong," Terry had said that day in my turquoise bedroom. "It's wrong."

Surely, I'd made some progress since 1964, hadn't I? Or maybe I had never dealt with it at all.

I pushed the questions out of my head, poured more wine into my glass. It was time to put the steak on the grill.

* * *

At 10:00 p.m., the tree frog chorus had reached its peak. So had the voices in my head.

I finished the wine in my glass.

Some part of my brain knew not to get in the truck. Another part told it to shut up and go for it. I'd been at the cabin practically all day. It would be good to get out, just for a little while.

* * *

I went 12 miles north, to a bar and restaurant near Lake Burton. Our Atlanta neighbors had taken us there a few times. The place was busy, the bar crowded. I found a seat and ordered a glass of wine. *It's Saturday night*, I told myself. *You needed to get out. That's all this is.*

A sexy guy with tortoise-shell glasses and thick, wavy hair was holding court at one end of the bar. He didn't sound like a local. He was probably a successful guy from Atlanta, an attorney or some such who owned one of the houses on the lake, maybe one of those trendy ones with a Bose speaker system in the boathouse. He caught me looking at him, didn't smile, went back to talking to the group around him.

I sipped my wine, then our eyes met again. He cocked his head to one side, drew it back slightly, an "I'm losing patience here" look on his face. The woman next to him noticed and shot me an unfriendly glance, too.

I raised both hands, as if to say, "What's the problem here?" She puffed out a laugh and turned her back to me.

Jesus, I hadn't been that obvious, had I?

I checked my watch. 11:05. I finished my wine and ordered another.

I went to the men's room. When I returned to the bar, my second wine was waiting for me at the spot I had occupied earlier.

"Thanks," I said to the bartender.

"No problem, man," he said.

I ended up feeling more isolated than if I'd stayed at home. I wasn't sure what I'd come looking for—someone to talk to. Someone to take home with me. Really?

I wiped condensation off the glass. Was I losing my mind? I wasn't about to take someone home to our little cabin in the woods. To do what? Meet the dogs? Check out the remote on the hammock? It was time to settle up and go home to my perfect life.

I finished my wine and asked for my tab. The bartender took his time ringing it up. It was nearly 11:30 p.m. when he handed me the check. I paid, left a tip and gave a quick, parting smile to the couple at the end of the bar.

The gravel parking lot swayed beneath my feet as I walked to the truck.

I stood at the driver's side door to get my balance, hoping the stars would stop turning above me. My mouth watered; I swallowed over the nausea that crept through me, took a few deep breaths. I hadn't had that much to drink, had I? Then I thought back to the bottle of wine I had opened in the afternoon while I wrote the letter to my parents. The day's count was not insignificant, and included hard liquor, something I wasn't accustomed to drinking. Still.

It sounds crazy to suggest that someone slipped something in my wine at the bar. I don't know what the motive would have been. Maybe the sexy guy who didn't like my cruising him did something to retaliate. Or the woman next to him. Maybe the bartender thought I was one of those gay guys who needed to be taught a lesson. Maybe he was a mountain homophobe who had developed a quick remedy when a homosexual started queering up his bar. But I was guilty of two innocent glances. Why would that be enough to tamper with someone's drink? And what would they use? Was there some sort of at-the-ready date rape drug to slip to objectionable customers? It was ridiculous even to consider it.

Nonetheless, whatever had happened, or not happened, something wasn't right. On the road, I'd never struggled so hard to keep the truck inside the lines. It was scary how drunk I was. Yet I tried to maintain a steady speed, thinking if I went too far below the speed limit, I'd be even more conspicuous.

I missed my turnoff and considered stopping and turning around, decided it would be better to keep going. Problem was, I was on the road that fed right into Clarkesville, where police were more likely to be.

Luckily, I made it to the town square without being stopped. I found a parking space, turned off the engine. Maybe if I sat there a while and sobered up, I'd be in better shape to drive the rest of the way home. My eyes felt heavy. I relaxed against the seat, struggling to bring into focus the blurred row of storefronts that faced me.

* * *

The square was hushed when I came to. I wiped my eyes, held my wristwatch to the light from the streetlamp overhead. It was nearly 1:00

a.m. There was a sour taste in my mouth. And an odd, cool feeling down below.

My pants were soaking wet… and something else. I felt between my legs. I had shit in my pants. Not a lot, but enough to raise a certain stink.

I'd blacked out at home after drinking but had never experienced anything like this. Had there been something more than alcohol in my wine at the bar? Or was my body telling me, "Enough. It's time to stop." I'll never know for sure.

I knew I had to get out of there before the Clarkesville cops came by on their nightly rounds.

I started the engine, backed out of the parking space. Thud. Thud. Thud.

I got out and walked around the truck. Sure enough, one of the rear tires was flat.

I pulled forward into the space and turned off the engine. Shit. I'd left the dogs outside on the deck when I left the cabin. I needed to get home to them. When the weather was good, they usually slept all night on the deck, but without me there? Max could get antsy. She might decide to go looking for me, go down to the lake where we'd walked that afternoon. Blue would undoubtedly follow. I didn't like the idea of their wandering along the road in our subdivision at night. People came home late, some of them probably in worse shape than I was. I had to get home. I wasn't sure I could change the tire myself, wasn't sure I could drive again tonight even with a good tire.

I knew of a convenience store with a payphone on Highway 115, the road out of town. It was just past the bridge over the Soque River. I got out of the truck again, locked it, checked that my wallet was in my back pocket and started walking. I was wearing one of the TravelSmith outfits I'd bought for Italy. A white T-shirt, a light gray fleece V-neck pullover and green pants made from a special quick-dry fabric that was supposed to wick moisture away from the body. I hoped that, by the time I reached the convenience store, the wet spot on my pants wouldn't be quite as apparent. The smell, however… maybe I could at least dump my underwear in the restroom.

"Are there any taxis around here?" I asked the clerk when I got to the store. In 2000, uber was just the German word for over, not a way home.

"Not that I know of. Not this late." She was plump, her unwashed brown hair pulled into a limp ponytail.

"Is there anyone who could give me a lift to Skyview? It's only about five miles from here." It was more like seven, but five didn't sound quite so extreme.

"No, sir. I'm here by myself tonight."

Today, now that I know Clarkesville better, I think a better decision would have been to hang out at the store and see if I could bum a ride home with the next customer. I had plenty of cash with me. It could be done. Still, I couldn't read the clerk's attitude. She might think I was loitering, call the cops on me. At any rate, I figured the best way home would be on my own two feet. I considered buying some water, using the restroom to clean myself up a bit, but I thought of the dogs again and knew I shouldn't delay any longer the long trek home.

I crossed the highway and continued up the hill toward the elementary school.

At 20 minutes per mile, it would take me two hours or more to get home. It would be after 3:00 a.m. when I got there. I picked up my pace, hoping a car would come along that I could hitch a ride in, hoping it wouldn't so I could avoid that risky decision—do I get in or not?

A car came over the hill up ahead, headlights bright and the shadow of some sort of rack across the top. It slowed as it approached me, made a U-turn and stopped next to me. The car was black with POLICE emblazoned in big white letters across the side. My heart sank.

"Whatcha doing out here, bud?" the driver asked through the open window. There was the trace of a grin on his face, as if he thought this was all a joke. But there was something arch in his tone, too. I'd heard it when I covered the police beat in Montgomery. It said, "I have all the power here."

"Walking home," I said. "My truck has a flat… on the square." I pointed toward town. "Could you possibly give me a ride to Skyview?"

He laughed. "What do you think this is, a taxi service? Get in the car."

"But—"

"I said get in."

* * *

"ID, please."

I pulled my wallet from my back pocket, unstuck my license from the plastic sleeve that held it and handed it to him through the open glass partition between the front and back seat.

"You visiting up here?" The address on my license was Atlanta.

"I bought a house in Skyview last year." I thought it best to leave Ted out of this discussion. "A weekend place."

"Been drinking?"

"I had some wine earlier."

"Hmm." I guessed he was mid-50s, not much older than I. He had pulled the car under a streetlight on the roadside. The back of his neck was wrinkled like worn leather above the collar of his uniform, his sideburns bushy and gray. "You sure don't smell very sweet."

"I got sick earlier. It was weird."

He radioed in my name, license number and birthdate. Then he handed a plastic contraption to me through the open glass.

"Breathe into this."

"A breathalyzer? I was walking—"

"Don't argue. Breathe."

I blew into the plastic tube on the machine. One breath, I thought, and your life literally goes down the tubes. But what could he charge me with? Walking under the influence? Then I remembered the people who were fined or given jail time for public drunkenness or drunk and disorderly conduct when I covered city court as part of my police beat responsibilities in Montgomery. The cases hardly ever warranted a story in the paper, but those charged were usually the most lost and pitiful-looking people in the courtroom. As lost and pitiful as I felt right now.

I handed the thing back to him.

He wrote on a clipboard in his lap. "So, tell me what you're doing out here at 1:30 in the morning."

"I was on my way home from Lake Burton. I felt sick when I got into Clarkesville, so I parked on the square to see if it would pass. Then my tire went flat."

"Why didn't you change it?"

"I wasn't feeling that great. And I had had some wine earlier, like I said. I didn't think it would be a good idea to drive even if I did fix the tire, so I started walking."

"It's a long way to Skyview."

"I know..."

"What's the make and model of your truck?"

"2000 Nissan pickup. Red. A King Cab." We'd opted for the larger size when we traded in the old truck earlier in the year.

On the radio, he asked the dispatcher to send someone to the square to check out the truck.

Then I waited. There were no more questions from the officer, only the squawk of the radio and the dispatcher responding to other calls. At last, a pair of headlights came toward us. Another police car. It made a U-turn on the highway and pulled behind us. An officer got out, walked toward us, this one younger, blond, fresh-faced.

"The truck's there with a flat tire," he said through the driver's side window. "No other visible damage." I supposed the suspicion was that I had been involved in an accident of some sort, or a hit and run.

"Are you going to tow it?" I asked.

The cop in the driver's seat gave a laugh. "This ain't Atlanta, bud. No, we'll leave it there for you to deal with tomorrow." He handed me my license through the open partition. "Now, this nice officer's going to take you home. But let me give you a warning. If you're ever out walking again at 1:30 in the morning with alcohol on your breath and shit in your pants, I will take you in."

* * *

The officer pulled into the driveway. "You take care, now."

"I appreciate the ride," I said. "Thank you."

I got out of the cruiser and closed the door behind me. Max and Blue tramped down the steps from the deck. They stood watching me, worry on their little faces. Thank goodness they hadn't gone looking for me, or maybe they had. At least they were safe now.

"I'm sorry, girls." I patted their heads, my heart full of shame.

It was nearly 3:00 o'clock in the morning.

* * *

Fuck!

I woke up at 7:00 a.m. in a panic, the sad facts of the night fully registering with the hangover that greeted me. I had blacked out in the truck. Lost control of my bodily functions. Been picked up by the police. Left the dogs alone until the wee hours. *Holy shit,* I thought. *What a fucking insane thing to do.*

And the truck! Was it safe on the Clarkesville square? How would I get to it?

I sat up, head throbbing, body feeling as if there were syrup in my veins.

And my driver's license?

I dragged myself out of bed, checked the wallet on the dresser top. Thank goodness. I remembered now. The officer had handed it back to me before I transferred to the other cruiser for the ride home.

"Come on, pups."

Max was still curled on the foot of the bed, Blue on her dog bed on the floor by the dresser. They followed me into the kitchen, out the back door to the deck. I filled their bowls with fresh food, rinsed out the water bowl they shared and filled it, too.

The phone rang on the liquor cabinet in the kitchen. I came inside, dried my hands on a dishtowel and picked up the receiver.

"Hello?"

"Hey, how are you?" It was Ted. "Did you have a good night?"

If you only knew, I thought. "Uneventful. Grilled a steak. Got to bed early. You?"

"Last night was okay. Rob (a friend of Ted's from high school) and I went out for a drink afterward since we hadn't seen each other in a couple years. He said to tell you hello."

"That's nice."

"Dogs all right?"

"They're fine. We just got up."

"You slept in." I was usually up by 6:00 a.m. on weekends. "You're sure everything's okay?"

There must have been something in my voice that unsettled him. I tried to sound cheerful. "Great. Having a lazy mountain weekend."

"I love you. I can't wait to see you tomorrow."

"I love you, too. How's your dad?"

"Good. We're grilling steaks tonight, too. It'll be nice to have the day with him."

After we hung up, I made coffee, then sat at the kitchen table and put my head in my hands.

* * *

I found a taxi service in Clayton, a town slightly larger than Clarkesville, about 25 miles north. Because it was Sunday, they couldn't send anyone to pick me up until noon. So, I waited. I made the bed carefully, smoothing out all the wrinkles and making sure the edges of the comforter with the blue and green geometric pine tree pattern hung just so. I made a piece of dry toast to go with the coffee. I would have walked the dogs to the lake but didn't want to leave the phone in case the taxi service called with an update. These were still landline days, and we had no answering machine at the cabin.

The driver arrived when he said he would. When we got to the square, I was relieved to see the truck where I'd left it.

"What are you going to do about that flat?" the driver asked.

"The spare is one of those miniature things. There's a scissor jack, so it's pretty easy to change. But sometimes the lug nuts are hard to get started." He seemed amiable enough. "Could you give me a hand?"

"I was going to offer to change it for a little extra."

"Deal." I could have hugged him. I gave him a 20 for his efforts.

I drove 30 minutes south to the mall in Gainesville, where the Sears store's recorded message had told me they were open on Sundays. While they put a new tire on, I went to the cafeteria in the mall and assembled the most nutritious meal I could think of—liver and onions, white rice, a green salad without dressing, a glass of low-fat milk, a glass of unsweetened iced tea, a Jell-O salad for dessert. Jell-O was good for you, wasn't it? Soothing to the insides. Mine felt as if they'd been scraped with a wire brush.

By the time I got back to the cabin, new tire on the truck, jack and tire iron neatly returned to their respective storage spaces behind the seats, I was beginning to feel the heaviness leave my bloodstream. My heart was beating more calmly, like any other Sunday afternoon.

In fact, all the neat appearances were back in place. Body intact. Record clean. Truck undamaged. Dogs safe. The only evidence was the plastic bag of dirty laundry I'd put together after the policeman brought me home last night. Once back in Atlanta, I'd throw the soiled clothes in the washing machine and take care of that evidence, too. I'd mail the letter to my parents. I'd get the dogs settled in the house, feed Lucy and Jessie and be at my glass-topped desk at the agency by 9:00 sharp on Monday morning, as if nothing had happened.

Once again, the ice on that frozen pond in Columbia had held beneath my feet. But this time, I didn't deserve it.

* * *

I made a peanut butter sandwich and poured a glass of milk for dinner. No wine tonight. No Jack Daniel's. I took the meal to the deck, sat at our green metal table.

I had always liked how the silhouette of the mountains to the north turned an unusual shade of blue some evenings as the sun set. This was one of those evenings, the mountains a deep turquoise as the sky glowed orange behind them. Colors that belonged more at the beach than north Georgia.

I picked up half the sandwich and started to take a bite, then put it back on the plate.

The mountains.

In the evening calm, I felt their steady presence, listened to their silence. They had witnessed what I'd done this weekend—dangerous behavior, childish behavior, dishonest behavior—seen it, shit and all. Yet they didn't turn away. Unlike some people in my life, they didn't flinch at the sight of the real me. There they stood, silent and still.

How did the saying go? "I lift my eyes to the hills." For a moment, I couldn't recall where it came from. Rodgers and Hammerstein? Shakespeare? No, the Bible. It was a Bible verse that had come to mind.

"I lift up mine eyes unto the hills, from whence cometh my…?" What was the rest of it?

"From whence cometh my… strength?"

Something moved me to get off the chair and down on my knees, my eyes on the view of the mountains through the deck railing, taking in their calm. Their majesty. That was it. Their majesty.

Blue ambled up next to me, licked my ear.

"Hi, girl," I said softly.

I put my arm around her. She sat and looked in the same direction with me. She seemed captivated, too.

I said aloud, "I lift up mine eyes unto the hills, from whence cometh my…"

But "strength" wasn't right, was it? It was "help."

I said the full sentence, this time correctly, the way I remembered it from my church-going days in high school. "I will lift up mine eyes to the hills, from whence cometh my help."

I don't know whether I called it God that evening. But there was something in those mountains beyond the trees, something expectant, waiting for me to say more. I thought of the long night that had begun 24 hours earlier, how privileged I'd been that the police had let me go free and brought me home, how things could have easily turned out differently, with me in jail, or injured, or dead. Maybe others dead, too. That's how it would end next time if I didn't... if I didn't...

"Help me," I said to the mountains. "Help me, please."

I rested my forehead on Blue's head. I stroked one silky ear. I closed my eyes and, for the first time since long before Amy died, I wept.

Chapter Twenty-One: Yes

Back on track: Ted and I in Victoria, BC, June 18th, 2003

In Alcoholics Anonymous, I learned to be comfortable with the concept of God.

There were gay AA groups in Atlanta. I attended some of their meetings. But I learned that people of all sexual orientations were welcome at any other AA meetings, too.

"I could say, 'I got blitzed and had sex with 12 guys last night before I lost count,' and no one would bat an eye," I told my therapist, Brenda, one afternoon after I'd started seeing her again. It was true. There isn't much of anything someone who has been in AA hasn't heard.

So, I went to the meetings at a long-established club only a few miles from Embry Circle. I got a sponsor. In the year that followed my night with the police, I went through the Twelve Steps. It was one of the best experiences of my life. It got me through 9/11 sober. But that was only one of the benefits.

This new God—well, new to me—was different. In church growing up, I had been taught about a God that wanted to be studied, that wanted to be obeyed, that wanted to be worshiped. Maybe I wasn't listening, but I never got the message that God just wants to have a relationship with us, no matter who we are. Maybe that's why I hadn't felt much of anything when I left the church in my college years, a break that lasted for decades. The old God I had known was a source of constant anxiety. The new one was an ocean of peace. I dove in.

And with my spiritual boundaries newly widened, I began to consider a new image of the God I had grown up with. Not a heavenly father. Maybe not any sort of being at all. Maybe something we make together here on earth when we love and support one another, when we abide by a certain set of humanistic principles, when we do unto others what we would have them do unto us. Maybe God is as simple as that.

In one early-morning AA meeting on a rainy Wednesday, a long-haired fellow in a shabby motorcycle jacket told about his young daughter's death in a fire while he slept off a weekend drunk in another part of the house. He didn't make it through the end of the story. As he wept, everyone got to their feet. Those nearest him put their hands on his shoulders. The rest of us laid our hands on the person next to us. We were one connected body, 30 or 40 of us, a circuit channeling something electric, something bigger than all of us. Rain drummed louder on the roof, as if affirming our prayers.

"God forgives you," people whispered. "God loves you."

I knew God, whatever God was, loved all of us in that room that morning.

The next order of business was to learn to love me.

* * *

Working through the steps to recovery taught me to look at myself and make positive changes.

It showed me how the connection I had made between our commitment ceremony and Amy's death was grandiosity—a classic characteristic of alcoholic behavior.

It showed me that God's love isn't part of a bargain we enter into, a quid pro quo, a "do this and you'll get that." No, God's love is always there. All we have to do is ask for it.

It showed me how easy it is to be brought down by circumstances if you are already inclined to look down on yourself, as many gay people do.

It showed me how strong gay people must be in this world.

It showed me how having a relationship with God can help. It might not be everyone's cup of tea, but it worked for me.

On another level, I knew my newfound relationship with God was a kind of payback to my sisters. At a time when I needed them most, they had said there wasn't room under God's shelter of grace for Ted and me, or anyone like us.

I had news for them. There is.

* * *

My newfound stability gave us confidence. And confidence is good for the real estate market.

At one point in the early 2000s, Ted and I owned three houses while the paperwork was shuffled. When the dust settled, we had sold the house on Embry Circle and bought another nearby with a smaller yard. Because we were spending more time in the mountains, we wanted to deal with less yard maintenance at our place in the city. With Max and Blue, it just wasn't practical to consider a condo in a high-rise somewhere—though we would have liked that—so we compromised.

We also sold the small cabin and bought a larger one in the same mountain neighborhood, Skyview. The new place had even more privacy but was less primitive. It had central heat and air, a dishwasher, a screened porch, while maintaining that mountain feel. There was also a wood-burning fireplace.

I had only one criterion: The new mountain house had to have a view of the same row of Blue Ridge Mountains to the north that we had at the other cabin.

The window over the sink in the kitchen in the new mountain house had the view, so I could enjoy it when I did the dishes or poured our morning coffee. For me, the mountains were a reminder of God's grace. Ancient. Constant. Inspiring peace. And peace was what I wanted more than anything in the days after my run-in with the police.

In the house with the smaller yard in Atlanta, in the bigger cabin in Clarkesville, Ted and I became the couple people know today. There were external challenges to come—namely, deaths in our families—but internally, I was stronger than ever. Calmer. Happier. More confident than I had ever been. Those self-improvements made our relationship better, too.

Even though I left AA after a year, the experience gave me a stronger foundation for living. I learned to keep my drinking within moderate limits—no more 1.5-liter bottles of wine in an evening. I know some couples are fine with one member being a drinker and the other a teetotaler, but I didn't want that for us.

I wanted us to be the couple in the letters from 1977. An older but wiser version, granted, but with the same fire, the same spirit of discovery, the same love of the newness of it all we had in those days—the days before I let my own insecurities, and my family's curses, come between us.

* * *

In 2005, after Char closed the ad agency in Atlanta, I went out on my own. I started my own business as a marketing contract writer for technology companies. After more than 12 years with Char, I had developed a wide network of colleagues, people who had moved up the ranks to lead their own marketing departments in successful companies or founded their own marketing agencies with a focus on the technology industry.

Two of those contacts helped my young company get established. One of my first gigs was managing a team of writers to develop the copy for a new website for a major business software vendor (and competitor of SAP) based in Atlanta. The other was a plum that didn't pay as well but added new elan to my portfolio. A friend's marketing agency had scored as a client the construction firm that was building the new aquarium in downtown Atlanta. The firm wanted to produce a book commemorating the challenge of building the structure and the enormous saltwater tanks it housed. I was chosen to write it.

"We're looking for an almost *New Yorker*-style piece," said my friend. "Readable but with real substance."

He had me at the *New Yorker*.

My friend scheduled a tour with the lead of the construction company's building project management team. I hadn't counted on the noise in the 440,000-square-foot structure as we walked through it, but there was no time to stop the interview; the building was on the fast track to go from design to finish in three years—half the time a project of that size would normally take. Its benefactors, Bernie Marcus, co-founder of The Home Depot, and his wife, Billi, wanted the aquarium completed by Thanksgiving 2005.

I wasn't sure I was getting half the detail I needed on the microcassette recorder I carried with me, nor did I count on the end of the tape breaking away from the reel once I got home to my desk and rewound it.

"Jesus Christ!" I said. Fear snaked through my stomach. *It's over*, I thought. *I'm done for.* There was no way I could call my friend and say we had to do the tour over again.

Hands trembling, I gingerly put a piece of Scotch tape on the reel, fed the end of the microcassette tape to it with my fingers, then used a pencil to turn the reel carefully until the tape caught. Success! Another ice-holding-beneath-my-feet moment, only this time it wasn't my life on the line, but the life of my fledgling business.

The tape was good enough to help me capture most of the details to tell the main story. From the quiet of my desk, I conducted follow-up phone interviews with other construction team members to fill in the gaps. Those interviews were also the basis for 10 short sidebar stories, one on each double-page spread, including one about the delicate setting-in-place of six 24-inch-thick acrylic panels to support the 20 tons of water in the living quarters for Ralph, the aquarium's whale shark. After setting, the six panels were bonded together at 179-degree-Fahrenheit temperatures to create a seamless, 238,000-pound whole.

Full of photos that accompanied my narrative, the thick coffee-table book was a success for the client. A success for me, too. I had never written about building construction—let alone aquarium construction—and had little knowledge of it when I took the assignment, yet I had produced a major piece on the topic in just a few weeks. I was proud of that.

Tape recorder emergency and all, my young business was off to a promising start.

* * *

That same year, my mother was diagnosed with bone cancer. I was making frequent trips to Nashville, helping get her and my dad situated in an assisted living facility, while Ted was back and forth to Anderson, South Carolina, on similar duties with his father.

Gene was not doing well, struggling with congestive heart failure, still living at home but tethered to an oxygen generator. The long breathing tube gave him mobility across most of the length and width of his small house in Anderson, but it just didn't seem right to see him so restricted. He had never been one to be tied down.

When he went to college on the GI Bill after WWII, Gene got a job as a spear carrier in the Chicago opera. He was pursuing a degree in physical education; the opera frequently recruited well-built young men from his program to play soldiers or palace guards in its productions.

It sounded like perfect casting to me. In his 50s when I met him, Gene was a short, stocky linebacker of a man. The family breadwinner, he fit the manly hunter prototype, too.

In the early days of my relationship with Ted, while Gene was still working for General Electric in Greenville, South Carolina, he'd come home at 6:00 p.m., set his briefcase by the kitchen door and sit down to the dinner Ted's mom had prepared. The first time I witnessed it, I was surprised by how "Ward and June Cleaver" it was. And so unlike Bob and Beulah, who usually had a leisurely cocktail before Mom put dinner on the table.

Gene was a man who carried a fully stocked toolbox in any vehicle he drove. He brought his own power saw and took command of the building of the deck outside our first cabin. He could shuck oysters, plant a backyard garden that produced vegetables in profusion every summer, build a kite and fly it on the beach. He could stop a fussy great-grandchild cold by smacking his hand with his fist, twisting his face into a grimace and growling, "I'll give you a knuckle sandwich!"

I loved my father. But I loved Gene because he was so unlike my father. My even-tempered dad never threatened to give anyone a knuckle sandwich.

Gene died in February 2006 at age 80. We'd had a big birthday party for him the previous November, when all the family came to our house in the mountains. Though he quit smoking in 1971, the year he'd had heart bypass surgery (one of the first procedures of its kind in Atlanta), his death certificate listed smoking as the cause of death. I guess we never outrun our mistakes in life, but Gene gave his a run for their money.

After Ted's mom died and Gene and a neighbor lady started living together (they never married, though they told everyone they had), the dinner schedule loosened a bit. We saw a new side of Gene. He started drinking single malt scotch. To Ted's dismay, he'd drop hints about his and his new friend's healthy—nay, lively, to hear him tell it—sex life.

He even took cooking classes at the local technical college. "That's not like my dad at all," Ted would say, pleased that his father was branching out. On one visit, Gene proudly demonstrated how to turn a radish into a rose with a few scores of the knife. He developed a signature dish: mushroom caps stuffed with breadcrumbs, butter, onion and parsley. (They were fabulous. To this day, Ted tries to replicate them but never gets the combination exactly right.) He talked at length about the importance of a good mirepoix.

He redid the kitchen in the house in Anderson to accommodate his new skills as a chef, replacing the old harvest gold color scheme with a bright red and white one. The new design included an ingenious triangular island that worked perfectly in the small space. He used the new stovetop and the grill it housed nearly every night, and proudly showed off the extra storage space the island afforded, along with his extensive new collection of pots and pans hanging from the ceiling rack overhead.

He also got serious about wine—an expertise that Ted and I appreciated far more than radish roses. Kendall-Jackson's oaky chardonnay was his favorite. At cocktail time, he'd pour a big glass and bring it to me wherever I happened to be, at the kitchen table over Christmas or on the screened porch of the house the family rented on South Carolina's Edisto Island over Memorial Day weekend. "Here ya go, Mister Mike!" he'd say in his booming voice.

Gene always accepted me, though our nephew Chris reminds me today that there were times he wasn't exactly happy to have me on the scene; he just never let me see it. "He listened to Rush Limbaugh, for Christ's sake," Chris says about Gene, as if that is all you need to know to understand the challenge Ted faced as a gay son, to appreciate the leap Gene took to make room in his heart for me. Chris' words make me love even more the softer side of Gene that emerged in his later, Kendall-Jackson years.

There was one tense evening, in the early 1980s, I believe, when we all stayed with Ted's brother and sister-in-law in their house outside Charleston before their son, Beau, was born. We were there for the Spoleto music festival. After a long, hot day in downtown Charleston, Gene was not pleased that Ted and I were quietly availing ourselves of the downstairs bath's grand walk-in shower. (I don't remember how he knew we were in the shower together. It wasn't as if Ted and I were moaning in ecstasy in there.) He had no problem with Ted and me sharing a bedroom, but the idea of our showering together got under his skin.

He only showed displeasure with me one other time. In 1991, during the family's vacation on Edisto Island the week before Memorial Day, Ted's Aunt Denise and I were kidding around, trying to do a synchronized swimming routine in water that was far too rough for careless swimming. In our silliness, we got too close to one of the groins, the boulder structures that reach like long fingers into the surf, designed to prevent erosion. A surging wave lifted us, sent Denise up one side of the groin and me up the other. I no sooner caught my breath than another wave took me in its foamy grip, flipped me over and slammed me on my back on one of the barnacle-encrusted rocks. I remember thinking, "This is the end."

Fortunately, "the end" didn't come. Denise and I managed to pull ourselves off the rocks and sit, bloody messes, on the sand. Ted went to get the car to take us to the only doctor on the island. Gene drove us to the clinic. I could see the disapproval in his eyes, knew it lurked beneath his silence. I was the stronger swimmer. I should have been watchful and kept Denise and myself out of danger. I don't think anyone in the family had ever gone to the doctor during our many vacations on Edisto; we were blots on the family record.

Denise and I had cuts on our backs, arms, legs, hands and—the worst part—on the bottoms of our feet. Unfortunately, the doctor told us that barnacle wounds couldn't be stitched. She gave us tetanus shots and sent us home. We showered, put clean clothes and socks on and settled on the sofa in the living room, totally miserable. Ted brought us Tylenol and stiff cocktails. (Gene didn't offer to pour any Kendall-Jackson for me that night. He also made little *phtt* sounds at the bloody footprints we left on the linoleum all evening.)

I managed to bake a fresh peach pie the next day, bloody feet and all.

"How are you doing today, Mr. Mike?" Gene asked, putting a fresh bag of ice in the freezer and eyeing the pie. "Ooh, that looks good."

"Better," I lied. The muscle soreness had really settled in overnight.

"It could have been worse. We were lucky."

I took the "we" to mean I had returned to his good graces. He did pour me a glass of wine that evening. He couldn't resist, however, calling Denise and me the Dynamic Duo every chance he got through the rest of the week.

We learned our lesson. In all our subsequent years on Edisto, we've kept a generous distance from the groins, even when the Atlantic's surface has been glass-tabletop smooth.

My favorite memory of Gene: On one of the many weekends he came to visit Ted and me in the north Georgia mountains (we were only an hour or so west of Anderson), Gene helped me install a new faucet in the upstairs bathroom. I think the year was 2002 or 2003. The drain stopper installation involved my getting on my back on the floor and scooting backward so my head and torso were inside the vanity. Standing, Gene straddled me so he could access the sink above my head.

"I haven't been in this position with a man in a long time," I joked.

"You haven't?" he replied, as if to say, "Why the hell not? What's the matter with you?"

For a moment, I wondered if there might have been a fellow spear carrier who had offered his services to Gene long ago in Chicago. I'd seen pictures of Gene when he was younger; he was a sexy man. But the image dissolved as he and I successfully completed the faucet installation and went downstairs for a well-deserved glass of Kendall-Jackson.

I guess we never know the full story of our parents. I guess it's best that way.

Gene was a parent to me. There wasn't any other term for him at the time. Ted and I weren't married yet, so he wasn't my father-in-law. But even if we had been, he was more than an in-law. More than a friend. He was a father to me, too.

After his death, we scattered his ashes on the beach on Edisto, where Jean's ashes had been scattered, too. We knew she was there. Ted's brother, a career police officer, one of the sanest, most level-headed persons I have ever known, said he had seen a shadowy figure in a trench coat walking in the rain one evening when he and his wife had visited the beach some years after Jean's death. From a distance, the figure turned and looked at him, then continued down the beach.

"It was Mom," he said.

No one dared doubt him. Jean loved that beach.

The day after we scattered Ted's father's ashes, Ted took me to Charleston, where I caught a flight to Nashville to visit my parents. Mom was not doing well. Her femur had broken during her chemotherapy. She'd had surgery to repair it and was slowly convalescing in a rehab center.

It wasn't until I got back to the mountains that I got to mourn Gene properly. Ted was working in Atlanta. I loaded a beach chair, a blanket and a bottle of Kendall-Jackson in the truck late one afternoon and drove to the other side of the neighborhood, to the first cabin we had owned in Skyview. We knew the guys who had bought the place; both young professionals, they stayed in Atlanta during the week. I didn't think they'd mind my being there for a little while.

I pulled the truck into their driveway, set up my chair on the deck Gene had helped us build, poured a little wine in a Solo cup, wrapped the blanket around me to ward off the February chill. Someone in the neighborhood had a fire going. The homey scent of woodsmoke laced the air. I sat facing my favorite view, the row of mountains to the north. They were purple in the winter light.

I raised my cup to them. I had learned, after all, that they were good listeners.

"Thank you, Gene," I said to the mountains, for he was there, wasn't he, a part of their eternalness? "Thanks for everything."

Chapter Twenty-Two: A Whole New World

Ted and Mom, Embry Circle, mid-1990s

My mom died two months after Gene. Her funeral was April 14th, 2006. Good Friday.

The eulogy by the minister of Old Hickory Presbyterian outside Nashville, where my parents had gone to church since Dad's retirement in 1976, was beautiful. I was even more impressed when I asked for a copy after the service.

"I don't have it on paper," the minister said.

"You did it off the top of your head?" I asked.

He shrugged. "I always do."

What I liked most was the way he captured my mother so accurately, so specifically. Her paintings, especially the Monet-ish sunflowers that hung in the Smithsonian a few years earlier in an international art exhibit.

Her pride in her Canadian roots. He told how she had come by her name, how my grandfather and grandmother were at a loss to name the baby that was due in late November 1915, how, after attending a church service where one of the hymns was "Beulah Land," my grandfather announced, "If it's a girl, we'll name her Beulah," and that was that.

The pastor mentioned my mom's delight at being the center of attention. "Who else would have their funeral on Good Friday?" he quipped from the pulpit.

He also said my mom was sneaky. I don't remember the example he gave, but I could have added several.

Some evenings when I was growing up, when my sisters and I would be watching an episode of *Twilight Zone* or *Alfred Hitchcock Presents*, we'd look up from the TV to see Mom peering around the doorway at us, wearing Dad's brown fedora and a pair of sunglasses. It would scare the hell out of us; then we'd laugh and laugh. The three of us loved a good scare. One Valentine's Day, Mom made a card for my father and taped it under the toilet seat lid, so it greeted him first thing in the morning. I still have the photo she proudly took of the card in its hiding place.

Ted once described my mother as "huge." By that he didn't mean her physical size—she was quite small—or that she had a loud voice or laugh. She was just a big personality. The cliché fit: She lit up a room. True, her Yankee accent often did stand out among the southern drawls around her, but it was more than that.

In the eulogy, the pastor told the story of Hurricane Beulah, a major storm that moved from the western coast of Africa in early September 1967, gained level four status by the time it reached Puerto Rico and made landfall September 20th near Brownsville, Texas. I was in high school that year.

"Some of us here today might remember that storm," the pastor said. "Beulah Coleman certainly did. In fact, she often enjoyed referring to herself as Hurricane Beulah. But she wasn't a destructive force. To the contrary, she was a powerful force for good in the life of this church."

I had held up pretty well in the days since Mom's death, but the Hurricane Beulah story was my undoing. I wept until my shoulders shook in the pew that morning, so much so that several people seated around me gently laid their hands on me.

I wept because I'd forgotten the story about Hurricane Beulah. It was such a surprise when the pastor mentioned it; memories came flooding back as I sat between Ted and his Aunt Denise in the pew that morning. It summoned my mom's voice so vividly: "Here's Hurricane Beulah!" she'd say with a twinkle in her eye. I had forgotten what a kick she got out of sharing her name with a hurricane.

I wept for another reason, too. Hurricane Beulah was a memory from the good days with my mother, while I was still her golden boy. The days before I came out, before that evening when she told me to go to hell. Things were never quite the same between my mother and me after that.

Sure, it had been years since I had accepted the fact that an apology was not forthcoming, that I was, with or without it, a person loved by God, a person loved by my parents. Still, I wept because some hurts never go away.

Some might wonder why I never asked Mom for an apology—maybe she had forgotten what she said that day? But what good is an apology if you have to ask for it? So, I let it go. I know deep down that the weekend-long 50th anniversary party we hosted for my parents in 1988 was an elaborately roundabout way of seeking that apology. It didn't work, though I hoped it might. Today, I regret never having talked with her about it directly, about how it hurt to know the curse remained in place through the years. Today, I think I would have been perfectly within my rights to ask her. I should have, but I didn't.

Maybe every parent and child go through a similar awakening, the moment they discover the beloved is not the ideal they thought. The break must come eventually, so the psychologists tell us. It is more jarring for some of us.

That's not to say that things weren't good between us in Mom's final years.

She really did love Ted. And in her own way, I know she loved me, too. The detailed flowered border she painted on one of the invitations to our 20th anniversary celebration is testament to that. It hangs in Ted's and my bedroom today.

The Old Hickory pastor and I had agreed on a "let the pros do it" approach for Mom's service; there wouldn't be a time for attendees to stand and voice reminiscences of my mother. I certainly wasn't in any shape to deliver a eulogy myself. But there was one story I silently added to the pastor's remembrances that morning.

A few months earlier, I'd been with her and my dad at the hospital the day the surgeon put the rod in to repair the broken bone in her leg. Dad had gone somewhere, to get coffee or go to the restroom. It was only my mother and I in the room before they began the sedation prior to surgery.

"Thank you for being here," she said, taking my hand.

Even when the nurse came in to get things started to take Mom to the OR, Mom held my hand tight.

Sure, there was unfinished business between us, but the memory of this moment helps me close the gap. For the sake of my own health and sanity, I have to say it is enough.

* * *

Life is a cycle of love and loss, tears and laughter, pain and healing. And so, as life would have it, after the deaths of my mother and Ted's father, as we mourned their passing, Ted and I found the best gift this life has ever given us.

We were exhausted from the years of trips to Anderson and Nashville. We were tired from the time we'd spent apart.

And now that that period was over, we wondered, "What do we do now?"

We knew we needed something. We just weren't sure what.

Ted didn't want to go to counseling, but I did. I found a grief counselor in Clarkesville. He and I talked about the possibility of my going to church. He recommended Nacoochee Presbyterian, a place Ted and I had passed dozens of times on the way to Lake Burton.

When I got home that day, I checked the church's website. I liked the fact that they didn't only say they were welcoming; they spelled it out. I don't remember the exact wording, but they made it clear that sexual orientation wasn't an issue at Nacoochee Presbyterian.

So, we went the next Sunday.

We entered through the bright blue doors of the white frame building. Someone handed us bulletins for the service. We greeted others gathered in the narthex. Then an official-looking woman in a long, beautifully pressed robe and colorful clerical stole met us at the entrance to the sanctuary, her arms outstretched, her kind eyes bright. I could tell she had summed us up in an instant: We were a couple. We were hurting.

"Welcome!" An angel in silk, she hugged each of us. "We are so glad you're here."

* * *

Nacoochee Presbyterian is a mainstream church, affiliated with the Presbyterian Church (U.S.A.), which has 1.3 million members and is the largest body of Presbyterians in the country. Yet it was just unchurch-y enough for Ted and me to feel comfortable.

There was no booming organ. The music director played a simple piano. Outside the sanctuary windows during Sunday services, we could see cows wandering along the fence between the church property and a wide pasture. (Have you ever experienced the inner peace that comes from watching cows?) Best of all, we never felt we were being preached at. The sermons by Rev. Bob Prim were beautifully crafted reminders of God's abundant grace. And there was so much hugging! Hugging was not part of my religious experience in grade school and high school—but then, neither was honesty about my sexual orientation.

Our past behind us, we relaxed in the church's embrace.

We said, "Let's stay here." And we threw ourselves into its welcoming arms again and again in the 12 years that followed.

* * *

As the church became part of our Sunday morning routine, we learned there were deeper reasons why we felt at home there.

Nacoochee Presbyterian had a growing statewide and national reputation as a gay-friendly place. It was sometimes described as "Presbyqueerian," either derisively or affectionately, depending on the point of view of the speaker. Sure, it was housed in a small, 1927 building nestled in a rural valley in the north Georgia mountains, but looks were deceiving. With 300+ members, it was one of the largest churches in its regional presbytery. Many of its members weren't country folk but well-to-do retirees and professionals who'd fled Atlanta and other cities for a quieter life.

We knew the Sautee-Nacoochee community, where the church is located, had a history of attracting artists, musicians, aging hippies and others who made the area a pocket of liberal thinking in one of the most politically conservative counties in the country, but the evolved perspective by a mainstream church on the topic of homosexuality was something we hadn't expected.

How had it happened? We learned that in the early 1990s, a lesbian elder in the church had struggled with her desire to be more publicly "out" in the face of PC(USA)'s prohibition against ordaining "self-affirming" gay and lesbians as elders. She ultimately resigned her position rather than challenge the church's rules, even though her resignation was itself a kind of challenge. In solidarity with her, the other elders on the session, the church's governing body, left her position unfilled. As described in Priscilla Wilson's lovely book, *Gourd Girls* (Mt. Yonah Press, 2005), the session led the church in a study of gay and lesbian issues in the years that followed, inviting Biblical scholars and theologians on both sides of the fence to speak at the church.

A few years later, Rev. Prim's predecessor, a married man with children, came out to the congregation. While most members embraced Rev. John Hobbs, others left the church to worship elsewhere. Those who stayed grappled with the issue of God's acceptance of homosexuality in a way that other churches hadn't at the time—and came to terms with it.

When Rev. Hobbs announced he would be leaving the church, its leaders made sure that the new pastor was as open-minded on the topic of gay rights as they were. They found one in 1998 with Rev. Prim, who became not only Ted's and my spiritual guide, but also a good friend in the years we were active in the church, from 2006 through 2018. Bob had been in high school in Montgomery, Alabama, while I worked there, and, like Ted, got his undergraduate degree at Furman University in South Carolina. There was a Vanderbilt connection, too. Bob obtained his divinity degree there in 1986, so we had some common bonds for starting a friendship that still thrives today.

A fit, big-hearted family man with close-cropped brown hair and a winning smile, Bob won us over with his lack of pretense, his love of books—authors like Wendell Berry, Jon Hassler, Marilynne Robinson—and his sly sense of humor. Most of all, we were grateful for his refusal to brook any argument that gay people had no place in the church.

How wonderful to find a mainstream church with such a history of enlightenment! It truly fit our picture of how a church was supposed to be. From time to time, we had considered attending services at Atlanta's Metropolitan Community Church, but we always felt that it wouldn't be quite the right fit for us.

"It's like separate but equal," I told the session of Nacoochee when we joined the church some months after our first visit in 2006. "Why should gay people have to have their own churches?"

No one at Nacoochee Presbyterian disagreed.

* * *

The church needed a volunteer to update the website and coordinate other communications for a growing membership. I charged into those projects; it felt good to have something productive to focus on in my spare time other than my grief over the loss of Gene and my mother.

Largely because of that work, in 2008 Nacoochee Presbyterian's nominating committee invited me to serve on the session.

It would mean I'd be ordained as an elder, something I wasn't sure I was ready for. It also would be in direct opposition to the PC(USA)'s requirement, adopted in 1997, that candidates for the position of elder, deacon or minister live in fidelity in a traditional marriage or, if single, in chastity in order to be ordained. Yes, it was called the "fidelity and chastity" clause. Nowhere did it say that gay people couldn't be ordained; you could as long as you stifled yourself. In other words, the door was locked.

It was a big step, but I accepted the call. I must admit it was thrilling. I was not only flouting the rules of one of the nation's largest denominations, but I also had a whole church cheering me on. With butterflies in my stomach and a smile on my face, I was ordained one Sunday morning to serve as an elder on the Session for a three-year term, from 2009-2011.

I felt honored by Nacoochee's invitation to become an elder—honored to be part of the church's maverick tradition of inclusiveness. But at Nacoochee, it was all taken in stride. Members joked with me, asking if I knew what I was getting into by taking on a leadership job in the church. I laughed along with them. But I also quickly learned what ordination meant the first Sunday I served as chalice bearer during communion.

Standing next to Rev. Prim at the front of the church with a smooth pottery goblet in my hands, repeating the blessing, "cup of salvation," to the dozens of people who dipped their chunks of bread into the cup I extended to them (the process is called intinction), I could barely get the words out a time or two. But I made certain to look in the eyes of every parishioner that day. One of them, a woman with certain right-wing leanings, even put her hand on mine while she dunked her bread into the cup. Blessings come from the most surprising places.

Pride, love and a feeling of complete unworthiness mixed inside me as one by one, people took communion from me. It brought tears to my eyes and a lump to my throat. There I was, an openly gay man, reviled by many and often disliked by my own self, presenting God to my brothers and sisters in a mainstream church, not a "separate but equal" one.

It was something I had never, ever expected to do in this life. The ultimate gift.

I took my seat next to Ted in the pew when the ceremony was over. I felt completely wrung out and yet, mirabile dictu, more alive than I'd felt in a long time.

Thank you, I whispered to God, my new friend whose presence thrummed all around and inside me on that bright blue morning.

* * *

It was encouraging to see that the denomination I had grown up in, and later run away from, was changing, too. PC(USA) was considering Amendment 10-A, a shift in the ordination standards to allow openly gay people to serve as leaders in the church.

At Rev. Prim's request, I prepared a brief talk in 2009 to present to our regional presbytery in northeast Georgia in favor of the amendment. I didn't keep a copy of the statement, but a key theme was "I don't have a lifestyle; I have a life."

I believe another line was: "We pay our taxes. We walk our dogs. We stand in the checkout line at the grocery store just like anyone else."

Giving the address in the face of vocal opposition from many of the churches in the local presbytery, I was terrified that Saturday morning. Yet Nacoochee Presbyterian's faith in me and Ted gave me confidence. I took confidence in our longevity, too. Ted and I had celebrated our 30th anniversary in May 2007. We did the math and realized that our relationship was six years older than he and I had been the night we met at the Other Side in Nashville. Put another way, we had spent more days on this earth together than we had apart. (It's the only time I've ever enjoyed doing math.) The numbers gave our relationship credibility and my argument legs. Our relationship wasn't some one-night stand after a drugged-up night of dancing at the clubs. Is that really who these people thought we were?

My goal was to break down the stereotype of gay men, to show that Ted and I—and most gay people—are just ordinary people. Sinners, yes. But sinners whose sins are no worse than anyone else's. Rev. Prim liked my statement so much that he asked me to read it at both services at Nacoochee Presbyterian the following morning. Many hugs followed.

* * *

In 2011, a majority of the presbyteries of PC(USA) approved Amendment 10-A to adopt the ordination standards (even though the Northeast Georgia Presbytery, consisting of 50 churches including Nacoochee, was a holdout). Granted, we hadn't been able to sway our local presbytery, but it felt good to have added our voices to a movement that brought historic change to the denomination.

The new standards are a wonder of reason and enlightenment. Scrapping the old requirements of heterosexual marriage or chastity for single people to be ordained as elders, they simply require that candidates for elder be examined for their capabilities, talents and suitability for office.

In full compliance with the new rules of the church, Ted was ordained as an elder and served from 2012-2014. Afterward, he continued to lead the church's finance committee. After my term leading the communications committee, I served as clerk of the session from 2011-2016, and later helped produce the monthly online newsletter in a blog-style format that the church still uses today.

How did two guys who had had their share of frayed ends in their lives become such devoted churchgoers?

Why wouldn't we? Why shouldn't we?

It made sense to us.

It was time.

"You look so normal," said a friend of mine years earlier, a fellow I'd met at the Green Hills YMCA in Nashville in the mid-1980s. We sometimes met for coffee and donuts at a local cafe after my swim and his gym workout. One day I told him frankly about Ted and me.

I was in my mid-30s at the time, still struggling with being open about my sexuality. I considered being told I looked normal a supreme compliment.

At Nacoochee some 25 years later, I didn't care so much whether Ted and I looked normal.

We were accepted. That was all that mattered.

* * *

Joining Nacoochee brought me closer to the self I wanted to be. It put a greater distance between me and the person I was in 2000 in the back of that police car on Highway 115 in Clarkesville. Getting reacquainted with the Bible at Nacoochee since I'd abandoned the book after high school, I was reminded of the apostle Paul's moment of conversion on the road to Damascus.

Highway 115 didn't go to Damascus; it went to Cleveland, Georgia, the seat of the next county over, but it was good enough for me.

As I wrote this memoir in 2020, the interim associate pastor at our church in Atlanta said during the lesson one Sunday, "We are better than our worst moment." It was a reference to the discord in our country in the weeks following the death of George Floyd in Minneapolis, but I think it fits well here. At Nacoochee, I knew I was better than my worst moment, too.

* * *

We learned a lot from Bob Prim.

One November, Ted and I and our friend Francois, a Project Open Hand buddy who'd built a weekend house near our mountain place with his partner Alan, traveled with Bob to Houston to attend a conference organized by the Covenant Network, the organization within PC(USA) that worked for passage of Amendment 10-A. The group also supported a change in the church's definition of marriage to include same-sex couples—a move that ultimately would succeed, too.

At the conference, one speaker presented the results of research on the fraternal birth order effect, which suggests that if a boy has older brothers, he is more likely to be gay as a result of a buildup of antibodies in the mother's system—antibodies thought to play a role in shaping sexual orientation. The comments hit home with us. We knew a real-life probable example of the effect: Francois' partner, Alan, whose work had kept him in Atlanta while we traveled. Alan is the third of four boys in his family. The two older sons and the youngest are straight. Alan, as he once described himself to me, is "gay, gay, gay."

"Alan should hear this," I whispered to Francois during the presentation.

"He's the poster boy," Francois quipped, his brown eyes gleaming.

Back at the hotel after the presentation, Ted, Francois, Bob and I stopped at the bar for a drink before heading upstairs to our rooms to rest and change for dinner.

I made a remark about the research presented that day, how it offered more proof that homosexuality isn't a choice. I thought the research represented a step forward in the gay equality movement, but Bob offered a different view.

"What if it is a choice?" he asked. "Who cares? What if you want to be gay just because you like it? What difference does it make?"

I set down my wine glass and sat back in my chair. Here was a straight man, married with two children, pastor of a church in one of the reddest counties in the U.S., yet he was light-years ahead of me in the debate over gay rights. I had nothing to add.

"That's the best way to look at it." Ted sipped his scotch. "Isn't there enough finger-pointing already? I agree, Bob. Why should people care?"

"Here's to letting people be," Bob said, and we all raised our glasses.

Chapter Twenty-Three: Father to Son

Dad at his 96th birthday party at our cabin in Clarkesville, Georgia
Photo courtesy of Becky Gibson Portwood

Since my mother's death in 2006, Dad had lived with my sister Pat in Hephzibah, Georgia, outside Augusta. Pat and her husband had built a nice addition to their house that gave Dad his own bedroom and bath with a walk-in shower. But after three years, Pat was exhausted.

Dad was mobile and his mind sharp, but he had grown increasingly fragile since my mom's death. I had been amazed at the resources of strength and energy he found to be her chief caregiver in her final days, but those stores were gone now. He needed someone to prepare his meals, to manage his medications for rheumatoid arthritis and a heart condition, to take him to doctors' appointments and generally stand guard to keep him from falling and be sure he was happy and comfortable.

In early 2009, when he was 95 and I was 56, we moved him to Clarkesville to be with us.

The configuration wasn't ideal. Our lot at the edge of a deep ravine in Skyview didn't allow for easy house expansion. Ted and I gave Dad the only bedroom downstairs—our bedroom—and moved our things to one of the small bedrooms and bath upstairs.

As we spent more time in the mountains, we had taken another downsizing step in Atlanta, sold the big three-bedroom house and bought a condo that had only a half bath, a living room, dining room and kitchen on the ground floor. It wouldn't have worked for Dad at all. I found myself wishing we had kept the big house, but that's not the way it happened.

So, we made it work—Ted staying in Atlanta during the week so he could go to the office every day, Dad and I in the mountains.

My business was going great. The crazy days of getting it established were over—when I'd be working on copy for two client websites, go to bed at 2:00 in the morning and set the alarm for 4:00 so I could meet our agreed-upon deliverable times. My workload was solid and more reasonably balanced when Dad came to live with us.

I had bought a 10'x12' prefab greenhouse at Lowe's and had it reconfigured as an office a short walk up the hill from our cabin. From my desk inside, I could see my favorite view of the mountains through the generous skylight that sloped nearly to ground level. Before the building went up, I had taken a chair to the site one snowy morning and, with stakes, string and hammer, had carefully marked off how the building should be positioned so I could see the mountains while I worked.

For the first week or so after Dad was with us, I continued to use that office as my main workplace. We'd have breakfast. I'd help him get dressed and situated for a few hours of reading on the living room sofa while I worked in my office up the hill. But I felt uneasy leaving him alone in the house, had visions of him falling in the bathroom or the kitchen while he got himself a second cup of coffee. So, our dining room table became my office again.

I hired a friend and fellow member of Nacoochee Presbyterian to run errands for me, to make quick trips into town for groceries, check our post office box and make bank deposits. (This was when my clients were still mailing checks, before automatic deposits became the norm.) It helped immensely. I didn't want to leave Dad alone while I did those errands myself, and if I took him with me, especially if we went to the grocery store, what would have been a half-hour trip could easily stretch into the 90-minute zone. My friend helped me balance my work with the things that needed to be done to keep our home life running smoothly.

It was mostly fun having Dad with us.

On nice days, we'd have lunch on the covered deck we'd built—without Gene's help this time—in the backyard, perched on the edge of the ravine where coyotes, bears, deer and foxes lived.

"It's a regular park back here," Dad said, gazing at the mountains in the distance.

I had started taking singing lessons as a diversion from the at-the-desk posture in which I spent my working hours, and Dad seemed to get a kick out of it when I'd run through my warm-ups with him.

"I wish your mother could hear you sing," he said.

I wished she could, too.

We'd go for long drives down country roads. While we enjoyed the scenery, he'd tell me stories I hadn't heard from his childhood, often involving summers spent on his uncle's farm near Port Allegheny, Pennsylvania. Dad had been born in Port Allegheny, but his family moved to Buffalo, where Dad went to high school.

"We had some good times on that farm," he said.

Still, I knew having Dad with us wasn't a perfect solution. Ted and I didn't mind giving up our bedroom and living upstairs for a short time, but Dad was relatively hale and hearty. "What if this goes on for years?" we wondered. In addition, I had acquired a new gig with a technology company in Atlanta that hired me for writing and consulting while it rebranded itself after an acquisition. The project required my being in the city from time to time, which meant hiring a sitter for Dad, which inevitably led to an argument in which he insisted he didn't need a sitter and I insisted he did. I wasn't so much physically as emotionally tired from playing the heavy with my father.

We knew it was time to choose an assisted living center near Clarkesville for Dad. He looked at it with us and agreed it was a pretty nice place. It was nine miles from the cabin, so I'd be able to visit frequently.

Despite all the positive vibes, when moving day came in May 2009, he did not want to go. I'll probably hear his hopeful "Couldn't we wait and go tomorrow morning?" until the day I die, but once he got settled in the place, he accepted it graciously, with his usual chin-up spirit and good humor.

Nonetheless, he persisted in calling his neighbors down the hall and the small group he took his meals with "the inmates." It was his way of reminding me that this was not where he had hoped to spend his final days.

But… you do what you have to do.

During the 11 months he lived at the assisted living center, he phoned nearly every night to wish me pleasant dreams. At first, I turned it into another guilt trip, telling myself "if I were a better son" I would have been the one to start the tradition, the one to make the calls. But then I came to understand that it gave him a sense of control at a time in his life when I was making many decisions for him. It harkened back to the days when I was in college or working in Montgomery and he'd phone "just to check in and see how you're doing." I loved those calls. Even as he neared the end of his life, Dad was still Dad.

He joined our church and came to Sunday services.

"I think you're the oldest new member we've ever had," Rev. Prim told him.

Dad was proud of that.

For his 96th birthday in November that year, we had a party and invited as many new church friends as our cabin would hold. While I finished preparations for the party, Ted drove to the assisted living center, picked Dad up and brought him to the cabin. The cigarette-smoking cake lady baked three beautiful cakes for the occasion. I put a "3" and a "2" candle side by side on top of each.

One church friend who is a wonderful photographer took many photos that day, but I have a favorite. In the photo, Dad sits on our sofa holding a glass of champagne. There is a look of total contentment on his face.

Since Dad's death of a heart attack in his room at the assisted living center in April 2010, whenever doubts begin to gather about how well I handled his final days, what I could have done differently, how we might have reengineered our house and our lives to make room for him, I think of that photo. In fact, I keep it handy, on the top of the stack of family photos in the plastic box in my office closet.

Don't ask me why I haven't framed it to keep in a place where I can see it more frequently. Maybe it brings too much back. But I know where it is when I need it. And now it heads this chapter of my memoir.

* * *

"Bob Coleman would say that heaven is a well-stocked bar," Rev. Prim said in his eulogy to Dad on the day of his funeral in April 2010 at Nacoochee Presbyterian. The church was nearly full.

I had told Bob of Dad's habit of having a glass of Jack Daniel's in the evening through his '70s and '80s. But he still enjoyed wine in the years that followed. We also told Bob about Dad's perennially delighted surprise when Ted or I would say, "How about a glass of wine?" at cocktail time while he stayed with us. Even though it had been a nightly treat for months, he'd respond as if we'd just made a first-time offer to fly him to Bermuda… or Buffalo for a real roast beef sandwich with horseradish on a kummelweck bun.

I think I had also told Bob the story of when Dad and Mom were visiting Pat in Johnson City, Tennessee, and having their usual cocktail time while watching the local news. When the middle-aged male anchor read the story about the alarming spread of gonorrhea in the county, the headline at the bottom of the screen read "VD Rampant." With drink in hand, Dad entered from the kitchen and remarked, "VD Rampant? Don't tell me that's his name!" Mom and Pat nearly choked on their cheese doodles.

If Bob didn't tell the story in the eulogy, I should have insisted on it. Or I should have told it after the service. But, as we did for Mom's funeral, we let the pros handle it and didn't build in time for comments from friends and family.

During the service, I knew how much better it was having it at Nacoochee, how disconnected I would have felt if we had somehow found a way for Dad to stay in Nashville after Mom's death and then had his funeral at the Old Hickory church.

At Nacoochee, a close friend read John 14:1, "Let not your heart be troubled," and looked right at me when she said the words.

At Nacoochee, Ted could put his arm around me in the pew without fear of any raised eyebrows.

At Nacoochee, a great blue heron flew up from the creek that flowed through the pasture behind the church. It circled overhead as we scattered Dad's ashes in the memory garden after the service.

At Nacoochee, everyone took a scoop of the ashes and sprinkled them in the flowers and on the grass that bordered them. After brushing the dust off their hands, they hugged Ted and me. By the end of the service, our dress shirts were smeared with gray handprints. We were literally covered with Nacoochee Presbyterian's love that day.

* * *

I could write so much more about Dad.

When I was a kid and Dad was back home from his assignment in Newburgh, it was increasingly obvious that I did not favor the sports that most boys loved. No problem. Dad found an alternative. Having grown up in Buffalo, he could both speed skate and ice skate. Home of the Dixie Flyers hockey team in the '60s, Nashville had an ice rink in the new Municipal Auditorium downtown. Dad took me skating at least one night a week during my junior high and high school days. I even had my own ice skates, which gave me a certain cachet among my classmates.

"This is something we can do together," he said early on in our skating days. He said it proudly, as if he'd made a discovery. I was fine with it. I loved our times at the skating rink.

As I've mentioned in an earlier chapter, my mom and a friend's mom had a conversation in our presence in which they wondered why our Boy Scout troop couldn't have more activities for "boys who aren't all boy." Unlike Mom, Dad never put my lack of all-boyness into words, at least not within earshot of me. I appreciate him for that, as well. I never felt "lesser than" when we were together.

I have friends whose fathers had trouble accepting their homosexuality, whose mothers were fine with it. That wasn't the case with me.

Why? I think Dad always knew I was gay. My mother didn't have to tell him about my kissing Luke McCoy for him to figure it out. I think Dad was always okay with it, or at least knew there was nothing he and Mom could do to change it. Dad might have been more vocal about his acceptance of me had it not been for Mom's vehement opposition in the early days. It must have put him in an awkward position. But he waited patiently, and the ship righted itself in time.

The summer before my junior year in college, I had stayed in Knoxville, ostensibly to get some courses out of the way because of my increasing involvement in the student paper. My private reason: I stayed to carry on the affair with Griff before he got his diploma and went home to Canada.

The morning after our last night together, Mom and Dad stopped to get me at Griff's. They were driving to Florida and were taking me with them for a week at the beach and a break before fall quarter began.

Dad came to the door of Griff's apartment, his Old Spice aftershave sharp and familiar in the sweet summer air. I wore the mint green, impeccably wrinkle-free Ban-Lon polo shirt I'd bought for the trip and shabby bell bottom jeans—an outfit that suited my dual nature that radiant morning: part free-loving hippie, part collegiate conservative. On the front stoop, I introduced Dad to Griff. All smiles, shirtless, his jeans slipping below his narrow hips, revealing the trail of dark hair that ran down his tight belly to his pubes, Griff shook hands with him enthusiastically. Dad got a kick out of his "oots and aboots."

"Mike's mother is Canadian," Dad said.

"He's told me." A devilish glint in his brown eyes, Griff sized up the two of us. "I would have known you were Mike's father," he said to Dad. "You guys have the same smile."

"Thank you," Dad said. "That's a compliment, I guess."

"Yes indeed."

I could feel myself blushing. Was Griff flirting with my father? That rascal. Yet I admired his chutzpah.

He and I had already said our goodbyes. I had come close to telling him I loved him the night before, but I didn't. I thought it would end the summer on a heavy note. We were two guys who'd enjoyed our freedom, had a good time together. That was it.

I got my suitcase, gave Griff a handshake. I thought at the time that he and I had done a good job putting something over on my father, giving him nary a reason to suspect that something untoward had gone on between us.

In retrospect, however, I think it's highly likely that Dad had our number. How could he not? Granted, the lease had run out on my apartment down the street from Griff's. I told Mom and Dad that was why I was staying with him for a few days, but surely Dad saw that there was more to the story. Hadn't he seen my eyes tear up when Griff shook my hand a second time and winked at me before closing the door between us? Didn't he notice how quiet I was on the drive out of Knoxville to Gatlinburg, where we stayed a night before heading on to Florida? Why did he offer to buy me a second drink before dinner that night—something Dad hardly ever did when paying restaurant prices for booze? Why did he say before bed how much he enjoyed meeting my friend that morning, what a nice fellow he seemed to be?

In my mother's collection of family photos, there was a picture of a young Dad with another extremely good-looking young man. They were laughing, their arms draped around each other in a pose I thought oddly intimate for the 1930s. Ted and I had never held each other so affectionately for the camera. The photo could have easily been titled, "Young Queer Love in the Great Depression." Only it wasn't a young queer. It was my father.

"Here's Daddy with his girlfriend," Mom said when she showed it to me one Christmas.

"That's a guy," I said.

"No it isn't."

"Of course it is." I held the photo out so both of us could see it. "There is no way this is a girl."

"Oh, heavens." She took back the picture and put it in the box.

Of all the photos she gave me in the downsizing she and my dad did before they moved into the assisted living facility in Nashville, the photo of Dad and his friend is not among them.

I wonder today if she was trying to tell me something by showing me that photo, something she couldn't put into words. Surely, she didn't believe the guy hanging on to Dad's neck was a girl.

"In my day, it was okay to have boyfriends. I understand that, but…" Dad had said when he and Mom learned the exact nature of my relationship with Ted. I'd wondered about the statement when he said it that night at Tony Roma's, but today it's even more of a puzzle to me. Did he mean platonic boyfriends, or did he mean it was okay to have sexual boyfriends, as long as the relationship didn't morph into something permanent, something public, something like Ted and I had? I'll never know because I never asked. Part of me is glad I didn't. Some mysteries are best left unexplored.

I met my friend Blake's parents on spring break sophomore year. Blake and I drove to New York to pick up the new car his father had bought him (his dad wanted to restore the Mustang). In the new car, we plowed through a blinding snowstorm on the New Jersey Turnpike and drove all the way to Daytona, Florida, for the week. Before the adventure, Blake's parents couldn't have been nicer or more gracious to me in their stunning home on the Gold Coast of Long Island.

I wonder sometimes, if my parents had met Blake, what their response would have been. I feel certain they would have detected the glow of their young son in his dazzling presence. Mom might have wanted to overlook it or pretend she hadn't seen what she'd seen. Dad would have accepted it as the unalterable truth about me, just as I am 99 percent sure he accepted the truth on Griff's front stoop that summer morning in 1972 in Knoxville, Tennessee.

* * *

If my mother was described as sneaky, my father could be described as cagey. I bet he also knew that if he had broached the subject of homosexuality with me in my high school and college days, I would have denied everything.

Sometimes I wish I had talked with him about it when he was with us in Clarkesville. But just as his work on the Manhattan Project during World War II was a topic he preferred not to discuss, I suspected a straightforward talk about my homosexuality—about that Canadian guy Griff he met in Knoxville— would have fallen in the same category. He never did ask to read *Loving Someone Gay,* either. He hadn't wanted the book in his house.

But he had welcomed Ted… into his home and his life. That was better than a book any day.

Chapter Twenty-Four: Can't Stop the Beat

Me as Edna Turnblad in a musical number from Hairspray at the Sautee Nacoochee Center's Shubert Alley in the Valley, September 2016. And to think there was a time in my life when I didn't like the idea of doing drag.
Photo courtesy of Becky Gibson Portwood

The obligations of caring for ailing parents had bound Ted and me for more than five years. We missed our parents terribly, but it would be less than the truth to say that we didn't feel a new sense of freedom along with the loss.

We traveled more. We'd gone to South Africa with our friends Alan and Francois after my mom's death. (Born near Durban, Francois had grown up in South Africa and was a perfect tour guide.) After Dad's death, Ted and I explored Spain, Morocco, Portugal, Peru.

With my singing lessons, my long-dormant love of performing began itching. I had time to scratch it. In the summer of 2010 a few months after Dad's death, I played Uncle Henry in a pair of black overalls in the Clarkesville community theater's production of *The Wizard of Oz.* In the stage production, the actor playing Uncle Henry also plays the Emerald Guard, the comic character who has the "horse of a different color" line and who leads the big number that opens Act II, "The Merry Old Land of Oz." My costume for the guard was a top hat, a green bow tie with sequins, white shirt, black pants hemmed just below the knee, and a pair of green Converse high-tops. I loved it.

I was no longer the shy guy I was in high school. Sure, it still makes me nervous to get up in front of people to speak or perform, but I've learned not to let that stop me. I'm happy to report I'm not shy about much of anything these days.

I went on to do several other shows at the theater over the years, including performing the hefty role of Adult Ralphie (with cameos by cowboy Red Ryder) in a sold-out, 12-performance production of the non-musical version of *A Christmas Story.* As narrator of the show, I liked Adult Ralphie's bemused but loving view of his parents. I enjoyed telling the story of a family that didn't have any problems more serious than a father's bad taste in lamps and a mother's limited cooking repertoire (meatloaf and red cabbage again, yum!). But I also used the show as a template, overlaying my own family's experience on it, seeing how my family and Ralphie's obviously were different, but shared similarities, too. The show reminded me that I, like Adult Ralphie, had plenty of good memories of my childhood and an enduring love for my parents—with my dad gliding across the ice on his skates and my mom posting her nude sketches all over the living room— despite the rough patches we went through. And like Adult Ralphie, the good memories are the ones I hold onto.

I also took part in performances in the black box theater at the community center across the road from Nacoochee Presbyterian Church. A musical-theater-loving lesbian couple and close friends of ours started a Broadway-style review there. We named it *Shubert Alley in the Valley: Where Broadway Meets Sautee.* Over the next eight years, I became known as the guy who found the most obscure Broadway songs to sing. One year I did two songs that baritone Alfred Drake had sung in a 1940s musical called *Sing Out, Sweet Land!.* Another year, "Somebody, Somewhere" from *The Most Happy Fella.* My favorite was "The Best in the World," the song Jerry Herman wrote for the 1980s Broadway musical *A Day in Hollywood/A Night in the Ukraine.* The song was written for a female and sung by Priscilla Lopez in the original show. I slightly altered a few of the lyrics and found it worked fine for me. It told the story of a movie-house usher who thought he was going to make it big in the movies; he returns home after his brief, failed stint in Hollywood to be the best movie-house usher in the world. A local dancer who had performed in the original Broadway cast of *42nd Street* had an enormous warehouse-style storage area for costumes in her home. She kindly loaned me an usher's cap for the number. Another reason I chose the song: It was very much a story about a son wanting to make his father proud of him.

Bob Prim started a Prairie Home Companion-style show in an intentionally corny radio format that ran every winter for 10 years at the community center. As part of the show, I wrote skits about a struggling community theater company and played the director most every year.

Each cast member got to pick a song to perform in the show. Over the years, I sang songs by Guy Clark, Tom Waits, Cole Porter. I considered it another step forward in my "outness" to sing "People Will Say We're in Love" from *Oklahoma!*. It was written as a duet for a man and a woman, but I did it as a solo in 2019 and 2020, the final year of the show. The song seems almost as if it were written for two men to sing to each other—two men who are discussing just how out-of-the-closet they want to be. In fact, it was Bob Prim who suggested I sing it after reading about a production of *Oklahoma!* in Oregon featuring a same-sex couple in the leading roles.

I prefaced it with this intro, a reference to my early romance with Blake:

I had a boyfriend in college.

One of those fraternity boys we hear so much about.

Whenever Blake and I went to the movies, he would insist on keeping an empty seat between us.

Sit side by side at the movies? Oh no, no, no. It just wasn't done.

Not in Knoxville, Tennessee in 1972.

Not on Saturday night. DATE NIGHT!

God forbid anyone should think this was a date.

I was thinking about those days while I looked for a song to sing tonight, and I found one.

You're probably familiar with it. It's from the Broadway musical *Oklahoma!*, which of course was made into a movie.

The song was written in 1940. A duet. Sung by a man and woman in the musical and the movie.

I thought I understood this song, but when I looked at it again a few weeks ago, I thought WOW.

This song could have been written for any couple afraid to sit side by side in a movie theater on Saturday night.

***

There were many people in the 80-seat theater that night who knew Ted and me, but just as many unfamiliar faces. Still, I didn't sense any stirs of discomfort when I started my intro: "I had a boyfriend in college." I'd performed in drag in some of the Shubert Alley shows, including the role of Edna in our rendition of "Can't Stop the Beat" from *Hairspray* (my lime green, brown and turquoise sundress cost $7 at our local Goodwill store) and one of the dancers in "Raise You Up" from *Kinky Boots.* Our performances were well-received, but how could they miss? They were splashy, colorful comedy numbers. My gender-bending rendition of the *Oklahoma* song was different—designed more to make people think than to laugh. I think it succeeded. Another indication of positive change in the new millennium.

I also sang in a revue of Frank Loesser songs—a performance that was a come-full-circle moment for me. In the early 1960s, my mother bought the original cast recording of *How to Succeed in Business without Really Trying* for my father for Father's Day. I loved all the Broadway recordings we had at home, *The Sound of Music* with Mary Martin, an album of songs from *Kiss Me, Kate* sung by Gogi Grant, Anne Jeffreys and Howard Keel. But *How to Succeed* sounded like something from another planet to my ten year-old ears. The music was so clean and crisp, so modern. And so funny. I loved every song. My favorite was "Happy to Keep His Dinner Warm," the secretary Rosemary's sardonic dream of being a New Rochelle housewife when she's married to the hero of the piece, J. Pierrepont Finch.

One summer day after we got the album, I was peeing in our downstairs bathroom and singing "Happy to Keep His Dinner Warm" with gusto. My mom rapped lightly on the door and said, "Honey, maybe it would be better if you sang another song from the show. How about 'Coffee Break'? That's a good one."

Though today some might describe my mother's response as a textbook example of microaggression, I didn't argue the point. I was a good boy. I did what my mother asked. And I think deep down I knew it was an odd choice for a 10-year-old boy to be singing. Still, I loved that song!

I threw my reservations out the window when I sang the song in the Frank Loesser review some 50 years later. We performed in a dinner theater-style setup. I made sure Ted, Francois and Alan sat at a table near the stage. I put a moose-head oven mitt on my hand and sang to Ted how happy I'd be to keep his dinner warm. I think I embarrassed him a little, but the audience loved it. They laughed and laughed.

I wish Mom had been there that night. I think she might have laughed, too.

Chapter Twenty-Five: Getting Married Today

Wedding Day with Best Man Rob Curry at Nacoochee Presbyterian, October 19th, 2013
Photo courtesy of Adair Soderholm

Two years later, I married the man whose dinner I was happy to keep warm… twice.

The first wedding was in August 2013. It was more a matter of practicality than anything else. As we increased our international travel, we had had our wills redone and thought it might be a good idea at the same time to make our relationship legal, to take advantage of the growing number of states that had approved same-sex marriage.

As Ted put it, it was time to make an honest man of me. We'd been lovers for 36 years.

(This was a few months after the U.S. Supreme Court overturned the part of the 1996 Defense of Marriage Act that prevented the federal government from recognizing same-sex couples, but state bans on recognition of same-sex marriages were still in effect. It wasn't until two years later that the Court ruled, in *Obergefell v. Hodges*, that all states must license and recognize same-sex marriage. During the period between the two rulings, Georgia was one of the states that held on to its discriminatory practices, so we still couldn't get legally married at home, but other states were letting freedom ring.)

We considered Minnesota, where I have cousins. But the state required a three-to-five-day waiting period between applying for a marriage license and getting it. We were hoping to complete the process over a long weekend.

Ted did some investigating and found Delaware to be a contender. The state had a 24-hour waiting period. It also offered Rehoboth Beach, where we had vacationed in 2001. Another plus was the Rehoboth area's proximity to Norfolk, Virginia, where our friend Rob lived, Ted's best friend from high school and college (not my friend Rob from the ad agency). We could fly to Norfolk, drive to the Rehoboth area, get married with Rob as our witness and best man, and then go to the beach to celebrate.

It worked beautifully. We came home with tans and a marriage license from Georgetown, Delaware, the seat of Sussex County, where Rehoboth Beach is located. I wasn't sure how the Sussex County Clerk of the Peace, a poker-faced fellow about our age, felt about performing our ceremony in the small park in the center of the town square. But after the ceremony, after Ted and I kissed surrounded by downtown Georgetown's rush-hour traffic, he told us how honored he was to be performing a similar ceremony for two cadets from the nearby air force base the following weekend. We realized we had been in good company all along.

It was also the moment that I realized our country had passed a turning point in attitudes toward LGBTQ+ people—and I had catching up to do. I'd gone through much of my life assuming that most people disapprove of us. That was my assumption with our clerk. Now, it was time to start assuming the opposite—that most people are okay with us; those who disapprove are the exception to the rule. What a lovely discovery to make at age 60!

As we left the sunny square, I wanted to apologize to the clerk for underestimating him. And to thank him for the unexpected flash of enlightenment. Our country had made big strides, I thought.

* * *

Once we got home to north Georgia, Bob Prim insisted we have a church wedding in addition to the civil ceremony in Delaware.

At that time in 2013, there was growing support within PC(USA) to update its official definition of marriage to include same-sex couples. The proposed new wording was carefully crafted to give the boat only a gentle rocking, describing marriage as "a unique commitment between two people, traditionally a man and a woman." But the new definition wouldn't become effective until June 2015.

So, even though our ceremony wasn't in compliance with the current policies of the church, in the view of Nacoochee, it didn't matter. The wedding went ahead just as we wanted. Nacoochee was being a maverick again. At my request, the church's music director even found a piano version of Donna Summer's "Last Dance," the big song from our early days in the 1970s, to play as our exit music.

My Minnesota cousins attended; so did my sister Pat, who stood up at the reception to apologize for the pain she caused when she refused to attend our 20th anniversary celebration and commitment ceremony in 1997. THAT was a great surprise. I was so pleased about it, and sorry for all the years of cold war between us.

More than 100 friends and relatives attended. We had a wonderful time. I am eternally grateful to everyone who celebrated with us that afternoon and into the night, who offered toast after toast and hug after hug.

Besides Pat's apology, there was another big surprise that day.

Do you remember the movie *Making Love*? Released in 1982, the mainstream film featured a passionate kiss between stars Michael Ontkean and Harry Hamlin. When Ted and I saw it in Nashville, there was a chorus of "ewwws" from the audience during the scene. Harry Hamlin later said the movie ended his film career.

Well, at our wedding at Nacoochee 31 years later, there was applause from the attendees at the end of the ceremony when Bob said, "I now pronounce you husband and husband."

Then he said to us, "You may kiss."

There was a moment of silence. Then Ted grabbed me and kissed me hard on the lips.

The applause and cheers and whoops from the crowd put the previous ovation to shame. I really had not expected that. What a grand reversal of my lesson from Terry at age 11! On this day, in this north Georgia church, two males kissing was exactly right.

We had worked hard to be accepted by the church. Even though we were embraced the very first day we entered its sanctuary, we wanted to prove we were worthy of the leadership positions the church had granted us.

Was it our hard work that brought the cheers that afternoon?

Or had the world changed that drastically around us, regardless of what we said or did, or what kind of example we set?

Maybe it was a bit of both.

I wasn't going to question it too much. I was going to enjoy it.

Getting married in our church made a difference for me, for us. I didn't think it would, but it did. I had always thought a big public wedding was frivolous, unnecessary… not to mention an unnecessary expense. I was wrong. Having an entire community say it supports your union is an incredible, life-affirming thing. Something settled in me that day. Something bloomed. Love for my husband. Love for the acceptance we had found. Love for my life.

At last, it not only looked good from the outside. It felt good on the inside, too.

* * *

When Ted and I got home after our Nacoochee wedding and celebration, arms loaded with gifts and cards from people we loved, it felt like a new life was starting for us. A new life as we began our seventh decade on the planet. How lucky we were. How blessed to be able to give it all a go one more time.

Front door locked, porch lights off, we walked out back in the cool autumn air.

"It was a good day," Ted said, taking my hand.

"A good day? Can you believe what we just did!"

"I know," he said. "It's pretty amazing, isn't it? Who knew, all those years ago."

We were quiet for a moment, looking up at the bright, silent stars above us.

"Want anything?" Ted asked, pulling me from my thoughts. "A nightcap?"

"No, thanks." I turned to him, buried my fingers in the hair on the back of his head. It felt a little silkier, not as bristly as it had our first night together at the apartment on Rosewood Avenue in Nashville in 1977. But it still felt wonderful. Marriage is loving the way you are. Loving the way you were. Loving the ways you've changed.

I rested my forehead against his and let out a long breath.

"I just want to go to bed," I said. "With you."

Epilogue: The Best of Times Is Now

At the annual Emancipation Celebration, when we visited friends from my Alabama Journal days

Writing a memoir is as much an activity of leaving things out as putting things in. "Less is more" is the rule. There are so many events, so many people I've left out of this manuscript. But my story is about two men carving out a life for themselves in times of extreme external and, often, internalized homophobia, so I've focused on the experiences that directly illuminate that narrative.

As much as we loved the mountain community where we had planned to retire, Ted and I moved back to Atlanta in 2019—six years after our marriage. While the Sautee community around Nacoochee Presbyterian Church will always be home in our hearts, we missed the diversity, the "bluer" political environment, the culture and the food of Atlanta.

Now that we're back in the city, we know it was the right move for us. As we watch the disturbing trends in our country to undermine the rights of individuals based on gender identity and sexual orientation, we feel a need to be closer to the state's political center. Ted has become active in the Democratic Party here, and it's good to be part of the effort to thwart those toxic initiatives. Yes, we do feel threatened by them, but we know our best line of defense is to stay strong together.

Another good thing about our move to Atlanta: We are ten minutes away from the hospital where I had my heart surgery in November 2019. (My recovery has gone very well, by the way.) We've found a Presbyterian church where we feel at home, too.

How is our relationship doing? Ted says that if you're with someone long enough, your arguments become like the cartoon of the prison inmates who've been together so long they have their favorite jokes numbered, and only need to say the number to get everyone rolling in laughter. Marriage is like that.

While we've left the big issues behind, the everyday bugaboos are what they've always been. Ted is a Taurus. He has a bull-in-a-china-shop approach to many household activities, when kitchen drawers are left open to gather crumbs from the counter while he's cooking, lids on bottles left loose so the contents freely spill in the refrigerator if knocked over. I am an unrelenting Virgo, with OCD planted at a young age by my dear father, who had the role of safety engineer for many years with DuPont. Milk cartons are not to be left on the kitchen table during breakfast where the contents are likely to sour more quickly. Pans are not left unattended on a hot stove. Scissors are always handed blade-side away from the recipient. We've grown wise enough to laugh at most of our differences. It makes life much more enjoyable.

We don't have many "if I could do it over again" moments. When I do, I imagine going to college without a Blake in the picture. He was the first person I fell in love with. I loved the comfort and, yes, the sweet agony of our friendship. Nonetheless, my devotion to Blake consumed two years of my college life, during which I passed up other romantic opportunities.

I wonder how my life might have turned out differently if I'd accepted them. Or, at the very least, how my college days might have been a little friskier. But then I would have missed an extraordinary friendship. I should mention that I regret having lost touch with Blake in the years since college. I can't find him anywhere on Google today. In real life, he had a most ordinary name (the only ordinary thing about him), which decreases the chances of an online reunion. I'd like to thank him for offering his friendship so freely to me, and for pouring the perfect foundation on which Ted and I built the best of both worlds for us—an erotic, let's-do-it-all-night brothership. We have never kept an empty seat between us at the theater.

As for other characters in my story, my sister Marsha's views have mellowed about Ted and me. She's accepted the fact of us, and we get along pretty well. I see no more "abomination" pamphlets.

Maggie and her husband are happy in their retirement in Nashville. She and Bud Rose are friends these days, and since I'm friends with Bud on Facebook, he let it be known while I wrote this memoir that Maggie would be willing to reconnect with me. So, I sent her an email. As a result, we have struck up a pleasant correspondence online. That feels really good. Both she and Bud have said they bear no hard feelings toward me. That feels good, too. I like knowing that this memoir started that healing for me… for us… after all these years.

Bud is also married. He and his husband have a good life in the Pacific Northwest. He is a published author and a popular, well-liked figure in his hometown. When my friend Alana read our story, when I told her Bud turned out to be gay, too, she said Maggie "got a double whammy, didn't she?" Indeed she did. If ours is not a cautionary tale about the pain caused by hiding one's true self from the world, I don't know what is. Thank God we all survived it.

Terry and I are also in touch on Facebook. He's a grandfather now with a beautiful wife and family. After we reconnected several years ago, we've made sure to acknowledge each other's birthdays every year. We've never talked about that afternoon in my turquoise bedroom in Columbia. We don't need to. In our own 11-year-old way, we were simply declaring who we were that day.

Sadly, Matt and Sharon drifted away from us in the years following Amy's death, but our strong friendship with Buddy and Alana continues, including our tradition of celebrating every Thanksgiving together. I will always be grateful for their love and support, especially in the early days of Ted's and my relationship, when we needed a sound, unconditionally loving rock to hold onto.

When I look back on my life, at the clippings from the now-defunct *Alabama Journal* and *Nashville Banner*, the work I did for the healthcare association, the hundreds of brochures, websites, position papers, bylined articles, ads and blog posts I wrote with Char and as the owner of my own business, it all seems so random. So do the unpublished manuscripts. The common thread, I suppose, is a talent for writing and for making money at it. But I don't see much continuity. I wonder what sense it all makes.

That's when I understand that Ted is the continuity, the common thread. Or to give credit where credit is due, my life makes sense with Ted.

The 1977 letters opened the door to this memoir for me. I wanted to get them out of the closet, so to speak, and bring them to life. (I keyed in all 16,000 words on my desktop computer.) Reading the letters now, I see two young men aspiring to something, something they couldn't quite picture because they'd never seen it, had no model for. We were certain of one thing, however: Our love was "special and wonderful," as Ted wrote in that August 11th letter in 1977. That was really all we needed to know.

We never did build that house, the one Ted drew the plans for. We came to dislike A-frames as we got older, didn't think their design would be practical for us, so the sketch sat in the box with the other letters for four decades while our lives went on around them, while we bought and sold and bought houses, upsizing and downsizing along the way. We've owned six houses and two condos in our years together and were fond of most of them, but part of me wishes we'd given those plans a try.

And then I realize, we've had features of that house in all the places we've lived. It's been reflected in all of them in some way. Besides, I don't believe Ted's invitation to share the A-frame with him was a literal request; I think he was asking me to share this house of life with him—for better, for worse and everything in between—regardless of the angle or color or location of the four walls around us.

The four walls around us at our condo in Atlanta, incidentally, are being prepared for a fresh coat of paint as I write this, now that we're vaccinated, relaxing and stretching out somewhat as the worst of the Covid pandemic appears to be behind us. Later, there'll be new flooring and other updates. We love it here, love being able to walk to so many places—restaurants, the library, the post office, the light-rail train to the city—and we intend to stay a good long time. For now, though, the place is a bit of a mess as we get ready for the renovations. Life goes on, as they say. So, thankfully, do we.

And so do the cowboy cookies. Ted bakes them quite often these days. My mom's recipe.

July 30, 2022
Atlanta, Georgia

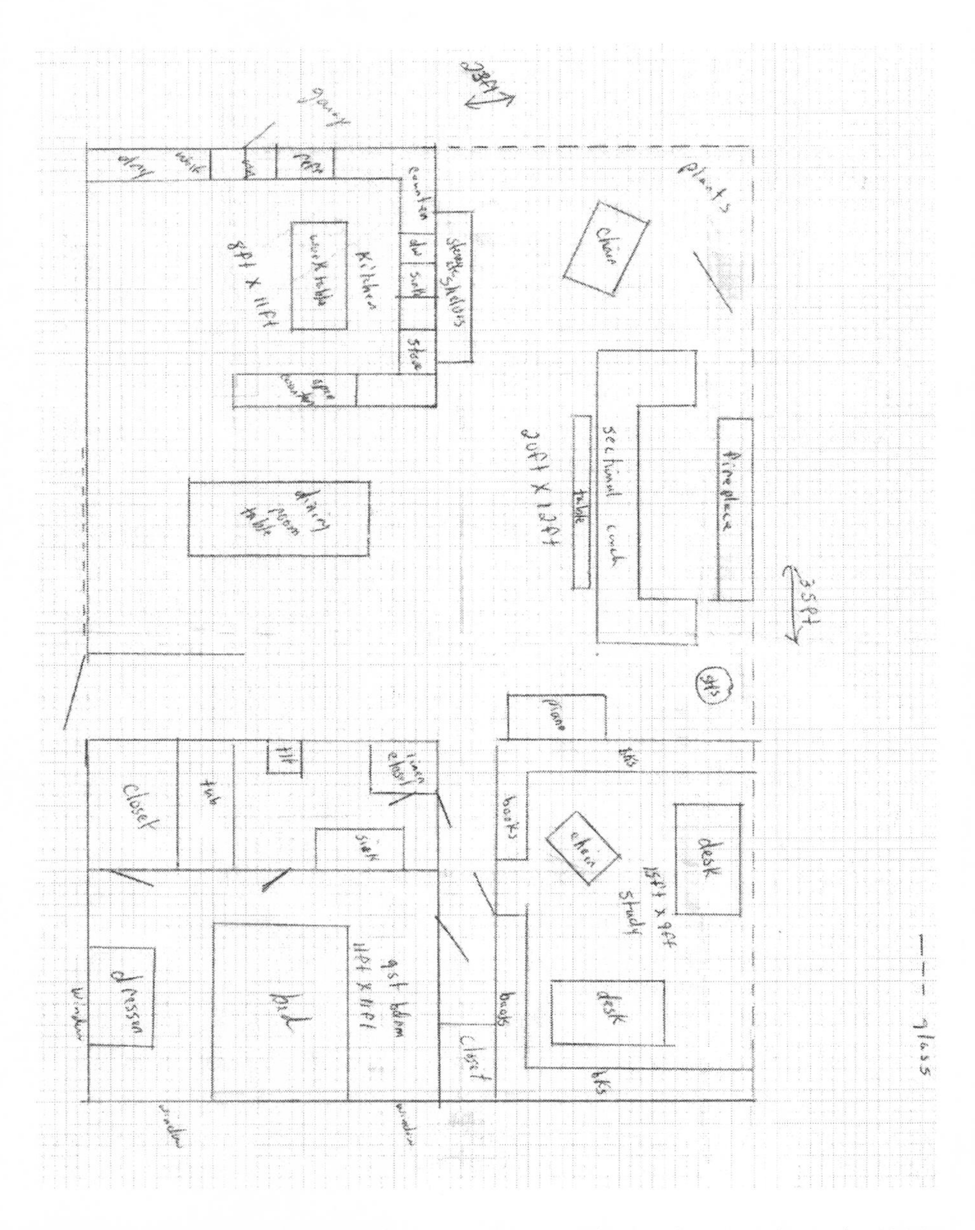

The first floor of the house plan Ted drew not long after we'd met in 1977

The Cowboy Cookie Recipe

Ingredients

2 cups old-fashioned rolled oats
2 cups all-purpose flour
3/4 teaspoon baking soda
1/2 teaspoon baking powder
1/2 teaspoon salt
1/4 teaspoon ground cinnamon
3/4 cup (1-1/2 sticks) unsalted butter, softened
1/4 cup vegetable shortening
3/4 cup brown sugar
2/3 cup granulated sugar
2 eggs
1 teaspoon vanilla extract
2 cups semisweet chocolate chips
3/4 cup chopped walnuts

Putting It Together

Combine oats, flour, baking soda, baking powder, salt and cinnamon in a large bowl.

In a separate bowl, beat butter, shortening, and sugar for 2 minutes with an electric mixer. Beat in eggs, one at a time. Add vanilla. Gradually stir in dry mixture. Add chocolate chips and walnuts. Cover and refrigerate for 1 hour.

Preheat oven to 350°F. Lightly grease two baking sheets.

Using 1⁄4 cup of dough per cookie, shape dough into balls and place on the baking sheet, leaving 2-1/2 inches between. Flatten balls lightly with your fingers. Bake one sheet at a time on the center oven rack for 13 to 14 minutes. They should be lightly browned when done.

Makes about 24 cookies.

About the Author

A professional writer for nearly 45 years before retiring in 2020, Mike Coleman won awards for news reporting and writing for nonprofit organizations and businesses in the technology industry. He has also had a lifetime interest in creative writing. His short story *Worse than Murder* took Honorable Mention in Writer's Digest's 74th annual writing competition in 2005. Another story, *The Night Watch,* is featured in the "Stories Worth Talking About" section of the children's story site Bedtime-Story.com. He and his husband live in Atlanta, Georgia. Read more about them at https://mikecolemanauthor.com/.

Other Riverdale Avenue Books You Might Like:

In Bed With Gore Vidal: Hustlers, Hollywood and the Private World of An American Master
By Tim Teeman

Best Kept Boy in the World:
The Short, Scandalous Life of Denny Fouts
By Arthur Vanderbilt

Hollywood Gays:
Conversations with Cary Grant, Anthony Perkins, Liberace, Cesar Romero and Others
By Boze Hadleigh

Inside The Hollywood Closet
By Boze Hadleigh

Deeply Superficial: Noel Coward, Marlene Dietrich, and Me
By Michael Menzies

Playing by the Book
By Chris Shirley

Wasn't Tomorrow Wonderful?
By Kenneth Walsh

Made in the USA
Columbia, SC
02 October 2023